WHAT MY DAUGHTERS TAUGHT ME

WHAT MY DAUGHTERS TAUGHT ME

JOSEPH WAKIM

ALLEN&UNWIN
SYDNEY • MELBOURNE • AUCKLAND • LONDON

Allen & Unwin
83 Alexander Street
Crows Nest NSW 2065
Australia
Phone: (61 2) 8425 0100
Email: info@allenandunwin.com
Web: www.allenandunwin.com

Cataloguing-in-Publication details are available
from the National Library of Australia
www.trove.nla.gov.au

ISBN 978 1 76011 392 6

Set in 12/17 pt Fairfield LH Light by Post Pre-press Group, Australia
Printed and bound in Australia by Griffin Press

10 9 8 7 6 5 4 3 2 1

MIX
Paper from
responsible sources
FSC
www.fsc.org   FSC® C009448

The paper in this book is FSC® certified.
FSC® promotes environmentally responsible,
socially beneficial and economically viable
management of the world's forests.

Dedicated to Daughters

'For when I am weak, then I am strong' (2 Corinthians 12:10)

Contents

Prologue: Earthly paradise   1

How to act my age   7

How to carry on   19

How to be a complete parent   32

How to grieve   41

How to hope and pray   48

How to keep their hair on   55

How to lose a rabbit   65

How to party   72

How to dispatch spiders   77

How to rock   88

How to do the morning scramble   95

How to come clean   103

How to do their assignments   113

How to be a 'dance mom'   121

How to smash stereotypes   131

How to weave magic   137

How to buy pads   151

How to compete with a screen   165

How to satisfy the style police   176

How to wear a formal dress   187

How to say goodbye   202

How to get things straight   215

How to be busy   226

How to make quality time   235

How (not) to drive   246

How to let them date   250

How to let myself date   265

How to break free   275

Acknowledgements   279

PROLOGUE: EARTHLY PARADISE

Once upon a time I lived in my hometown of Melbourne with my young family: my beautiful wife Nadia and our three little girls—Grace, Michelle and Joy. Ours was a house of music, dancing and laughter. And, as Lebanese Christians of the Maronite Church, ours was a house of faith. I was the hardworking king of the Dad-pun, and Nadia the ever-calm domestic queen. After all, we were 'crowned' during our marriage ceremony to have authority over our mini-heavenly kingdom of home and family.

After a career in psychology and social work, I was completing a Master of Business degree in the hope of becoming a better breadwinner. Nadia, a graphic designer, was studying to become a teacher and she taught at the Arabic Saturday school. We were both changing professions and pursuing our dreams. We loved and were loved. We were happy.

I met Nadia in 1988, on my first 'pilgrimage' back to my birthplace in Lebanon, courtesy of my father's pledge to all of his eight children. I was a puny 'street worker' wearing op-shop jeans. The first thing I noticed was her down to earth appearance and demeanour.

She did not dress to impress the 'Australian' bachelor. Her denims were a refreshing sight amidst the lovely ladies who fluttered their eyelashes and flashed their sequins. Unlike the layers of etiquette that other women used to obscure my view, with Nadia there was neither smoke nor mirrors.

Her shoulder-length brown hair formed a halo around her face, and her brown eyes sparkled with the promise of hidden treasures. She had an infectious smile that reminded me of Julia Roberts, and her speaking voice was warm, never affected. When she parted her luscious lips and sang in Arabic, French and English, I was instantly captivated. Her angelic voice was more intoxicating than the *'aaraq* (alcohol spirit) that my uncle used to anoint me upon my arrival in Beirut. No coffee cup ever predicted that in the chaos of war-torn Lebanon our two hearts would find peace. I knew immediately that I wanted to marry her, to spend the rest of my life with her.

We were a match made in heaven. Nadia conducted the church choir in her local village and led the Fersen el 'Aadra (Knights of Mary) children's group at the Sunday school. I played the guitar and sang my own songs. During that life-changing trip, I wrote a song in Nadia's honour and recorded it, with her cousin singing harmony in the chorus and playing the *dirbakki* (Lebanese bongo). Soon, Nadia and I sang in harmony. Our hearts were in harmony.

Nadia and I developed a repertoire of favourite songs in three languages. She sang perfectly in pitch while I accompanied her on guitar and tapped my feet. I always had a guitar in the boot of my car, as many of our family visits culminated in singalong celebrations that lasted well into the night.

We loved music so much that our three daughters were named after songs. Grace was named after 'Amazing Grace'. During Nadia's first pregnancy, whenever we had friends over, I would strum the chords of this hymn while Nadia sang the words. After her birth,

Grace became animated whenever she heard this song. Her nickname was Goochi (as in 'Goochi, goochi, goo'), because she squirmed whenever my tickling hands approached her. As she grew, Grace fulfilled her mother's dreams and became a petite and elegant devotee of ballet, attending several classes a week and travelling far and wide to perform and compete.

Grace is not only her name but also her virtue. She is protective, affectionate and forgiving, with no heart for grudges. She is a replica of her mother and has grown up to become a mother figure to many. Grace has a more olive complexion than her sisters and her brown eyes exude a quiet confidence.

Michelle was named after the Beatles song, 'Michelle, Ma Belle', echoing Nadia's love of the French language, and of a cousin she had taken under her wing back in Lebanon, Michel. Throughout Nadia's second pregnancy, our visitors played prophet, insisting that this baby was a boy. They based their certainty on old wives' tales such as the shape of Nadia's bump and the way a chain moved when dangled over her belly. They were all 100 per cent sure and they were all 100 per cent wrong, so I nicknamed our second-born Boo-Boo. In a way, though, they were right.

Michelle grew into a tomboy, and until the age of thirteen, she almost never wore skirts or dresses. Rather than dancing, Michelle became another family musician, playing the *dirbakki* while I played the guitar, Nadia sang and Grace danced. She has crystal-blue eyes, an inheritance from both sides of the family. As a child, Michelle was bouncy in every way. How she walked, the melody of her voice and her love for ball games. She has her mother's voluptuous lips, once puckered by being our only baby who slept with a dummy, preferably honey-dipped! When she wore her favourite baseball cap above her bouncy hair, people often assumed Michelle was my son, which she resented. While Grace was easy going, Michelle was a

3

fuss pot, sometimes changing her clothes several times in one day, except for the runners, which stayed on.

Joy was named after the Christmas carol 'Joy to the World'. During this third pregnancy, Nadia scratched her nose whenever she saw or craved strawberries. This was our only explanation for the strawberry-shaped birthmark on Joy's nose when she was born. I nicknamed her Zuzu because the J sound becomes a Z sound in Arabic when we are speaking endearments. Although she could only sit in my guitar case and watch the family's music-making back in those Melbourne days, in later years Joy, too, joined her sister Grace in ballet classes. Joy also has the family's blue eyes, and as a child her round face was framed by a halo of silky blonde curls. Joy was placid and picture-perfect. When her large eyes gazed up, her snow-white face was illuminated. My mother compared her softness to a marshmallow.

Lebanese visitors made the sign of the cross when they saw her, invoking God to protect her. Some insisted we should pin the blue eye amulet on her chest to ward away the evil eye of jealousy. But our faith taught us that the crucifix was the protector and did not need any help. After all, Joy already had blue eyes as clear as glass.

Joy squinted in the sun and burnt easily. She waddled in her sisters' shadows; Grace and Michelle fast-tracked her growth while I tried to slow it down. Her name also defined her: a malleable doll everyone wanted to embrace and photograph.

One happy summer, a national dancing competition took us to Surfers Paradise on the Gold Coast. We could not deny Grace the chance to take part, so we treated the trip as a family holiday. It blew our budget, but it was worth every cent.

The curtains opened for act one on the high stage and we all beamed as Grace appeared in her Minnie Mouse costume along with the other Disney characters. As she hopped backwards in her dance routine, she reached the back of the stage, hopped into the rear curtain and slid downwards, disappearing from view. Nadia and Michelle grabbed my arms, their fingernails digging in, while I held my breath, poised to make a scene myself and dive in after her.

The crowd gasped, then laughed at this cartoon-like spectacle. Where did my daughter go? Was anyone running to her rescue? As if nothing had happened, Grace hopped back onto the stage without a limp and continued the routine with a wide smile. We exhaled, hands on hearts. It certainly was not funny at the time, but we all laughed hysterically later. And we were very proud of her professionalism.

It was not long after Australia's first six-star hotel—Palazzo Versace—had opened. We popped into the foyer for a look around and we were in awe, but we knew that it was a luxury we could not afford. I saw the glint in Nadia's designer eye as she dreamt of being queen for a night and waking up just once in this majestic palace.

The magic of making my wife happy had no price tag, so I asked Grace to keep her mum occupied while I slipped away 'to the bathroom'. Upon my return, I announced my surprise—that we would all be sleeping in one of the hotel's luxury apartments that night.

Nadia was in raptures and the children were ecstatic. Our video camera chewed up every chandelier, every gold tap and every embroidered pillowcase. Our luggage swallowed up as many complimentary perfumes and shampoos as it would take. And I bought Nadia a gold Versace bathrobe and slippers, to remember her one night as a queen.

I know now what I did not know then about my daughters. This spontaneous gift was etched into their memory as a gesture of love. 'I love how you noticed these little things then gave her a big surprise,' Grace said years later.

The video camera could never capture the love we all felt for each other, but it trembled each time I felt a lump rising in my throat. Neither my hand nor our life could keep still during these magical moments.

But then cancer crawled its way into our lives and changed everything.

HOW TO ACT MY AGE

'So what are you ordering, Dad?' asked a twenty-one-year-old Grace, as the young waitress stood by smiling.

I glanced at the fancy font on the menu in the candlelight. It looked exquisite. There was only one teensy problem: I could not read a thing. I squinted, picked up the menu and extended my arm. Still a blur. I was nearing 50, but I was in denial.

'Grace, I trust you with my eyes closed.' They might as well have been! 'Surprise me.'

The young waitress tilted her head. 'I wish my dad trusted me with his eyes closed.'

'Don't ask Grace,' jibed eighteen-year-old Michelle. 'She takes half an hour to decide for herself!'

I grinned at the waitress. 'What's your fish of the day?'

She pointed to the blackboard on the far wall. I saw the word 'SPECIALS' but everything beneath it was a bloody blur again. Why do they assume that 'romantic' customers in a dimly lit restaurant have infrared vision? Don't they want us to savour the true colours of their food? Don't they know that as hunger increases, vision decreases?

I pretended to read the specials. 'What do you recommend?'

'Well, there's barramundi and—'

I decided to accept this first offering to end my misery and escape the spotlight. 'Perfect.'

'But you don't normally like barra—' began Michelle.

'I do today.' I put down the menu and breathed a sigh of relief.

My subterfuge had been useless. 'Dad, you seriously can't read that?' Michelle asked, squinting and pointing at the blackboard.

'Of course I can!' I yelled over the music. 'Specials.'

Michelle turned to Grace and raised her left eyebrow. 'He's in denial.'

'Don't worry, Dad,' consoled fourteen-year-old Joy. 'I need my eyes checked too. At least you can read that blackboard. I struggle at school when I sit at the back. The whiteboard looks all fuzzy.'

'Me too,' added Michelle. 'Maybe that's why I don't enjoy reading books.'

'Oh, how cute!' exclaimed Grace, clapping. 'We'll book the whole family in at the optometrist!'

'The what?' I put my hand to my ear to hear over FUN's 'We Are Young' blasting away in the background.

'And the audiologist!' Grace raised her glass as if we were toasting.

'What did you say about family?' I asked.

'See, all those years in rock bands made you deaf!' Grace said, pointing to her ears.

'It's selective hearing,' Joy argued, shaking her finger. 'He hears me talking to my friends from the other side of the house well enough. And he wonders why we prefer to text!'

'Rubbish!' I defended myself. 'It's just the music here. Too loud! They don't want us to see or hear properly.'

'It's just old age,' Michelle said, slapping me on the shoulder.

'Fifty years ago, 50 was old age,' I waved my finger at all of them and raised my voice to be heard over the music. 'Now it's common for people to live more than a hundred years. The second half of my life hasn't even started yet.'

'Hear! Hear!' came a shaky voice from a nearby table.

'Mind your own bloody business!' I muttered, and my daughters convulsed in fits of laughter until Grace nearly fell off her chair.

The next day, we made a block booking of optometry appointments for Joy, Michelle and me. Michelle needed reading glasses, while Joy had some issues with certain colours on the classroom whiteboard. As for me, I was long-sighted, which suited my personality. I always aspired to be the parent who saw the curve of the horizon.

It also explained why I struggled so often with labels on medicine bottles and their expiry dates. When I had restless nights and reached into the medicine cabinet, admittedly my eyes were tired and my vision blurry, yet even in broad daylight I found the vital instructions tiny and nearly impossible to read. The difference between one and two tablets could be the difference between life and death. Pharmacists should either use a larger font or provide free glasses!

'So, Dad, you need glasses,' smiled Grace. 'Let's choose something stylish that really suits you.'

There was no escape. 'No, I don't need glasses,' I protested, swinging my arms forward to eye height. 'I just need longer arms so I can read at the right distance.'

Joy laughed. 'You look like an orangutan.'

'Thanks, I feel better by the minute, monkey!'

It took time for the reading glasses to grow on me, and I resisted hanging them around my neck as a permanent reminder of my 'disability'. When I left them on and walked about, I felt like Alice in Wonderland as objects shrank and expanded around me. It was a bad idea to wear them when nature called. When I looked down, the much-magnified technicolour view revealed far too much information!

When we took family 'selfies' at restaurants, I noticed that something else disconcerting was happening. My eyes disappeared when I smiled.

'No good! Do it again!' I insisted. 'My eyes look closed.'

'Don't smile so much,' suggested Michelle. 'Your mum has the same problem.'

So *that's* why my mother always widened her eyes for photographs. She was compensating for her raised lower eyelids by raising her eyebrows. It looked ridiculous.

I checked my younger photos. I was always smiling and my eyes were always open, effortlessly. It was as if some of my facial muscles had retired and been replaced by a single lever: every time the ends of my mouth moved upwards, so did my lower eyelids. Was this why older people never smiled when they posed for those olden-days black-and-white photos?

My daughters were relentless.

'Open your lips.'

'Show some teeth.'

'Relax your eyebrows.'

'Just smile naturally!'

'Stop!' I pleaded. 'This is torture! There's nothing natural about posing!'

'We're only trying to help because you keep complaining about your photos,' retorted Grace.

I sighed. 'Nothing that a bit of Photoshop can't fix!'

When I needed headshots for a publisher, I went to a photographer friend. Once the photo was taken, he performed cosmetic surgery without botox, enlarging my eyes and airbrushing my wrinkles. It was something Nadia used to do in her job as a graphic artist.

As he zoomed in on a large screen, I noticed feral hairs protruding from my ears like a lynx cat's. 'What the hell?' I cried, pointing to the unsightly tufts. 'They've got to go.'

He removed them on the screen and it did not hurt a bit.

'Man, our hormones are out of whack,' I added, placing my hand on my thinning crown. 'Why do we lose hair where it belongs then grow hair where it doesn't?'

I was never one for vanity or mirrors, but what I saw in my reflection no longer reflected how I felt. I had noticed that my daughters were experimenting with hair colours and rinses. I had also noticed that many grey-haired men dyed their hair jet black and looked ludicrous. Could I at least hide those grey strands that belied my darker eyebrows? Maybe then my daughters wouldn't find me so mortifying when I did cartwheels on the beach.

I was already familiar with the shampoo aisle of the supermarket and guessed that my natural hair colour was medium brown. Although I was never in the least embarrassed about buying sanitary pads for my daughters, I buried this product in the trolley, paranoid that anyone who saw it would know my secret. That way, if someone told me after I had dyed my hair that I looked good for my age, I could accept the compliment graciously.

I was busted by the checkout chick, who recognised me as the man who buys pads. She couldn't find the bloody barcode, and as she turned the burgundy box around she gazed up at me and grinned. The box had a man's face on it, so there was no point pretending it was for anyone else.

'My daughters . . . their idea.' I blushed.

'If you buy the pads for them, why don't they buy this for you?' she suggested.

After I closed my bathroom door so I would not be interrupted, I donned the prescribed gloves, mixed the two bottles together, shook vigorously and massaged the 'solution' into my problem. But then I made the classic mistake: I lost track of time. The instructions warned 'DON'T GUESS: USE TIMER'. The longer I left it before rinsing, the darker the result would be. As soon as I realised, I leapt into the shower, and was relieved to see the dark colour washing onto the floor.

I presented myself to my daughters as a new man, curious to see how long it would take them to notice. I had all my defences lined up if they attacked, but it was not my hair colour they noticed.

We had been sitting together on the sofa in front of the television for about ten minutes when Joy said, 'What's wrong with your forehead?'

'Nothing,' I shrugged. 'Why?'

She stood up and turned on the bright downlights. Michelle and Grace gasped and raised their hands to their mouths.

'What have you *done?*' asked Grace.

'Did you put colour in?' accused Michelle.

'Have you checked the mirror?' continued Joy.

They marched me to the mirror like a handcuffed criminal. I, too, gasped when I saw what they saw. The colour had stayed on my scalp too long, and ugly blotches had leaked downwards, staining my forehead, ears and neck.

'That's okay,' I said suavely, pretending to be confident. 'It'll wash off in the second rinse.'

They were having none of it. They sat me down on my bed for the cross-examination.

'Why would you dye your hair in the first place?' smirked Michelle.

'Because it had gone grey too early.' Then I deployed an answer I had prepared in case I was found out: 'And because I was forced to age well before my time.'

'But you always said we should accept the way God made us,' continued Grace, 'and whatever he dishes out to us. "Thy will be done", remember?'

'And you always said that if something's bothering us, we should talk about it,' Michelle added, raising an eyebrow.

As they patronised me, they highlighted my hypocrisy.

'And what about "Your body is a temple of the Holy Spirit", huh?' Joy asked now, wobbling her head.

'This is different!' I shook my head. 'I'm not ready for . . . grey.'

Grace gazed at me in pity. 'You know that white hair goes with blue eyes. Your dad had that combination.'

I shook my head.

'Dad's in denial again,' Michelle said, raising her palms as if she was going to strangle someone. 'Haven't you always said that it's not what's on the head, it's what's in it that counts?'

'Well, what's in my head is that I want to look the way I feel.' Then I played the trump card: 'Your mum needed to have her hair brushed and be prettied up so that she could feel fantastic when she looked at herself in the mirror.'

'What's that got to do with you, princess?' mocked Michelle.

'Yeah, Dad,' frowned Grace. 'You shouldn't compare. This isn't an illness, it's just natural.'

'Your mum dyed her hair to make herself feel better,' I sulked. 'Haven't you dyed your hair?'

Michelle looked at Grace, horrified. 'So now you're comparing yourself with *girls*? Rewind and listen to what you just said.'

'We just don't want you to look like those . . . woggy men,' concluded Grace. 'You used to make fun of them and how they try to look half their age.'

I had a second shower and scrubbed with a coarse loofah and Solvol, eventually replacing the black blotches with red scratches. I had a third shower with soft soap in the hope that it would destroy the evidence, but no longer distracted by my hair, I became aware of another unwelcome change. My belly had grown into a breakaway republic through a resistance movement that craved sugar. It is apt that the Lebanese call a diet a 'regime'; in my case it was an attempt to bring the republic back into the federation. I could no longer see my toes without leaning forward or pulling in my tummy. I used to look straight down at my feet but now this republic obstructed my view. My eating and exercise habits had not changed, but my metabolism obviously had.

I figured I would be less likely to burn off anything I ate in the evening. 'You need to help me, gals,' I pleaded. 'Light at night. No more heavy food in the evening.'

'Why?' asked Joy.

'Let's just say, double demerit points after 6 p.m.'

'Why, are you speeding?' teased Michelle.

'No, I'm slowing down. It just sits there,' I explained, pointing to my stomach. 'If I eat one ice cream after 6 p.m., it's like eating two.'

'Okay, we'll book you if we bust you,' laughed Grace.

Were these the early warning signs of male menopause? Is it a time when men pause in front of the mirror and take stock of . . . everything? Now, each time a photographer called out 'cheese', I had to raise my eyebrows and tuck in my tummy.

When we visited Lebanon, it was common for people to have dinner at ten o'clock, but they had a saying: *Ta'aasha w tmasha* (Stroll after dinner). Back in Australia, if it was too wet to walk at night, I worked out with a skipping rope until I collapsed in exhaustion. As I bounced, I felt like I needed a man-bra. Why were my breasts suddenly so happy to do their own skipping? They were supposed to be firmly fastened to my ribcage, not free-floating! When I was younger, the 'Skeleton Dance' taught me that 'dem dancing bones' were all connected. Now I felt like my anatomy was disintegrating!

As if this were not enough, I felt a lump near the nipple of one breast.

What the hell? I rushed straight to Google and realised that male breast cancer does exist. Learning from Nadia's experience, I made an appointment with my GP and tried to sound calm. I should have told my daughters but they would have been petrified. This time I could not practise what I preached about bottling up secrets.

While waiting for the results of a biopsy, I clung tightly to the rose-scented rosary I used as my conduit to heaven and spoke to Nadia. 'Please . . . tell me this isn't serious. Will I share the same fate as you?' Then I realised how stupid this sounded. I imagined my epitaph: 'Here lies Joseph Wakim, beloved husband of Nadia. Both died of breast cancer.' It was too tragic, too epic, too Hollywood.

When the GP sat me down and reassured me there was no malignancy, I nearly passed out in relief. In gratitude, I squeezed the rosary in my pocket.

'Oh, doctor, you have no idea . . . I haven't eaten or slept properly since—'

'I know,' he said, placing his hand on my shoulder, 'but I do need to ask you something else.'

'Anything!' I was so relieved he had not delivered a death sentence.

'Have you done anything different lately?'

'Like what?'

'Anything on your body? A new soap?'

The penny dropped. 'Does hair dye count?'

He looked up the active ingredients of the product and when he said 'Aha' I knew that some allergic chemical reaction had caused this scare. He explained which ingredient I had to avoid and I left the surgery feeling like skipping, and did not care if my breasts felt like skipping separately. I had a new lease of life.

Days later, I told my daughters. They were horrified by my private torment but thought the story was hilarious.

'Please don't mention it to anyone,' I pleaded. 'I don't need this sort of attention, with all the talk about me needing a wife.'

Michelle dropped her jaw. 'Why would we? The moral of the story is that you shouldn't bottle things up.'

'No, the moral of the story is that you should check what's in the bottle!' argued Grace.

'No, the moral of the story is that I went straight to the doctor without delay.'

While some parts of my plumbing slowed down, others sped up. I acquired an appetite for coffee but there was no warning about the race to 'waterloo', every 30 minutes. Suddenly, my body became impatient. When nature called, I had to go. Any delays strained the walls of my bladder until I broke into a sweat.

If I was washing dishes, the running water was torture. My daughters would recognise my 'busting dance', where I swayed from foot to foot like a lizard on a scorching road.

'Dad, go to the bathroom,' Grace would offer, 'we'll finish them off.'

If I was driving and the urge took me, I had to find a tree to avoid an accident. Never had the golden arches of McDonald's looked so welcoming. Never had the sign 'restroom' been so apt.

My fancy footwork during the 'busting dance' may have contributed to secondary symptoms: hard skin on the soles of my feet. This I inherited from my father, who had leathery hands and feet.

I once read that the hardness forms to protect the skin from more friction, especially as the body gains weight and the poor soles have more to carry. After trying for a few weeks to use sandpaper to smooth out these rough surfaces before my shower, and rubbing in Sorbolene cream after it, I realised it was making no difference.

While Joy and I waited for my car tyres to be changed one day, we wandered through the local shopping centre. She fancied a manicure at the nail salon. While I watched the masked ladies at work, I learnt a new word: shellac, a high-gloss varnish that hardens under ultraviolet light so that the nail polish is more durable. The glazed nails look like a Red Delicious apple, thanks to the secretions of lac bugs.

'You want to try?' asked the lady leaning over the cash register.

I grinned, shook my head and took a step back.

Joy turned to face me. 'Dad, what about your feet?'

'Your feet?' asked the shrewd lady.

'Do you have those fish that eat off the dead skin?' I hoped that would end the conversation.

'Illegal in this country, but we can shave.'

She ushered me towards an empty back-massage chair and virtually thrust me into position. My feet landed in a spa, which was suddenly filling with blue water. I was being seduced.

'First try, then talk,' she smiled.

A short lady waddled towards me and sat on a low stool in front of my feet. She snapped on her rubber gloves and I felt very vulnerable. This was happening too fast! Joy, in hysterics, grabbed her phone and pointed it at me.

'No Instagram, Joy!' I insisted. 'Don't you dare share this!'

'Dad, who said men can't be pampered? Don't your feet deserve it?'

Before I could answer, sensations ran up from my feet to my head as I began to experience my first pedicure. After trimming my nails, my stooping pedicurist applied moisturising cream and a razor, one sole at a time.

'Aah!' I opened my mouth to cope with the ticklish treatment. The ladies who were reading magazines or their phones looked up and giggled at me.

Joy's mouth was agape. 'Dad, you should *see* how much stuff is falling off your feet!'

Shreds of dead skin flaked off my feet until I was surely two sizes smaller!

'You must come back every month to be better,' instructed the pedicurist.

'Of course,' I smiled.

Joy was right. My feet deserved this even if I didn't. Why replace my car tyres and yet never do anything to look after my feet? A pedicure is a seriously great surprise gift for men who think they carry the world on their shoulders but ignore their feet, which carry everything. I would accept this as a birthday present any year, even if it meant being surrounded by pampered women for an hour—and admitting I was 50.

Clearly these girls of mine had a thing or two they could teach me!

HOW TO CARRY ON

Who would ever have thought the stars would align in such a way that the day Nadia was handed the keys to heaven was the same day I was handed the keys to our new home, the dream home Nadia had designed but would never enjoy? All the tea leaves, coffee cups and palm readers failed to predict this cruel joke. No one ever gasped, 'I see a white dove with a key in its mouth.'

Immediately after Nadia died, I knew that my daughters and I needed to move in to our new house—we needed to be together more than ever. From her wheelchair, Nadia had directed the transformation of the abandoned Sydney house we had bought into a liveable home for our family. Her design was simple and modern, with white walls and comfortable open spaces. But our freshly painted home needed cleaning before my children could move in, so they slept at their Aunt Lola's house that first night. Her husband is my oldest brother James—two brothers married two sisters. He is my only sibling in Sydney—the other six are all in Melbourne. James buffered me during this painful period, guiding me through dreaded but necessary decisions about funerals and cemeteries. He allowed me to grieve while neglecting his own need to do so.

Grace was nearly twelve, Michelle had just turned nine and Joy was only four. They had been forced to carry on without their mother as her relapses overshadowed her remissions. We had not told them that their mother was terminally ill—they were too young and Nadia could not bear the pain of telling them. Their memories of their mother were happy ones and would forever be enhanced by the magical moments preserved in our family video collection. They had no memory of their mother in pain, probably because every time I ushered them into her room, at home or in hospital, she had radiated a smile that assured them everything would turn out all right.

That fateful night, once they were asleep, I rushed to our new home to assemble our furniture. My old friend Scott, who had flown up from Victoria, stayed with me to help. At midnight, we were still turning screws and setting up beds. It was Easter Saturday. At midnight on that day, we would usually be at church, celebrating. *Al Masih Qaam!* (Christ is risen!) is our traditional Arabic greeting. *Ha'kkan Qaam!* (Truly He is risen!) is the reply. As the phone calls and condolences poured in, some consoled me with this thought: 'It is a great honour that Nadia has truly risen with Him on the third day.' Easter would never be the same.

I hung up all the clothes in our new built-in wardrobes, including Nadia's. What else was I supposed to do while her body was still warm?

Scott tried to teach me a few rudiments of cooking, but I had no appetite to learn. Survivor guilt choked me and stopped me from swallowing . . . anything. How dare I eat when she could no longer breathe? The more I sacrificed, the more I felt content.

'Come on, Joe, you have to eat.' Scott handed me a sandwich of whatever he could muster from my fridge.

I clenched my fists and crossed my arms. 'My stomach is in a knot.'

It must have been after two in the morning when we finally collapsed on the sofas, exhausted. Scott had no idea how much his presence was helping me. He did not need to say anything. He just needed to be there.

I said this was not the way it is when someone dies in the movies. And so we started to compare the most sentimental movies of all time.

'What about *Stepmom*!' I recalled. 'Stupid me, I watched that sob story on my own a few months ago, after the children had gone to sleep. I thought it might toughen me up and help me prepare.'

'And did it?'

'No way! I didn't hear any violins in the background at the hospital, did you?'

Scott bit his lip. His eyes squinted and his shoulders shook to hide his laughter at my furious sarcasm.

'These movies lie,' I continued to rant. 'They just keep prodding and poking you until you cry. As if a dying mum can sew a photo tapestry! Where was the smell of morphine and the sick bags? Where were the tubes on every limb?'

'I can't believe people pay money to cry!' Scott said, encouraging me to go on venting.

'Hire the video and we throw in a tissue box!'

'Or a beach towel for those who bawl their eyes out!'

'Or a steak knife!' and I motioned slashing my wrists. My grief had morphed into anger, then into parody, then into comedy and then into guilt.

As Scott helped release the emotional pressure valve on my choking heart, I released a heavy sigh. In my bedroom I lit a candle to signal Nadia's presence and turned out the lights. What Scott did not know was that I then embraced and inhaled Nadia's socks.

I tucked my rose-scented rosary under my pillow, which I had decided would allow me to communicate with her directly, just in case she phoned. Her presence was my oxygen. I saw her shadows dancing on the wall. I could still taste her on my lips. I could hear her whispering my name.

What I did not know was that Scott was nursing his own fears for his wife, who was being tested for breast cancer while he left his family in Victoria to be with me. He set a fine example to his children through this sacrifice: when a friend is in need, we should always do the deed. I was so relieved that his wife was later cleared of any malignancy and they did not need to go through the ordeal we were enduring. I was also relieved for myself as I could not handle any more guilt.

I reached for the rosary and dialled Nadia's number on this hotline to heaven. 'Did you arrive safely?' I asked. 'Do you miss me? Can you see me?'

I hesitated to extinguish the candle and stared at the still-flickering flame. 'Our bedroom is ready. I've hung up your clothes. You finally have your en suite bathroom with a spa. I even hung your gold Versace robe there. Now, when are you coming home?'

'It's the saints. It's all their fault!'

As the condolence calls continued on Easter Sunday, some mourners seemed to have a crisis of faith and needed someone to blame. Theirs were the same voices that had prayed for a miracle and promised their favourite saint would not let them down. Other callers politely paid their respects, as is customary in our Lebanese culture, even if they did not know us personally. My mother, Souad, raised us to observe these *waajbaat* (duties), just as she had learnt them from her own mother and expected me to pass them on to my daughters. My father, Jalil, was less interested in public appearances and preferred to visit personally after the *waajbaat* rush was over.

'One day, it will be our turn,' my mother used to explain, 'and people will return the respect. Whoever sees you with one eye, see them with two.' We were raised in humility and to reciprocate favours twofold so that we were never in debt.

But I never recall my parents cursing the saints. My father revered St Charbel Makhlouf, who hailed from his own village, Bekaakafra, which is the highest in Lebanon. He told us stories of when he was the security guard at St Charbel's tomb and the saint's body was exhumed in 1950 before he was canonised. He watched to prevent believers collecting saintly relics as 'miracle makers'.

I should not mock them. In desperation, Nadia and I had knelt at the shrine of medicine before the men in white gowns and prayed for miracle makers in the form of chemo. Eventually, though, they threw up their hands and told us their chemo cupboard was bare.

We'd ended up with our own 'shrine' in the rental house when we first moved to Sydney. In reality, it was our fireplace, crammed with candles, incense and two rows of saintly figurines: some were our own, some had been presents and some had been lent to us. I knelt in front of the crowded shrine now, not to pray this time, but to pack away all those figurines. Those received as presents had to be wrapped carefully in newspaper and laid to rest in cardboard boxes for storage in our new home. Those received on loan had to be returned to sender, but what on earth should I write in the thank you note? Good try? Better luck next time?

Some of the senders shook their heads and asked their saint: 'All our lives we've never missed Sunday mass, we've put money in the collection plate, we've been to confession, we've fasted during Lent and we've prayed by your statue. But when it was our turn to receive a miracle, where were you?'

As they listed the offerings they had made to their saint, they pushed their fingers into their palms, one by one, until they formed a fist. Is a saint a life-insurance salesman? Are we really to expect a return on our investment if we pay all our instalments on time?

'The saints depended on each other to do the job!' nodded another disillusioned supplicant. 'It's our fault. We should have prayed to only one saint to intercede for Nadia, but we relied on too many saints, and they relied on each other.'

Oh, ye of little faith, I thought. Were all our prayers to be reduced to some generic email addressed to many saints, hoping for one of them to reply and say to the others, 'I got this one'?

The owners of these disappointed voices did not know their own faith. Our parish priest at the time, Father Maroun, once explained that prayers are for our immortal soul, not our mortal body, so who of us left on earth could say that a miracle did not happen as a result of their prayers? Only Nadia knew that now.

I examined the red-faced statues before wrapping them. Did each one really cry out, 'So sorry, my son, but I thought St [insert name here] had your wife covered.'?

As I buried each statue in a box, I smirked: 'Covered? I'll show you covered.'

It was lucky for those statues that we were moving house. It meant they were spared the baseball bat. They could have been smashed in one angry swing at the shrine by any of the disillusioned faithful.

Thank God, my children were oblivious to these saint-bashing tirades. They knew that 'Thy will be done' means God knows what is best and when it is best. I explained that prayer was not a McDonald's drive-through, where you order at one counter and collect at another one around the corner.

Once the shrine was deconsecrated to a fireplace, I recalled our visit, one Saturday two years earlier, from the chimney sweep, during our first winter of renting this home. My inexperience in fire-laying meant that the smoke from burning wood constantly drifted into the house rather than up the chimney. As we waited for him to arrive, I asked my children to watch the Disney musical classic, *Mary Poppins*. I paused after the scene where the chimney sweep Bert sings, 'Good luck will rub off when I shakes hands with you.'

I crouched on the floor and looked my girls in the eye. 'And guess who's about to knock on our door?' I said.

'Bert?' asked Michelle.

'No, a real chimney sweep!' I replied, enlarging my eyes.

They leapt on my back and kept checking at the window, asking impatiently, 'When's he coming?' When he finally arrived, the girls took turns shaking his hands then insisted he 'shakes hands' with their mum.

We were all desperate for any good luck. It had been a while since my children had smiled so much, and our puzzled visitor had no idea why cleaning a dirty old chimney was so welcome in this family.

Now my phone rang and jolted me back to the present. I dreaded more *waajbaat* phone calls, especially those offering to take care of my children. The condolence book was looking like an increasingly attractive alternative. Sometimes the callers did not want to leave voicemail messages but kept calling until they talked to me personally. Did they want a verbal receipt for paying their respects? I wondered how I could conclude these calls politely. After all, I was flat out emptying the rental house and preparing our new one. I was like a bird flying between the two nests, twigs in mouth.

But I was wrong about this particular call. It wasn't one to cut short.

'I know it's hard to hear Happy Easter,' the caller said, 'but can I come around and help in any way?'

'No thanks, you should celebrate with your family.'

'You *are* family.'

This caller was not alone. Several people sacrificed their Sunday to help me unpack boxes, set books in shelves and lay cutlery in drawers. It was the most bittersweet house-warming.

Every wall and ceiling in our new home was painted white, exactly as Nadia wanted, but the designer was not there to cut the ribbon and declare the house a home. I declared it 'Beit Nadia' (house of Nadia) and put up a plaque with those words near the front door.

As I tested all the lights, I recalled a phone call from Nadia only two days before, on Good Friday, when I was in the house with our builder.

'Joey, we need a safety switch,' she said urgently, 'in the electricity . . . for the children.'

How could someone about to switch off be so switched on to something our builder and I had overlooked? That was Nadia through and through. Selfless and pragmatic to the very end.

The emotional roller-coaster continued on Tuesday. It was Nadia's 41st birthday and the day for the final viewing of her body. The words 'happy birthday' sounded so silly. I fell to my knees and kissed her hand. Touching her hand felt chilling, but it was a relief to see her looking so peaceful, dressed in her favourite clothes. It replaced my last memory of her, tied down with tubes on every limb, gasping for air.

As I held her hand, I felt two hands land on my shoulders. Two old friends, nuns of the Antonine Sisters, Daad and Sayde, had arrived like angels from Melbourne. Among an ocean of unfamiliar faces, it was those two women from Melbourne who made the surreal real for me. They had known Nadia as a happy and healthy human in the BC (before cancer) era. They had dined with us, sung with us and laughed with us throughout our BC married life.

It was Sister Sayde who had given me the rose-scented rosary I carried everywhere. She never speaks in platitudes but has her own original sayings. 'You know, Joe,' she said now, 'the first hundred years of this life are tough, I can't deny it, but I promise you it becomes much easier after that.' She is more than a nun to me, a sister who loves laughing at herself and taught me to do the same.

In distilling the essence of my beloved in a eulogy, I wanted to remember everything and overlook nothing:

Nadia filled our homes with echoes of her laughter. The more she ridiculed us, the more we loved her, as the truth gives you peace and laughter lengthens your life. Nadia avoided being a burden to anyone. She preferred to carry her own cross rather than share it with others.

I thank Nadia for giving me fourteen and a half years of married life and three daughters who permanently remind me that life and dreams must go on, three daughters who have given me a rainbow in what could have been a valley of darkness, in more ways than they could imagine.

I only choked when I recited the lyrics from our favourite song by Fairuz, a famous Lebanese singer:

Do you see the ocean so vast? as vast as the ocean do I love you
Do you see the sky so far? as far as the sky do I love you

The Wednesday morning funeral filled Our Lady of Lebanon Church with a polite parade of people paying their respects. Family and close friends flew up from Melbourne and I reached out to them as if they were oases in a desert. The monks chanting in Aramaic, the incense rising to the heavens, the water sprinkled on the white coffin and the tall candle shining brightly all helped to connect us with Nadia, and connect heaven with earth.

Grace read one of the 'prayers of the faithful' and Michelle carried the bread for the offertory. At four, Joy was shielded so that this was not a traumatic experience for her.

On Nadia's tombstone, we inscribed:

Her wisdom was beyond her years
Her faith was beyond our fears
Her cross was beyond our tears
But her happy voice echoes in our ears

I was heartened by these consoling words from several men: 'I will always be there for you, like a brother.'

That night, the pain of my grief was excruciating. Survivor guilt had really kicked in now, and was kicking me to the ground. 'My daughters need their mother,' I lamented. 'It should have been me, not her.'

But in the white house Nadia had created, the sharp edges of my grief were cushioned by my children and their immediate needs. They anchored me to the present.

'Dad, I'm peckish.'

'Dad, can you test me on my spelling.'

'Dad, there's a spider in my room.'

'Dad, can you iron my dress.'

'Dad, I need toilet paper.'

'Dad, can you tell me a story.'

'Dad, I can't sleep.'

'Dad, I can't find my wheat bag.'

'Are you having a "boy look"?' I responded. The children had taught me that expression, meaning 'not thorough'.

When my daughters were with me, I could not lament the past—our happy marriage that was curtailed and our Melbourne life that was uprooted. I could not fret about the future or about being a lone rooster with three hungry chicks.

So why did I not just pick up the family, pack up our home and return to Melbourne? After all, we had rushed to Sydney because Nadia had needed to be close to her sister Lola, but now Nadia was gone. I would be lying if I said I was not tempted many times, but Nadia was buried in Sydney and my children had settled in quickly. I could not uproot my children again, especially when they had Nadia's devoted sister watching over them.

Each night we had a sacred ritual. Grace lit a candle for her mother and prepared the rosary beads. Michelle lit incense, which she waved through every room of our home. And Joy heated wheat bags for each bed as the cold nights were approaching. The ritual concluded with saying the rosary and prayers, then optional extras—bedtime stories and massages. I was their everything and they were my everything. This was 'do not disturb' time, and all phone calls were silenced.

To avoid stressful morning surprises, we learnt to lay out the girls' school uniforms the night before. Although Joy was still only four, the school had made an exception for her and allowed her to commence kindergarten a year early. This meant that Joy was protected from witnessing the worst of Nadia's pain. Our baby did not witness the gradual incapacitation of her mother. It also meant that she spent two years in the kindergarten class.

I checked how my daughters brushed their teeth and I turned this drill into a rhyme:

Little circles round and round,
Open wide then upside down.

When Michelle lost her baby teeth, I tiptoed in while she slept and snuck a shining gold coin under her pillow. In the morning, she squealed, 'The tooth fairy came!' Grace squinted at me and I winked. She grinned back at the revelation, proud to be colluding with a grown-up. Joy was mesmerised by so much talk of magic, fairies, angels and miracles in our home.

Each night, I sat with my precious daughters until they slept. I kissed them goodnight twice—once from me and once from Nadia, but there was probably no need. I sometimes felt Nadia's cool breath on my own neck, so no doubt she kissed the girls each night for herself.

'Why do you keep doing that . . . brrr thing?' asked Grace, imitating my shivering.

'I got chills, they're multiplying,' I said, baiting Michelle, who at the time was obsessed with John Travolta and *Grease*.

'And I'm losing control!' She took the bait and sang on cue.

'Shh!' I heard Nadia whisper in my ear. 'Are you trying to relax them or excite them?'

It was selfish of me to keep them up, but I felt as if I never had enough time with them. Once they slept, I craved adult companionship, preferably in person. Why did no one call now? I stared at the white walls and white ceilings that were never intended for a widower.

Too much time alone allowed my inner voices to hold conversations, even arguments. Sometimes I had to break them up, or they would give each other the silent treatment.

'They have their own families to look after,' my forgiving side would say.

'But can't they spare one phone call?' my less patient self would protest. 'On their way home from work?'

'Well, why don't you call them, then? They told you to call any time.'

'Because I don't want to impose.'

'Maybe you make them feel awkward?' This was my spiteful self.

'Me? How?'

'Sulking and feeling sorry for yourself.'

'Rubbish! They don't know what it's like!'

'See! There you go again! *You* don't know what it's like for *them.*'

'Ha! Easy! They just need to pick up the phone and say, "Hello, how are you?"'

'You say that now but you were exactly like them.'

'How do you know?'

'Because I've always been here with you!'

'Shut up, all of you, I'm trying to think!'

There was no remote control to mute these persistent voices or change channels, because we were trapped inside my head. They were dangerous company, and they never left me alone.

Fortunately, I had real company a month after Nadia passed away. My eldest sister Eva flew up from Melbourne for a week and kept me sane. She added a woman's touch to our home while I scribbled copious notes on cooking recipes, cleaning tips and gardening basics.

Just before we drove her to the airport, Eva took a photo of my family in height order as we stood in front of our conifer. Eleven-year-old Grace had her hair parted down the middle, nine-year-old Michelle wore her navy headband and four-year-old Joy wore her golden halo of hair. I felt that Joy was too far away and I hoisted her onto my shoulders. We all braved a smile for the camera—or in Joy's case, tried to—but our eyes could not hide our pain, so soon after losing Nadia. We looked like a family on a roller-coaster ride. We hung on tightly to each other and my arms became their seat belts.

HOW TO BE A COMPLETE PARENT

Although I now looked fondly upon the house phone as a lifeline, when Nadia was fading I had dreaded its ringing sound and the routine questions about her. Towards the end of Nadia's chemo cycles, I was caught off guard by one call.

'Hi, Joe, how are you?'

I rattled off the latest bulletin as if it were a weather report. 'Well, today Nadia had a scan and now she's asleep. Tomorrow, she has chemo and—'

'Joe. Stop—'

'—the kids nearly found out when this letter arrived in the mail and—'

'Joe. Please stop. Are you hearing me?'

'Yes, you wanted an update.'

'No, I asked how *you* are.'

I frowned. 'How *I* am?'

'Yes. How are you?'

A ringing sound amplified in my ears as if a rusty valve had just been turned and a tiny voice was screaming out. 'I don't even know *who* I am,' I replied, 'let alone *how* I am . . .' A lump in my throat choked me, preventing me from continuing. The ringing in my ears became so loud that it drowned out whatever wisdom the caller was offering.

As Nadia was melting, so was my identity. Her pain was mine. Her good days were my good days. I poured every drop of my hope onto Nadia and let her pour every drop of pain onto me. My moods synchronised to her rhythms.

In the BC era, I was a husband, father, brother, son, uncle, cousin, nephew and friend. After that, I was primarily Nadia's carer, hanging on to her life before she floated away.

In the white house, the monotonous ring of the home phone suddenly sounded melodic.

I would pounce. 'Hello?'

No response.

'Hello!' I would fast lose patience, as most of my callers were people conducting surveys or wrong numbers.

'Oh, good evening, sir.' He was clearly from a telemarketing company, calling from overseas. 'May I please speak to Mrs Vakeem.'

'Sure, sir, putting you through to heaven. Hold the line please . . .' I covered the mouthpiece, wanting to laugh and cry simultaneously.

The caller was probably used to people hanging up on him, but this time he had the opposite problem.

'Sorry,' I said quickly, 'please don't hang up. Look, I know you're trying to run a business and I'm trying to run a family, but maybe we can . . . talk. I wish Mrs Wakim was here, but she is de- . . . deceased.'

'Oh, I am so sorry to hear that, sir. Perhaps I should—'

'No, no. Stay on the phone. Do you have a wife?'

'No, sir. Sir, these calls are monitored and—'

'Well, what's the weather like . . . wherever you are?'

It was cruel to torment this innocent caller when I could have called Lifeline. I was a former social worker, after all. But I was worried the telephone counsellor would be someone I knew, which would have been awkward.

With my rosary and my faith, I never felt spiritually lonely, but I probably gave mixed messages about my social loneliness. Sometimes, after mass, when I saw those who had vowed to be 'like a brother', I wanted to vent.

'Oh, hi, Joe. I swear to the Virgin,' one said, pointing to Mary's statue, 'I keep asking about you. I just wanted to give you some time to be alone.'

Wow, what a gift, and what a big sacrifice it must have been to give it to me. I looked him in the eye, something my newfound friends struggled to do. 'Thank you,' I said, 'but I'd love to see you. I've had enough of being alone. Let me give you my phone number, for the tenth time . . .'

My stinging retort probably burnt that bridge, but I did not care. I did not need more sympathy cards, nor did my children. We just needed genuine friends who could look us in the eye, just enough friends to count on one hand.

The more I burnt my bridges, the more paranoid I felt that I was to blame for what seemed to be crumbling and short-lived friendships in our relatively new community.

Many Lebanese parishioners whispered, 'Aain al mahzoun day'a (The eye of the bereaved is narrow).' Was I squinting at people through a lens of intolerance?

One Melbourne friend sent me a copy of Λ Grief Observed, the 1961 book by Irish writer C.S. Lewis about his own widowhood and narrowed eye. In it he reflects on the uniqueness of each person's grief, and concedes that those paying their respects can find themselves in a no-win situation. 'I see people, as they approach me,' he wrote, 'trying to make up their minds whether they'll "say something about it" or not. I hate it if they do, and if they don't.' Was my friend trying to tell me that my aloneness was self-inflicted?

Sometimes, instead of making phone calls asking for help, I was receiving them.

'Oh, Joe . . . I don't know what to say . . . I don't know what to do . . . I can't sleep at night.'

'Just take a big deep breath. *Mitil ma Allah bi reed* (Whatever God wills).'

What I really wanted to say was, 'You've called the wrong number. Call Lifeline.'

'This is so unfair. Those poor children. I wish I could take care of them. Let me take them . . .'

'No need. It's best to keep to their routines.' The last thing my children needed was to feel abandoned by their father.

'This must be so tough. I can't imagine how you do it alone and still sound so calm.'

'I never feel alone,' I replied, 'and our faith teaches us to trust in God. He sends helpers. Just light a candle or incense, say the rosary, pray to your favourite saint, play relaxing music, have a cup of aniseed tea. They may help you sleep.'

'You think so? Will they work for me?' The helpless voice trembled.

Maybe I was counselling myself.

One night, I had palpitations. I kept checking on the children, worried that someone was going to take them away in the middle of the night. 'One man, three girls?' said a voice in my head. 'No way! This is a ticking time bomb. They need to be rescued from him . . . How can he ever measure up?'

I reached for the rosary and dialled Nadia's number. 'Please, Nadia, give me a sign. Am I going mad? Why can't I sleep? Why do I feel like a failure? Can you hear me?' I learnt not to expect immediate replies, especially as I was making long-distance calls.

The next morning was a Saturday and I was awoken by a knock at the door. My daughters were still in bed. There stood a silhouette resembling Nadia, carrying what looked like a tray. Our dear friend Sonya, my brother's next-door neighbour, stood poised like a heaven-sent angel, with some home-made cookies for my children.

'I am so sorry, Joe,' she said. 'I hope you don't mind me calling on you so early, but this couldn't wait.'

'You're always welcome, Sonya. We're always happy to see you.' *We?* I thought, *Who is we?* I was still speaking on behalf of Nadia.

'I love that plaque,' Sonya said. '"Beit Nadia", at the front of the house.'

When my children emerged to greet our visitor, she cried when she saw Grace, who most resembles Nadia. 'Joe,' she said, more urgently now, 'I have to tell you about my dream last night.'

My daughters sat down next to me, listening intently to our visitor.

'I saw Nadia,' Sonya continued. 'It was really her.' She rubbed her forearm to settle her goose pimples.

I felt the same chill tingle my spine as if a wind had just enveloped us. We were not supposed to believe in any ghost except the Holy Ghost. We were not supposed to believe that those in heaven could visit those on earth. But who are we to decide how heaven works?

'Her face was as bright as the sun,' Sonya continued. 'She looked so happy.'

'Did she say anything to you?'

'She said, "I'm fine. I kiss my children every night, but I am worried about Joey. Please visit him."'

My heart was racing. I had asked for Nadia to give me a sign, but this was too much. My daughters looked up at me, frowning, as if asking for an explanation. Instead, I asked them to make their breakfast.

Once they were out of earshot, I leant forward. 'Sonya,' I whispered, 'last night was horrible. I missed her so much. I asked her to show me that she was still with me, still hearing me or seeing me. And she sent you.'

Poor Sonya could not hold back her tears and crossed herself.

In case I thought it was a coincidence, another visitor came that afternoon, and he etched a life-changing picture in my memory. This time the silhouette at the door seemed to be holding a baseball bat. *Too late!* I thought mockingly, *I already boxed the saints!* In reality, it was a bearded priest carrying a long cardboard tube.

This time, my daughters reached the door before me. '*Abouna* (Father)!' was their delighted cry.

Somehow our parish priest, Father Maroun, already knew of my anxiety about failing as a father without me having to tell him. I had been meaning to tell him in the anonymity of the confession box, even though it was not a sin, just fear and self-doubt. Now I told him face to face. I asked the girls to play outside. This was a father-to-father conversation and we needed to be frank and open.

I told him my fears, but he had come prepared. He opened the tube and unrolled a large poster of Rembrandt's 1669 painting *The Return of the Prodigal Son*.

'Look closely at the hands of the father as he embraces his son,' he said.

I could not see his point.

'See how one hand is masculine and the other is feminine? God is both father and mother.'

This painting gave me so much comfort. It depicts the greatest father in the greatest parable, performing a dual role. It also shows the prodigal son resting his head on the bosom of his father as he seeks forgiveness. Perhaps the bosom is the next best thing to returning to the womb of the mother. I could relate to this father and to his arms enveloping his child.

This visitor did not swing a baseball bat at the saints, but he did free me from the rusty shackles around my ankles that were my ideas of what it means to be a man or a woman, a father or a mother. He taught me that I could be both.

'*Shukran Abouna* (Thanks, Father),' I smiled. 'I hear voices . . . every night,' I confessed.

'What do they say?'

'The girls need a mother. He cannot be both. He needs to let go.'

'Where do you hear these . . . voices?'

'In my ears. In my head.'

He frowned. 'And do you worry about what people say?'

I shook my head. 'My children need more of me . . . more than ever, not less.'

'And is that a problem for you?'

I shook my head again. 'I just don't want anyone to try to fill Nadia's space. It's sacred. I just want to . . . do my best. Just us . . . our family.'

I saw Michelle's blue eyes peer around the back door, checking on me. The whispering had probably made her suspicious. I smiled to reassure her and she returned to her sisters.

The priest did not notice. 'But if God sends you helpers,' he asked wisely, 'do you push them away?'

'Not if they respect me . . . and us. What we're trying to do.'

'Trying to be both father and mother?'

'Trying to be a full parent.'

He looked at the father's fatigued face in the portrait. 'You'll be tired,' he counselled.

I nodded. 'Nadia and I used to walk together and share every-thing. I feel like someone who suddenly has to walk on one leg. You lose your balance. You fall down. You make mistakes. But you need to get back up. Now I *can* look up . . . at *this* father, *this* parent. I can't see a mother in this picture.'

I felt I had his blessing and I did look up at that poster whenever I was down.

'See the hands?' I said later, pointing it out to my daughters. 'Father and mother.'

Grace rolled her eyes.

⟍⟍

That night, I heard footsteps approaching in the dark. My bedroom door creaked open. I reached out to the lamp switch.

'What's wrong, Joy?' The bright light forced her to squint and rub her eyes.

'Can I sleep in your bed?'

'Why?'

There was a whimper then a sob then trembling lips. 'I miss Mummy.'

I threw open the doona and she snuggled up to me. I tried to imitate Nadia's maternal touch, but my hairy chest was no match for a mother's bosom.

'Why now?' I asked. 'Did something happen? Did someone say something to you at school?'

But there was no answer because she had fallen asleep. Her snuffles soon morphed into cute nasal snores. She slept soundly, but I did not. I am a light sleeper, and the slightest noise or touch awakens me. Joy had a puny frame at that age, with many sharp edges. Her elbow jabbed my ribs. Her sweaty hand snaked around my neck. Her knees—yes, both of them—nestled into the small of my back. The more I rolled away in the queen-size bed, the more she rolled towards me. Maybe my weight created a slope. Later, her feet pushed against my hip and I ended up on the edge of the bed.

I tried to trick her by climbing out and curling up on the opposite side of the bed. 'All yours,' I whispered, waving to her from afar. 'Now I can finally sleep.'

Within minutes, she had gravitated back into my orbit and my bloodshot eyes had opened. The melodic birds of Baulkham Hills heralded that dawn was near. I crawled out, grumbled something to Joy and resorted to her empty bed to snatch at least a few serious snores. I should have thought of that earlier but I had been too tired. It was too little, too late. Soon the kookaburras joined the dawn chorus with their relentless laughter, as if the whole thing were funny. These birds had no mercy for men like me.

And the roller-coaster of emotional ceremonies had no mercy on my children. As if Easter, the funeral and Nadia's birthday were not enough for one week, now the Mother's Day hype was on the horizon.

HOW TO GRIEVE

One of the teachers phoned me from the school. 'All the students are making Mother's Day cards,' she said. 'Is there someone your girls could give one to?'

'Yes. Their mother.' This was something sacred. 'We can take it to the cemetery, and we have a shrine at home.'

We spent that first Mother's Day at the cemetery, among families who understood our new normal. There was a marquee, drinks and lunch provided by a funeral company. My daughters told me that they did not feel Nadia's presence there at the cemetery, but had they been among the rest of society that Sunday, they would certainly have felt her absence. Poignant images of children hugging mothers would have been in their face on television screens and in shopping centres.

I felt guilty phoning my own mother, who was alive and well in Melbourne, to wish her a happy Mother's Day. When we attended the 7 p.m. mass that night, our spirits were lifted. The church choir conductor, having been at the cemetery lunch that day, had spotted Grace and Michelle and invited them to join the other young singers upstairs. And now here they were, singing in church just as their mother had done back in Lebanon and Melbourne. Joy and I smiled at them from downstairs. We all most definitely felt Nadia's presence in the church that night. It was as if she were conducting a church choir all over again!

We found Mother's Day painful, but we need not have done. The church newsletter explained that the modern Mother's Day was founded by an American lady, Anna Jarvis, in 1905, in honour of her deceased mum. Perhaps we and this lady were kindred spirits before the retailers lost the plot.

But anyone who tells you that time heals is lying. The second Mother's Day was more painful than the first. The school held a Mother's Day mass on the Friday before, but the young priest who was presiding innocently assumed that the thousand or so children in the church all lived with their mothers.

He moved around the church pews with his cordless microphone and asked the obvious questions. 'So, on Sunday,' he asked one child, 'what will you give your mother?'

'A kiss,' the child replied, but it sounded like they were trying to be cute.

I sat at the back with the other parents, ready to soften the impact of these cruel words on my children as best I could.

'And what about you?'

'Breakfast in bed.' Many giggled at this.

'And what would you say to her?'

'I love you.'

He was twisting the dagger without realising it. My head bobbed desperately between Grace upstairs in the school choir, Michelle on the opposite side of the round church, and Joy sitting with her kindergarten class just metres away from me, monitoring their levels of distress. What I did not know until later was that my children were also monitoring each other.

'And what would you do together on Mother's Day?' the priest continued blithely.

At that point I noticed a girl in the choir embracing Grace. During a heart-wrenching Arabic song, dedicated to mothers, that Nadia used to sing, I felt a lump in my own throat. There was now a commotion around Grace, and then I saw them escorting her downstairs.

I panicked and rushed to intercept her. Grace was sobbing and two other girls were sobbing with her, perhaps out of empathy. I went to embrace Grace but the other twelve-year-olds threw open their arms for a hug, too. *This is ridiculous*, I thought, but I smiled. They all giggled, embarrassed, at how ridiculous it looked, then resumed their sobbing.

I held Grace firmly and diverted her grief into anger. 'What a clumsy priest!' I exclaimed, 'I'm going to make a complaint!'

'No, Dad,' she pleaded.

'Yes, Dad,' I insisted. 'What about the children whose mothers don't live with them?'

Just as her sobs subsided into whimpers, I saw Michelle marching towards us, straight-faced. *Poor kid*, I thought, *checking on her sister*. But no, Michelle had managed to bottle up her sobs to that point, but as soon as she saw me she burst into tears. At that, the others rebooted.

I cracked a smile and looked up at the sky to hide my laughter.

Soon Joy, her bottom lip shaking, was escorted out of church by her teacher, seeking the rest of the family. This was the first time all three had cried at the same time. I started to wonder if we should thank the priest rather than condemn him.

I had words with the parish priest, and every Mother's Day mass thereafter was dedicated to mothers here, mothers elsc-where, mothers in heaven and mothers to be. My children's tears washed away the clumsy mistake and ensured that no other children at their school would experience this ordeal ever again. Despite these changes, my daughters did not attend these school masses in the future. We discussed it each year and I respected their choice. I really could not imagine the anguish it caused them.

Each year, we slipped their Mother's Day cards into plastic sleeves and placed them either at our home shrine or at the cemetery. Again, I respected their choice.

'We're okay,' shrugged Michelle, 'as long as people stop feeling sorry for us. I hate it when they keep staring at us, as if we're about to fall over, as if they need to catch us.'

'Yeah, I hate sympathy too,' nodded Grace.

Joy looked up at her big sisters, her long eyelashes fluttering as she processed her sisters' words.

That second year, at twelve, eight and five, their combined age was 25 and I, at 41, felt way over 50. I did not want them to grow up too fast. The innocence of childhood must be cherished. And so I ensured that Friday-night tickle-a-thons on my bed became a weekly ritual that ended in heartfelt sighing or someone crying— with laughter.

Just as her mother had always done, Grace screamed at the sight of my wriggling fingers approaching—'Goochi, goochi, goo!' Michelle would roll into a ball like an echidna, while Joy jumped on my back like a marsupial, hoping in vain that she was out of reach. They laughed at each other's unique laughs.

'Stop, Daddy . . . I can't breathe!' panted Grace.

When they crawled under my doona to escape, I would slip off the bed and crawl in from the foot. The drama was enhanced by me singing the 'Duuun-dun' of the *Jaws* theme, faster and faster the closer I got. The pitch of their muffled laughter under the doona would rise ever higher. I would blindly tickle their kicking feet until I felt a whack to my head, at which point we would all emerge from the cave, perspiring and catching our breath. They were probably not the sounds our neighbours expected to hear from our family.

On Sunday mornings, before we went to church, my bed was a family gymnasium. I would lie on my back with my knees bent, then my daughters would take it in turns to grip my hands and 'plank' on the soles of my feet. As I straightened my legs and arms, they would be levitated and we would became a shaky balancing act. When they did lose their balance, they usually fell head first, hopefully on the bed rather than on the floor. They would compete to break the record for the longest suspension in mid-air.

I learnt so much from my father. The selfless love. Taking my children on a *mishwar* (outing). But I also learnt that playtime was precious. My father worked long hours, and I could not remember him ever diving on the floor and rolling around with his eight children. But I do remember that it was something I craved. I saw that his long working hours led to fatigue and little residual energy for us children. Is our parenting style inspired not only by what our parents did, but also by what they *didn't* do?

When my father collapsed on his sofa after work, he stretched his legs. This was our cue when we were children. We raced to be the first to peel his work boots and socks from his tired feet. Strange how they never stank. He would reward the winners with coins and sigh dramatically when his boots thudded to the floor. To us, his sigh was a crowd roaring after a 'touch down'.

I loved how he turned this ritual into a game so I continued this tradition with my own children—except they had to untie my shoe-laces first! When they graduated from shoes, I'd kneel down so they could loosen my shirt-tie. I'd swing the tie in the air like a lasso and cast it aside ceremoniously as I declared, 'Off with the noose! Let the games begin!'

My little family even invented a three-wheel cannon routine. Three of us would lie straight like sardines in a can while one of the girls would lie crossways on top. On cue, we three would roll in unison and the girl on top would be catapulted like a human cannonball, with arms extended forwards. Although we would try to contain the stunt to the 'trampoline' beneath, sometimes 'supergirl' would land on the floor in tears. The sacred space, the matrimonial bed, had become our one-ringed circus for daredevils and acrobats.

Nadia's eyes smiled down on us from the photos on my bedroom wall. Laughter was sacred. And some words were suddenly sacred. Words such as 'wife'. I once nearly bit someone's head off when he accidentally referred to Nadia as my ex. Others who only knew her as Lola's sister faced my wrath too, as I reminded them that she was my wife. Perhaps my stinging tongue pushed people away.

And words such as 'family'. Whenever I heard anyone inviting 'you and the girls', I found myself correcting them with 'You mean my family'. My children would notice but wonder why the fuss. It must have been that narrow eye of the bereaved again. 'But, Dad,' Grace explained calmly, 'you know what they mean.' Grace lived up to her name: she was the peacemaker who liked to keep the temperature down. 'There's no need to be rude,' she would say. 'They were inviting us . . .'

'*Us* is family. We're still a family. You're not orphans. You're not "the girls". You're my daughters.'

I was surprised by my own anger. Was I afraid that something else, something sacred, would be taken from me? 'The girls' themselves, perhaps?

Even though our home felt big to us, it was small compared to most other houses we visited. When we had guests, adults and children shared the one living space. We had bought a single-storey house because by that stage Nadia was already confined to a wheelchair. My children never complained or compared, but I felt them cringe when their friends made snide comments.

'I can ask my mum if we can have your birthday party at my house, if you like,' one friend suggested to Michelle.

It ate at me. 'Did you complain that our house was too small?' I later asked her.

'No!' she replied, offended. 'She just felt sorry for me, and you know how much I hate sympathy.'

I was determined to make our house a home. I invested in a trampoline, a dartboard, a basketball hoop, a swinging chair and totem tennis.

In our back garden, we set up a fountain with the inscription 'Holy Mother, pray for us'. Above it we added an encased shrine housing Nadia's framed photo alongside a statue of Mary.

'This isn't just a house,' I declared while the children watched me turn on the fountain for the first time. 'From now on, we call this our home . . . Michelle, please prepare the incense so we can bless this shrine.'

She was confused, as our incense ceremony was normally reserved for the rooms inside, but I wanted them to see that even the back garden was sacred, especially because the two mothers greeted us as soon as we stepped outside.

Nadia was ever-present, watching over us, surrounded by water and light, not tucked away in some dark corner. We felt that she was a part of us, not apart from us. I even combed through her hairbrush and taped her DNA to the back of her framed photo, as if this would make the shrine even more sacred.

HOW TO HOPE AND PRAY

'Oh, Dad, we clicked straight away.' Grace came home from school all excited about a new girl. 'We have so much in common. She's originally from Melbourne, too.'

'Why did they leave?' I asked. Her parents sounded like potential friends for me as well.

'Oh, her parents split up, so now we both have single parents and—'

'Don't you *ever* say that!' I snapped.

Grace raised a brow. 'Say what?'

'We're not the same. I'm not a single parent. We're not a broken family. *They* stopped loving each other. I *never* stopped loving your mum.' I twirled my gold wedding ring around my finger to remind her that I had never walked away from the sacred vow of marriage.

Grace had never seen me so judgemental. 'O-kay,' she nodded. She saw no point continuing the conversation and left the room.

Moments later, I realised I had overreacted and slapped my forehead. That evening, once I had finished my nightly chores, I went to kiss my children in their beds. I was hoping Grace would still be awake so I could apologise. When I saw her eyes closed and her mouth open, I gritted my teeth, but I kissed her gently on the forehead and whispered what I should have said hours before: 'Sorry I overreacted, Grace. I love you.' I hoped she was only pretending to be asleep.

For many men I knew, 'sorry' was not a word in their vocabulary, as if using it was a sign of weakness. My father, for example, used to apologise indirectly, through action or small talk or humour. But to me, saying sorry is a sign that someone has the strength to deal with the consequences of their words and actions. It would have been hypocritical of me not to say sorry. When I prayed each night with the children, we would talk about the difference between reciting the Lord's Prayer and having a conversation with God.

'What are the three most polite words we say to people we love?' I asked one night.

'I love you?' guessed Joy.

'That's three words. What about one word?'

'Please?' offered Michelle.

'Good girl, Boo-Boo.' I widened my eyes to dramatise my amazement.

'Sorry,' Grace said, quite sure of her answer. Perhaps she *had* been awake when I used that word.

'Yes, Goochi,' I winked. 'And how do you say thank you?'

'Thank you?' repeated Joy.

Her sisters giggled and I rolled my eyes.

'In one word, Zuzu.'

'Thanks?' Joy guessed.

'Exactly!' I celebrated. 'Now, these are the three pieces of the jigsaw puzzle.'

They looked at each other and frowned in confusion. I produced a pen and a printout of the Lord's Prayer.

'You look puzzled,' I smiled, but they were too young for this Dad-pun. I circled three sets of words and wrote our three words in the margin. '"Hallowed be thy name,"' I explained, 'is thanks. "Give us this day" is please. And "forgive us our trespasses" is . . . guess?'

'Sorry!' they deduced.

'So, when you pray, try this: say thanks for something good that happened today, sorry for something bad you might have done, and please for something you're asking God to give you.'

'Easy!' Grace cried, ticking the air with her finger. 'Can I go first?'

'No, me!' Michelle gasped, bouncing.

Joy was tired and playing with her ears, her eyes watery. When she yawned, it was contagious.

'Well, just for tonight, we'll do one each,' I suggested.

'Okay, thanks for . . .' And Grace looked up at the white ceiling for inspiration.

౨

When Joy turned eight, it was time for her Sacrament of Reconciliation and the Eucharist, also known as First Confession and First Holy Communion, respectively. While the 'sorry' sacrament was already familiar to her, this First Communion was challenging for all of us. All the other children had both parents standing behind them. We did not want to attract undue attention, and Nadia's sister Lola was the natural choice, given she cared for my children as if they were her own. By now, Joy's friends all knew that her mother was in heaven. Throughout the service, I felt Nadia's presence and held her hand via the rosary in my pocket.

Joy was beyond cute with her white gown, her floral crown and her wooden cross. When formal photos were taken, I preferred to stand alone behind Joy and leave a sacred space for Nadia.

'I saw you standing alone,' one man said as he approached me outside the church after the photos. 'Brother to brother, can I give you some advice?'

I knew where this was going.

'The girls need a mum,' he continued. 'You need a woman. Trust me, the longer you wait, the harder it will be, and you'll end up a lonely old man. By then, you won't need a wife, you'll need a nurse, or a nursing home.'

I twirled my wedding ring. 'They are not "the girls",' I began. 'They're my family. And they *have* a mum. Her name is Nadia. And our faith teaches us that we never die, but we—'

'Our faith teaches us that marriage ends till death do us part, remember? This is our sacred vow,' he said, flicking his head towards the church behind us. He put his hand on my shoulder. 'My brother went through this,' he continued. 'He waited and waited until his kids got married. Now it's too late. Nobody wants him. And remember—daughters marry into their husbands' families. They change their names.'

I thought of my three sisters in Melbourne and how they had all, for different reasons, ended up with the Wakim surname. My heart was racing. I shook his hand off my shoulder and showed him my wedding ring. 'I love my wife,' I said. 'You're asking me to commit adultery.'

He shook his head, shrugged and walked away.

'There you are, Dad!' called Michelle. 'Who was he?'

'*Haram* (Poor thing), he was confused.' I tried to sound calm. 'He thought I was his brother.'

'Come on. They need you for the group photo now.'

This would complete our family collection—all five of us now had a photo of our First Communion day. We could compare all the knobbly-kneed eight-year-olds at the same milestone moment.

That night, as I lay in bed sleeping, the burning issue of my wedding ring came back to haunt me. Her arms were wrapped around my neck. How I missed her gentle touch! She planted an ice-cold kiss on my forehead and chills ran down my spine. Our embrace tightened. I interlocked my fingers behind her back so she could not melt away.

My cold tingles were replaced by a hot flush. My hands became clammy. I kicked off the blanket and gasped for air. Nadia's arms around my neck were now burning. I was choking and gasping for air.

Then suddenly I could breathe. If this was only a dream, why was my heart pounding so fast? Was I having a heart attack? After all, I was named after my father's father, Yousef, who had died of a heart attack in his sleep not long before I was born, aged 55.

I opened my eyes and it was dark. The alarm clock read 3.33. It was not my neck but my ring finger that was throbbing. Something had changed. I felt my wedding ring in the loose clasp of my right forefinger and thumb. They had twisted it off my finger and now I had caught them red-handed.

I rolled over and I flicked on the bedside lamp. There was a red mark where the gold ring had been for eighteen years. 'Was that really you?' I asked Nadia, gazing around the room. She once joked to me that if I dared to remarry before the children were married, she would visit me in my sleep and strangle me. But I was doing the opposite: refusing to contemplate remarriage.

As I placed the gold ring on the bedside table, the light it reflected was blinding. My ring was my security, the only jewellery I wore. Our matching wedding rings were an engagement gift from my father's oldest brother, Uncle Tanios, in Lebanon.

Without the ring, I felt insecure. I crossed myself, just as I had the first moment I wore it. The Arabic word for wedding ring is *mahbas*, which also means 'prison', but I never felt trapped and never needed to be freed. Was this Nadia giving me her blessing to move on? As if I could ever do that!

'You're testing me!' I protested, waving my finger at the ceiling. Perhaps I outgrew the denial. After four years, her clothes still hung on her side of the wardrobe.

I slid open the door and touched her clothes, then pulled out a denim jumpsuit.

'Aah,' came a familiar voice. 'One of my favourites.'

I saw Nadia's reflection in the mirror. She was sitting on the armrest of the couch in our bedroom. She had her knees up to her chin, her hands on her ankles, and she was rocking back and forth gently. My heart skipped a beat and I held my breath. My gaze froze at the mirror. I knew that if I turned my head to look at the couch, she would be gone, forever, again.

'W-why don't you sit on the couch . . . properly?' I whispered softly to the mirror.

In the mirror, she smiled back. She tilted her head to one side, looking as young and healthy as she had when she last wore that dress.

'Joey, why are you so attached to my clothes?' she asked.

'I'm attached to all of you. But these are waiting . . . for when you come back.'

She smiled. 'I never left you, or our children. Give them to our children.'

'I'm going to. They're not ready for your clothes . . . now, but I'll keep them . . . for later . . . when they grow up.'

'Is my wedding dress there?'

'Of course.' I flicked through the hanging garments and pulled out her wedding dress. 'See?' I held it towards the mirror. 'I even have our wedding cake, with the horse and carriage on top!'

'Remember our wedding day, Joey?'

'How can I forget, especially seeing you glowing like an angel as you walked down the aisle.' I knew in my heart of hearts that she had now walked up a different aisle, glowing, to a reception of angels, but it was so wonderful to speak to her now, as if she were still here, that I didn't want to think about that too much.

'Joey, I see everything. Everything you do. Everything you think. I kiss you all goodnight. Every night.'

'I miss you so much.' I swallowed. 'Can we have a hug?'

'I'm so proud of you.'

'But can we have a . . .' I turned my head from the mirror to the couch. I wanted the real thing, the real touch, and not some reflection. But the couch was empty.

'No, *habibti* (darling)! Please come back. I promise I won't look.'

I searched inside the mirror. Nothing. I held up her wedding dress to the mirror, hoping it might make her reappear. Nothing.

Tomorrow, I would go through her clothes with my daughters, and they could choose and use what suited them now. The rest would wait, in case they grew up and had a change of heart. After all, fashions go in cycles.

HOW TO KEEP THEIR HAIR ON

It was time to progress as a parent from an L-plater to a P-plater, but without an experienced driver by my side. I pretended to know exactly what I was doing.

As I rushed the children to school (and myself to work) every morning, Grace and Michelle quickly learnt to be self-sufficient. I only helped them with their school ties, but like most men I could only do this while standing behind them as if it were around my own neck, not while facing them.

Little Joy needed more help. Grace taught me how to tie Joy's hair in a ponytail and secure it with a hair tie. It took me a while to realise that this morning routine was faster if I put the elastic around my wrist in preparation, rather than trying to reach for it with one hand while holding Joy's hair in place with the other. To my surprise and relief, this did not cut off my circulation and my hand did not turn purple as my mother had once warned. In time, I also learnt that the ponytail looked smarter if I tied it high on her crown; too low and it seemed to sag with gravity as the day progressed.

This was not information I could glean from textbooks. It was more like rock climbing up a cliff face on the *Discovery* channel—there was no time to look down and I was scared of heights.

'Dad!' echoed Joy from the valley below. 'It's not straight!'

I pulled on her ponytail as if it was my climbing rope.

'Ouch!' she cried. 'What are you doing?'

'Straightening it?' I guessed.

I stood behind her, with my head above hers, and looked into the bathroom mirror—which she was too short to look into without standing on tiptoe. Sure enough, this morning's ponytail was slightly off-centre. Rather than redo the entire routine from scratch, I tried to wriggle it to the middle by fiddling with the hair tie.

'Ouch! You're hurting me!' Joy reached back, undid the ponytail and handed me the hair tie to start again.

I tried to defuse her mood and cover my confusion by neighing and imitating a flustered horse—having trouble with a ponytail, see?—but she was in no mood to laugh. How was I supposed to know that you cannot drag a ponytail like a desktop icon without torturing the child?

The solution was staring at me: the water taps. I remembered that Grace and Michelle usually splashed some water on their hair when they were tying it into ponytails or plaits. Water was the gel that gave the hair a defined shape. So that's why Joy's silky blonde curls always ended up making a golden halo!

But I didn't quite get the water thing. I pumped some liquid soap into one hand and added some cold running water, then tried to turn it into a game. 'Have you washed your face, Zuzu?'

No answer meant no, so I gave her a face scrub, also splashing some water on her hair.

'Aagh! It's cold!' she shuddered.

I tempered the water to warm. 'The cold was to make sure you're awake!' I explained, pretending it was deliberate. Then I asked her to blow her nose into my hand, cupping her mucus so it would not squirt all over the washbasin, just like my mother used to do with each of us, lovingly, each morning. She used to say it would unblock our ears so that we would be able to hear the teacher. Now Joy would hear the teacher too.

'Yum! Organic hair gel,' I mused.

'Eeuw!' she protested, grossed out. 'Don't you dare!'

I washed it away with another dollop of liquid soap and now made sure that the sleep was removed from her eyes.

'Aah, Dad!' she cried, pushing my hand away. 'It stings!'

But the more I added warm water, the more the soap bubbled up around her long eyelashes. She squinted in irritation and I kept splashing and rubbing in frustration. Her eyes tightened, her mouth opened and her cries for help echoed throughout our home.

Maternal Grace came charging in. 'What's wrong?'

'Oh, just some soap in her eyes,' I shrugged.

'*Haram* (poor thing). Use the towel, Dad!'

Despite the tears and drama, in the end the soapy water did give Joy's hair a crisper contour and removed the halo. On special occasions, I graduated to plaits and braids, but only once I'd qualified for my hairdressing P-plates. When we shopped together next, Joy and I looked for blue hair ties to match her eyes and her uniform. On weekends, we used her fancier selection, which included ties decorated with butterflies.

When Joy's long hair became knotted, I knew it was time to untangle it with a nice hard brush. I ran a warm bath and added some bubbles, hoping to make it a pleasurable rather than painful experience.

'Turn around, Zuzu, and close your eyes,' I instructed. 'First, we crack the eggs!' I squeezed some shampoo onto her head and lathered it into her scalp with both hands. 'Second, the waterfall.' I poured bucket after bucket of water over her head (warm this time) to wash away the soap.

Then I held her head up with my left hand and brushed her hair down with my right hand. I had expected the shampoo to make the brushing easy, but if anything the knots seemed worse. The only solution, then, was to apply force. But the firmer I held her head, the more she screamed. I gritted my teeth and brushed harder and faster, all the way down, so that her pain—and mine—would be brief.

'Ouch, Dad!' she cried. 'You're killing me!'

I added more shampoo and rinsed thoroughly but it made no difference.

At this point, Michelle rushed in and gasped, 'Grace, have a look at this!'

As Joy heard her rescuers arrive, her cries became hysterical.

'Stop, Dad!' Grace exclaimed. 'Can't you see the red lines down her back?'

I lifted her hair and indeed there were scratches on her back from my vigorous brushing. Luckily, her skin was not bleeding, or I could have been arrested! Maybe our neighbours had heard her screams and already called the police. That's all I needed in my situation! 'But I used heaps of shampoo to make it smooth!' I pleaded innocently, shaking the now nearly empty bottle.

'No! You need conditioner to make it smooth!'

How was I supposed to know this silky-smooth secret? From that day on, Joy's hair would forever be an effortless pleasure to brush. Whenever I washed it, I cracked emu eggs of conditioner on her head.

Was I too paranoid, too protective or too private to take 'driving lessons' from experienced mothers? I could have asked my extended family or many others in the mothers' club who were always obliging. But at the time, I did not want to give anyone any ammunition to gossip about my family. I would imagine them chattering as soon as I walked away, or hung up the phone . . .

'Oh, Joe phoned me the other day. You wouldn't believe what he asked me. He said, "Sorry for the stupid question, but do I use shampoo or conditioner to remove tangles?" So cute, but those poor girls. How will they turn out with only a man to bring them up?' . . . Blah, blah, blah.

Yes, I was probably too paranoid and too private, but I soon learnt not to underestimate the wisdom to be gleaned from the treasures under my own roof—my daughters.

She might have looked like her mother, but Grace was completely unlike her in that she developed a revulsion for anyone touching her feet. Michelle, meanwhile, developed a fetish for using cotton buds in her ears.

'Careful you don't poke too deep,' I warned her one night before bed.

She simply rolled her eyes as if I was stupid for even suggesting she could be that stupid. She had hit double digits and believed she had graduated from childhood. 'How else can you clean your ears?' she asked sarcastically.

'Actually, Lebanese men grow the fingernail on their pinkie so long that it curls up perfectly as a shovel—'

'Eeuw!' Joy covered her ears in disgust.

'—for their ears and even for their—'

'Stop!' they squirmed in unison, utterly grossed out.

'—nose.' I sniggered under my breath.

'You men are so gross,' lectured Grace. 'If I ever see you grow your nail like that, I swear I'll—'

'Do you really think I'd ever do that? Imagine what collects under the nail . . .'

They looked very relieved.

'. . . but it probably tastes amazing,' I added, then ducked to avoid three pillows that came flying towards my head. 'Parent abuse!' I protested. Soon pillow feathers were flying everywhere. It was full-scale warfare, three against one.

It was a mistake to mock our culture if I wanted them to be proud of where they came from, but I hoped my behaviour would have a greater impact than my words.

My little chicks groomed each other and were never embarrassed doing it in front of this rooster, who watched and learned. I had never been curious about my three sisters, but I was intrigued by my three daughters. I looked at my hands and wondered if one of them was becoming more maternal, like the father's in the Rembrandt painting that stared down on me.

Just as I was gaining confidence, a new awkward moment, or hour, would arrive. One Saturday we went to the cinema as a family treat. I bought popcorn, ice creams and Jaffas—we were all set for a perfect afternoon. But ten minutes into the movie, Joy mumbled something about going to the toilet.

'Taking Joy to the bathroom,' I told Grace and Michelle with a confidence that turned out to be unwarranted.

As it happened, there was one tiny problem: this cinema complex had no parent rooms. Joy could not follow me into the men's toilets and I could not follow her into the ladies. So I waited outside the ladies and kept talking to her. 'Make sure you wipe the toilet seat first!'

'I know, Dad.'

'And flush before you—'

'I know, Dad.'

I leant against the wall near the ladies, but it was not a good look. Women gave me sidelong glances as they walked past to use the toilet, so I had to defuse any suspicion. 'Nearly finished?' I called out.

'I don't know.'

Now I wondered if I should run to check on Grace and Michelle, who were unaccompanied in a dark cinema full of strangers. But was it too dangerous to leave Joy alone?

'Finished?' I called.

'The more you ask me, the more you stop me.'

A whole hour passed before Joy finally flushed. It was such a glorious sound that I looked up and sang, 'Hallelujah!'

We caught the last few minutes of the movie together.

'What's wrong with Joy?' asked Michelle.

'Stomach ache,' Joy replied.

'We were worried,' Grace claimed.

'Well, why didn't you check on us?' I asked, wobbling my head.

They shrugged. 'But it *is* cold in here,' Michelle said, rubbing her stomach, her cardigan over her knees. Her growth spurts meant she was hungry every few hours, even after popcorn, ice cream and Jaffas.

Back home, I pulled out the beginner's cookbook my friend Scott had given me. So far I hadn't had to do much cooking. Having Nadia's sister living nearby was a saving grace, especially after school—by the time I picked them up from Lola's after finishing work, my daughters were fed. But it also meant that I was too late to watch and learn how to cook for them.

On weekends, as a last resort, I would find myself phoning mothers with quick questions. Do you boil the rice with the lid on or off? Do you use butter or oil? Why does it turn out gluggy?

It could be awkward when the husband answered. I would ask, jokingly, 'Can I borrow your wife for a minute?' Some would not see the funny side, but others would reciprocate with 'My wife is not for hire! Go find your own woman!'

That evening, spaghetti bolognaise looked pretty easy. I started off slicing and dicing the onions and soon my tears were welling.

'Mmm! Smells good,' smiled Grace. 'How soon?'

'Soon if you help.'

They all did their bit, but how could I be their cooking mentor while wearing L-plates myself? This was the blind leading the blind! I was pedantic about following the cookbook to the letter, using stopwatches and measuring cups. The result, of course, was usually clinical, and lacked the natural feel. Still, it was a start.

When it came to cooking, my mother and big sister Eva became my hotline for help. All my life, these ladies had never encouraged me to learn to cook and I had never shown any interest. Big mistake! My daughters must be encouraged from now on.

As I cried onion tears, my mind fast-forwarded to my daughters' future mothers-in-law.

'Son, how can you marry this Wakim girl? She can't even cook for you.'

Well, maybe I don't *want* my daughter to cook for him. Why can't he cook for her! But then again, she needs to know how to cook for her children, my grandchildren! Panic kicked in.

'Grace, stir the mince. Joy, boil the water. Michelle, pour some red wine.'

'You want a drink?' she asked.

'No, onto the meat. It says so in this book.'

'How much?'

'Just a lid full.'

Michelle was generous. The wine ignited in the pot and nearly singed her hair.

'Too much!' By now I was perspiring.

Grace made a salad. Michelle set the table. Joy lit a candle.

'This reminds me of our cooking show in Melbourne,' Joy said. She was the librarian and historian when it came to family videos and photo albums. She had an inbuilt search engine and a photographic memory. There was indeed a video from the BC era of the three of them hosting a cooking show. Making a salad, actually. Their lines were rehearsed and they wore tall white chefs' hats.

We sat at the dining table, said a prayer of thanks and enjoyed our first homemade meal by candlelight. Grace stood up to switch on the light. Like her mum, she dreaded darkness and loved the light.

'Mmm! *Bellissimo!*' Joy cried, kissing her fingers in keeping with the Italian flavour. She was also imitating Michelle in the home video she had memorised.

'It's the wine,' Michelle said, boasting about her tiny contribution. 'So tasty.'

After her first mouthful, Grace raced to the fridge and returned with the plastic bottle of tomato sauce. 'This will top it off.'

Michelle frowned. 'Dad already put in tomato paste.'

'Can't taste it.' Grace squeezed the bottle in a spiral above her serving.

Soon Joy reached out to copy her sister.

'But I thought you didn't like tomato?' I reminded her.

'This is *sauce*,' she corrected me.

'Read the bottle—*tomato* sauce,' Michelle said. It was what I was about to say, and it felt eerie.

Strange how that first pasta was the best we ever made. Perhaps it was just that our expectations were low. Perhaps we added love, an extra ingredient that was not in the book.

'Now we can invite people over,' Joy said excitedly.

'Just because we can cook one meal?' I laughed.

Maybe they craved coming home to the smell of cooked food. Maybe other kids took this for granted. I wanted to make what Nadia used to cook and I knew they craved Lebanese food. So I promoted myself to P-plates and turned to my Aunt Abla's cookbook. From beef, we learnt to cook with lamb, fish, chicken and even rabbit.

Which brings me to Jasmine . . .

HOW TO LOSE A RABBIT

'Free rabbits.'

It was a paper sign on the pet-shop window, beckoning to us. Joy and I and the shopping trolley with the dodgy wheels stopped in our tracks.

'Can we, Dad?' my helper pleaded, fluttering her spectacular eyelashes around her crystal-blue eyes. 'We always wanted a pet.'

Grace had been craving a puppy for as long as she could remember and had promised faithfully to take care of it herself, but I could not see this happening. In my childhood, we always had a pet dog and pet cat, but there were eight of us children. There was always someone at home to walk and feed the dog. By the time I picked my daughters up from Lola's house each night, it was dark. By that time a puppy back home would have been bored to death and have wreaked havoc.

Just before her cancer diagnosis, Nadia warmed to the idea of a labrador as a placid pet. I figured that a pet rabbit for her children passed the placidity test and would have met with her approval.

Could a pet rabbit be the consolation prize for my children? Sure, it could not fetch a ball, but it had four legs and was exceptionally cute. I certainly was not thinking of the rabbit as a fifth family member that could mitigate their maternal loss. I was just thinking of making our home more exciting and lively for my children and their friends.

'May I help you?' asked the shop owner's daughter. I asked her what we would need at home to look after a rabbit. A hutch, she explained, and hay, a water bottle and a feeding bowl (stainless steel, if you don't mind).

'That's all,' the trained teenager said, then shrugged and handed the grey rabbit to Joy for a cuddle, knowing that as soon as my youngest daughter held the rabbit to her heart, we would have reached the point of no return.

I rationalised it aloud. 'I suppose this will teach my children about responsibility and animal husbandry.'

'Exactly.' The teenager reeled me in effortlessly, and no doubt later boasted about her success with this pushover of a customer.

It soon became clear why the rabbit was free. Free rabbit plus five-minute cuddle plus accoutrements equals—ka-ching!—$150. Joy's smile was worth much more, but a thorny voice in my head still nagged: 'I tried to warn you: if it's too good to be true, there's a catch. But no, you were thinking out loud and drowned me out! Happy now?'

As the teenager swiped my credit card, she asked me if my back-yard was enclosed in case the rabbit escaped.

'But wait—there's more!' cried the sardonic voice in my head.

One hundred and fifty dollars plus a harness, chicken wire and wooden stakes equals . . . $220 . . . All on something that was not even on my grocery list!

In the back seat of the car, Joy nursed a cardboard box in her lap. She was only nine years old but in my rear-view mirror I saw her maternal instincts stirring.

Our homecoming ceremony resembled the entrance of a newborn baby into a family.

'Shh!' Joy insisted that everyone stay quiet to keep the rabbit calm.

But Grace and Michelle were lukewarm about this consolation prize. 'Dad, the whole idea was to have a dog so we could take it for a walk!' Grace reminded me. What she really meant was: 'I've been waiting for a dog since long before Joy was born.'

'Joy has you wrapped around her little finger,' added Michelle, meaning: 'I always help you with the shopping but *I* never get a treat like this.'

I rolled my eyes and ignored their bitterness. 'What shall we call her?' Really, I meant: 'Get over it, girls!'

Once Joy's elder sisters had a turn nursing the so-far anonymous, genderless rabbit, it grew on them. From Michelle's lap, the rabbit crawled up and buried its head in her armpit.

After watching our favourite Disney video, *Aladdin*, we decided to name the rabbit after the princess, Jasmine. None of us could deny the positive effect of this addition to our family.

'It feels so . . . normal,' smiled Joy, stroking Jasmine.

'Normal?' frowned Grace, raising her upper lip.

'Like normal families . . . who have a pet to come home to after school.'

'Since when do we come straight home after school?' Michelle reminded them.

Normal? I thought. *That word should be erased.* 'Thank God we're *ab*normal,' I insisted. 'Normal is boring.'

They turned their heads towards me as if I were abnormal. They had reached the age when peer pressure peaks at school.

When their friends visited, Jasmine was indeed a star attraction. They took turns nursing her.

'She's so nice and warm,' said Grace's friend as she cuddled Jasmine. 'I want to squeeze her.'

She must have over-squeezed.

'Is she normally this warm?' she asked.

I twigged and lifted Jasmine off her lap. The squeezing girl had been sprinkled with freshly squeezed Jasmine piss. A dark patch covered her skirt and my first thought was her pissed-off mother.

'What an irresponsible father!' she would say. 'Imagine letting a dirty animal like that inside his house! I bet his wife would never have allowed it.'

Grace lent her friend some dry clothes while I washed and dried the evidence. But while I fretted, the girls were pissing themselves laughing and rolling on the rug. I was worried they would really piss themselves and then the washing machine cycle would start all over again.

'So sorry,' I confessed to the victim. 'Jasmine isn't toilet-trained yet.'

'Oh, your dad is so cute,' she replied. I was worried she might try to squeeze my cheeks. She seemed quite keen on squeezing things.

The upshot of this incident was that Michelle was permanently grossed out and insisted that Jasmine 'piss off' outside. Each night, Joy hovered above her bunny's hutch, singing lullabies. We even took family photos, with Jasmine taking centre stage.

While Joy honoured her promise to help with the daily changing of water and of the soiled newspaper lining the hutch, I should have known that the excuses would soon begin: 'I'll do it later . . . I've got too much homework . . . But it's still clean . . . Can't someone else do it?'

Great! So now I was sentenced to housewifery inside and animal husbandry outside, happily married to Jasmine the grey-haired rabbit.

We soon realised the real reason Jasmine was a 'free' rabbit. She was wild and probably part of an abandoned litter. On Saturdays, Joy was always excited to take Jasmine out of the hutch and nurse her, but the wild rabbit had no interest in this human affection and would escape to the periphery of our back garden. Joy panicked and gave chase.

'Let her have a stretch,' I suggested from the clothesline to pacify Joy. '*Haram* . . . she's been caged up all this time.'

'Are you sure?'

'Of course. I've had pets all my life, remember.'

Joy brought her homework outside so she could keep one eye on Jasmine, but one eye was not enough. The search and rescue party was mobilised every two hours.

'There she is . . . hiding behind the shrine.' Grace finally spotted her.

Our shrine was a perfect shelter for Jasmine and therefore a perfect impasse for us. She had curled up under the basin of the fibreglass fountain, which contained more than 20 litres of water and was wedged up against a stone wall and another fibreglass rockery. I looked up at Nadia's smiling eyes in the shrine. What must she think of us, poised around her sacred shrine like this, chasing a rabbit, of all things?

Joy tried to lure Jasmine with lettuce from one side while Grace tried to scare her out by making rattling noises on the other. Michelle carried a blanket, poised for the ambush. I was wicket keeper in case the fugitive did a runner. I really hoped the neighbours were not watching our ludicrous backyard cricket match. They did not need to. Hours later, while our exhausted cricket team had a well-earned tea break, a neighbour knocked on our front door, nursing Jasmine.

'Yours?' they asked. The ungrateful traitor looked up lovingly at the neighbour, as if we'd caused our pet to run away from a good home. It reminded me of those awkward moments, back when I was a social worker, when I tried to return runaway children to their family homes. Now I felt like the embarrassed parents who embraced the child and cried: 'We gave her everything.'

The neighbours to our left, right and rear took turns knocking on our door. If you ever want to break down barriers between neighbours, my advice is to get a pet rabbit. Unless your neighbours like rabbit stew!

Jasmine provided free fertiliser for my herb garden of parsley, mint, rosemary and thyme, but the dilemma was that Michelle refused to put anything in her mouth that had been anywhere near Jasmine's rear end.

In a last-ditch effort to create a positive family experience, I googled the harness instructions.

'We're taking Jasmine for a walk!' I announced.

'Where?' asked Grace, raising a brow.

'The neighbourhood, of course.' I frowned as if her question was stupid. Had she not seen people walking their pet rabbits past our house every day?

'On a leash?' Michelle asked, her pitch rising. 'Like a dog?'

'Excuse me, it's a harness.'

Joy cracked a half-smile, appreciating my effort but clearly pitying me all the same. So off we went. Our little procession kept stopping so 'princess' Jasmine could chew grass. And poo. And poo. I tugged on the lead so we could move to the next station.

'Let me take over,' Joy insisted. 'She'll listen to Mummy.'

I shook my head, anxious about Joy's attachment to this creature, and the other girls' inevitable detachment.

Children walking past us had to do a double take. They shook their heads and chuckled. I held my head up with pride, but really I felt like Mr Bean when he casually behaves as if he is the normal one.

No matter how much I tried to sugar-coat the Jasmine affair, it was doomed from the beginning. Her daily abscondings exhausted Joy and broke her heart. She sobbed inconsolably the last time we 'let her go'.

'Aah! That's why they said "Free rabbits"!' I philosophised. 'They *want* to be free!'

My attempt to lighten the mood was greeted by Joy looking daggers at me through her tears. 'Why did she leave us?' she snuffled.

I did not like where this grief was going and worried that we were no longer talking about the rabbit. 'To get married . . . and have babies,' I said flippantly, shrugging to keep the tone light.

'There are no other rabbits around here,' she protested, wiping her tears.

'Of course there are. We live in the Hills and there'll be an . . . Aladdin.'

Years later, a grey rabbit 'lived' under the conifer in our front garden. Its large eyes would shine in my car headlights every time I drove in after dusk. It would not hop away, but always stayed put, 'at home'.

'See, Joy,' I boasted. 'Jasmine had babies and this one decided to live at her *tayta*'s (grandmother's) old house!'

'I'm not a *tayta*!'

'Not you—Jasmine!'

This 'descendant' of Jasmine needed zero maintenance and zero cleaning. We just welcomed her warmly as a free rabbit.

HOW TO PARTY

The menu for my daughters' birthday parties was much more than food. It was activities.

When the children were pre-teens, blindfolding their friends and playing piñata was the highlight of the party. Before we realised we could buy ready-made papier-mâché piñatas in party shops, we used to make them ourselves the night before by filling a balloon with lollies, then inflating it and covering it in layers of glued-up newspapers.

We used a broom handle to smash them. The youngest participants got first go, in case the older ones ended the game too early. An older boy once whacked the piñata so hard that we watched it ascend over our neighbour's fence and onto their clothesline.

Another homemade favourite was blowing bubbles. We would use the eye of a vegetable peeler to inflate a world of colours from dishwashing liquid mixed with water. At first I panicked whenever the bubbles landed on a girl's hair.

'Don't worry, *aammo* (uncle),' she would say, lathering it in. 'Free shampoo!'

But worse things happened when the bubble mixture was left unsupervised. Once, when I went to collect the clear plastic cup and top it up with more dishwashing liquid, it was nowhere to be found. Then I saw a three-year-old with his head thrown back, drinking the last drop of green liquid. It was not a good look.

His lips were green and I saw red. 'Did you drink it all?' Sometimes parents really do ask stupid questions.

'Cordigal!' he gurgled. As the child opened his mouth, a bubble formed between his lips. Smaller bubbles were inflating and deflating from his nostrils. He must have been thirsty, and the green dishwashing mixture in a clear plastic cup did indeed look like cordial.

I remembered from washing Joy's face with liquid soap that water increases froth, so I was reluctant to offer water to this child. As I panicked, I decided that first aid should be mandatory for all parents.

When I confessed the terrible truth to his parents, they exchanged sidelong glances and laughed it off: 'We always wanted to clean his mouth out with soap and water. Thanks a lot!'

Never again would I leave bubble cups in the hands of unsupervised children.

As my children graduated to the next level, we arranged treasure hunts with cryptic clues. 'Royal Air', for example, meant the clue was hidden inside a purple balloon. 'Golden Dozen' meant the next clue was hidden inside the body of a twelve-stringed guitar. There were two winners: the person who collected the most clues and the person who located the final 'treasure'. We even had a quiz with electric buzzers, as in *Sale of the Century*, with questions tailored to the children's age. Then as my daughters moved into secondary school, we decked out our garage as a dance party with sound-sensor coloured lights and a thumping sound system.

This birthday exuberance did not emerge from my own childhood parties, which were centred on birthday cakes. It emerged from my love for my children, and the pleasure it gave me to see them all have so much fun. It did not need space or money, but imagination to make the most of whatever we had.

The partygoers often did not want to go home. Some became such regular visitors that they helped themselves to our food, some of which was named after them. The Salim jar was named after a friend of Michelle's, who always made a beeline to our kitchen for this pottery jar and its never-ending supply of lollies. The partygoers would also 'camp' on our trampoline, lying side by side like sardines and watching the stars.

These parties gave me the perfect opportunity to watch my children and see how they engaged and interacted with their peers. As we packed up the marquees and string lights, we had honest conversations—what adults called debriefs. I would share my observations and ask questions, which gave me great insights into my daughters' moral compass, how they thought about things and what they found attractive.

I would also watch as their friends confided in them, which was often, sitting on the swinging chair as if it were a Freudian couch. Their friends would whisper and gesticulate with their hands, while my daughters would nod wisely.

'Dad, everyone comes to me for advice,' they would say, puzzled. 'I don't know why.'

It seemed cruel of their friends to burden my children, who had lost their mother, with more woes.

'Do they think you'll understand better than others?' I suggested. 'Because of what you've been through?'

Michelle shook her head. 'I love analysing how people think.'

'You're all natural psychologists,' I boasted.

'So you think we take after you?' Grace asked, rolling her eyes.

Even Joy piped up. 'But sometimes I laugh at what they say . . . on the inside.'

'Why?' I asked.

'Because they sulk over the smallest things, like not having the latest phone, or not having matching clothes, or having an argument with their mum.'

The sorority laughed loudly.

I would also watch them mother each other.

'Joy, your best friends in primary school may be completely different in secondary school,' counselled Michelle.

'Why?'

'Because people change. Quiet kids come out of their shell. Loud kids become quiet.'

'And what you have to watch out for the most,' offered Grace, 'are the kids who are the youngest in their family.'

'Why?'

'Because they watch their older sisters, and can act like they're already grown up.'

'Well, I'm the youngest in my—'

'You can't compare,' Michelle waved her hands airily and squinted. 'We just don't want you to copy the kids who are *jihlaneen* (unruly fools).'

﹏◎﹏

When Joy first invited friends to our home for her birthday parties, they were curious about our motherless household.

'Why were they so shy, Joy?' I asked as we took down the streamers.

She shrugged. 'One of my friends asked if we lived like the TV show *Full House*.'

I was vaguely aware of this American sitcom about three daughters raised by their widowed dad, but I also knew that he had his best friend and his late wife's brother move in with him. With three men raising three girls, no wonder the catchy theme song was 'Everywhere You Look'. Although I had no adults move in with me, our small home always felt like a full house. I pitied widowed men who were alone and lonely in an empty house.

My passion for party planning was one of my saving graces. I never wanted to be that miserable man smoking in the shadows. I craved to be as actively involved as my children allowed, without being in their faces.

Paradoxically, these happy occasions brought my saddest moments. Despite my façade of fulfilment, these celebrations always reminded me that someone special was missing. Perhaps this was why I became the go-to party guy and accepted so many invitations to MC happy occasions. I focused on the running sheet and the script, hiding behind the microphone rather than drifting like a lost soul. I was not interested in being paid, as the hosts were inadvertently doing me a favour. It was the best way for me to cope with celebrations.

HOW TO DISPATCH SPIDERS

'Nadia, have you seen my work shirts?' I once asked in the BC era. 'I've put all three in the washing but they never came back.'

There was no answer so I persisted. 'None in the laundry, none on the ironing board, none . . .'

'Check your wardrobe,' Nadia mumbled.

Sure enough, there they were, a mishmash of clothes, washed and dried. They peered at me in silence and humiliation from their prison cell. They were shoved onto a shelf: out of sight, out of mind.

Nadia may have been the domestic queen but she detested the futility of ironing. 'What a waste of time!' she explained. 'As soon as you wear them, they're creased again.'

I rescued them, untangled them, embraced them and ironed them with tender loving care. They spend so much time embracing our bodies, the least we can do is embrace them in return. And so, by default, I was sworn in to the Ministry of Laundry.

Doing the laundry was not one of those chores that required analysis. Or so I thought. I soon discovered that tissues left in pockets add beautiful snowflakes to all the black clothes.

'Girls, how many times have I told you to check your pockets?' I would ask.

The ironing board and I became buddies. In Arabic, it is called *jahash al qawi*, which literally means 'the donkey of ironing'. This is apt—it is a beast of burden, carrying all the weight of the iron and the pressure applied to it. I could relate to this donkey.

Now that it was just me, the marathon cycle of washing, hanging, collecting, folding and ironing became my routine. I would run between the washing machine and the clotheslines, completing the cycle in record time each day. The *Guinness Book of Records* could have created a new category for the domestic 'iron man' competition. I could hang a whole load in two minutes and iron ten garments in three minutes. I even learnt to drip-dry wet shirts on hangers to avoid ironing them later.

'Quick, kids!' I screamed once. 'It's raining!'

They joined my unpegging routine but squealed the whole time. They were more worried about their wet hair than our wet clothes.

As we collapsed inside among a mountain of rescued clothes, Grace panted, 'You are a machine! You looked like those Charlie Chaplain movies, everything in fast motion.'

'When you were a toddler,' I reminded her, catching my breath. 'I'd pop you on top of the clothes in the laundry basket and carry you in.'

'Wasn't that heavy?' Grace asked.

'And dangerous?' frowned Michelle.

'I only did it when your mum wasn't looking,' I confessed in a whisper, 'but you looked so cute, like a chick in a nest.'

My days were soon measured by spin cycles instead of sun cycles. If I could manage three cycles on a Saturday, it felt like I had earned a siesta.

On a windy Melbourne day in the BC era, I looked up at the

rustling leaves and widened my eyes. 'Let's go fly a kite!' I quoted, and we sang that song from *Mary Poppins*. As I skipped, my children stayed behind to dissociate themselves from the most embarrassing dad ever.

On a windy day in Sydney, I now heeded the call of the rustling leaves and sang out: 'Let's go hang all the bed sheets!'

My daughters could not hold back their laughter. 'Are you seriously excited?'

No, I was not becoming a clean freak, but the totally white house exposed every spot and belied all my hard work. Every Saturday I would hang out with the other clean-freak men, Mr Sheen and Handy Andy.

As my daughters stepped up to the Ministry of Laundry, my portfolio expanded to include Homeland Security, Defence, Border Protection and Foreign Affairs. And who was the foreign invader? Spiders, of course, those indigenous critters that have been here much longer than we have.

The way my daughters shrieked, you would swear there was a knife-wielding intruder in the house, like in the shower scene from *Psycho*. If the spiders could have heard it, they would have died of deafness on the spot.

'Dad! Quick!' screamed Joy. 'A *ginormous* spider!'

I ran into the bedroom and found Michelle and Joy standing on their beds, knees knocking, but no evidence of a spider. 'Where?' I asked, peering high and low.

They pointed to a tiny black spot crawling on the upper architrave of the window between their two beds. This poor spider had no hope of camouflage in our white house.

I hated killing innocent creatures, especially as we had invaded their territory in the Hills Shire. I pretended not to see this 'ginormous' spider. 'Where?' I asked again.

By now, they were jumping up and down on their beds. 'Just kill it . . . with a shoe or something . . . quick!' Michelle was hysterical.

'Oh, *that* tiny creature?' I said, pointing to the black dot. '*Haram*, it's doing exactly what we're doing: seeking a home, shelter and food.'

'*Yalla* (hurry up)! It's not funny.'

'But it's probably someone's mother and . . .'

'Quick, Dad, before it moves!'

I grabbed a couple of tissues, took off my shoes and mounted the bed.

'Sorry, Mrs Spider,' I said, 'but my children . . .' As I reached out to grab the animal with the tissues, it panicked and ran down the architrave towards Joy's bed.

Joy's eyes widened and she flung herself across the room to Michelle's bed. Amazing how much power we can muster when we're running for our lives! Now both of them screamed and huddled on Michelle's bed. I did not understand why they did not just leave the room instead. I presumed they would not trust my death certificate. They needed to be sure that the spider was gone.

'There's no way I'm sleeping there,' Joy announced, pointing at her bed. 'Dad, I'm sleeping in your bed tonight.'

Now I really was ready to kill this spider. If it was a choice between Joy's knees in my back all night or one dead spider, there was no contest. I crawled after it, on the floor, under the bed, armed with . . . tissues! I hunted it down and caught the critter, alive.

I emerged from the war zone under the bed, victorious and festooned with dust. I was careful not to squeeze so that I could release the spider outside and spare it from murder by toilet-flush.

When I approached with the culprit, shrouded in white tissues, they screamed and pressed themselves against the wall.

'Just get rid of it!'

I swung the front door open and flung the tissues into the nearest tree so the spider would have a chance of survival.

'No!' yelled Michelle. 'Now it will come back!'

'Along with thousands of others.' I teased her. 'It will tell its relatives on the "web" that we're hospitable people and—'

'And post it all over Facebook!' Michelle answered sarcastically with her fists on her hips. 'They'll say they should all have a party here because there's no death sentence! Great!'

'That's not very Maronite,' I frowned. Our Catholic faith entails respect for all creation.

Joy laughed at my response, which seemed to her completely random. 'What the heck have spiders got to do with being Maronite?'

I learnt to recognise each daughter's unique scream for different creepy-crawlies. And that the higher the pitch of their screams, the larger the size of the invaders. By listening carefully to these alarm codes, I would know just which ammunition to bring: tissue, shoe, spray or towel. Sometimes the tactics required were sophisticated, especially those for the tiny monsters hovering around the kitchen downlights. The ambush was a five-point plan: turn off the lights above the kitchen bench; turn on another light, away from the food preparation area, as a lure; spray like there's no tomorrow; watch them fall; mop up the mess. As the winged targets spiralled downwards, I made the sound effects of falling planes and explosions to satisfy my daughters that the mission had been accomplished by their Defence Minister.

Whatever you might be thinking, I did not secretly and hypocritically relish these heroic feats of death and destruction. But my daughters seemed simply unable to share our space with creeping, crawling, flying animals. Apparently, moths were always *chasing* my daughters personally, not just spiralling towards the light.

Cockroaches elicited a high C or even C sharp, but I always preferred to capture and release them.

'Eeuw, Dad! Just whack it with your shoe!'

'And release the babies?' I warned them.

A large spider hanging around in the shower was their pet hate, as if being naked rendered them more vulnerable.

When this innocent spider landed in the sink, it was tortured to death by boiling water and we watched it shrink. I was overcome with guilt for this primeval cruelty. In our family, the adrenaline response from my daughters was flight, leaving me to fight.

As I turned the hot water off, all three girls would lean in over my shoulder (at what they judged a safe distance) to confirm the cremation. Their pose as they did this—with extended limbs, elongated fingers and hairs standing on end—made them resemble the spider itself. Do arachnophobes ever see themselves in the mirror and scream?

One time, just as they were about to heave a collective sigh of relief, one of the spider's legs had a spasm and the screams blasted my eardrums. I sympathised with the spider and rolled it up in toilet paper to preserve its dignity. I tossed the entombed creature into the toilet, flipped the lid shut and depressed the half-flush button. But this was still not enough to satisfy the arachnophobes.

They ordered me to reopen the lid, then resumed their spider pose. What a sight it must have been for the spider looking up at this oval portrait of humanity: eight eyes glaring into the toilet bowl.

The tissue was gone but a couple of legs appeared to be wriggling on the surface. I blocked my ears in anticipation and recalled the opening scene of *The Party*, where Peter Sellers plays a bugler who is repeatedly shot but refuses to stop playing.

I applied the full force of the double flush. The end.

I could not understand how assertive young women could be reduced to a cowering heap in the face of a hairy visitor when they were already living with someone who wasn't exactly hairless.

But I was no man of steel. The real iron man of my life was my father, Jalil. He worked with iron and even had an iron rod in his leg after a near-fatal accident. Before he obtained his driver's licence, he was picked up each day on Heidelberg Road, Clifton Hill, just after the overpass, by a work colleague. On the fateful day, he was waiting there at dawn as usual, and thought he saw the car pulling in. He stepped forward but the car kept swerving without stopping and my father was thrown many metres by the impact. It was the wrong car and the driver had fallen asleep. My father saved a life that day—that driver could well have collided with a tree, but instead he hit my father and survived.

Jalil was a jack of all trades, nicknamed Jimmy-Fix by his work colleagues because of his fearless approach to all challenges. As a rigger for engineering contractors, he needed to move heavy machinery safely. With his biceps and barrel chest, he had the physique of a weightlifter, but his real specialty was his green finger. He was the 'tree whisperer' and believed that if you talked to the trees sweetly, they would bear delicious fruit. He learnt about grafting and gardening from his father, Yousef, and had hoped to pass on this green wisdom to his eight children.

From all that I had heard about my grandfather Yousef, a humble and gentle soul, I wished I were his reincarnation. But I showed no interest in horticulture in the BC era. Why bother, I thought, when the local supermarket could provide everything we needed.

Nevertheless, shopping for my family on my way home from work now took its toll. In the first place, I struggled to open the plastic shopping bags at the supermarket. I tried rubbing, blowing and even asking strangers. Then the bags sliced my hands as I carried them from the car to my front door. While juggling not only the shopping, but also my workbag, the mail, my lunchbox and the car keys, I could not open the door. The only way I could use my keys was to drop the bags, but I had a perfect grip on them all and it was only twenty more steps to the kitchen. Working in logistics, I was averse to 'double handling' if an action could be performed once instead.

I tried to use my nose to ring the doorbell. That sardonic voice in my head laughed. 'Your hereditary nose may be larger than life but it is still soft tissue, you fool!' When it finally worked, the chimes were music to my ears.

'I ran out of hands,' I panted to my daughters when they finally opened the door.

Was I trying to be a heroic father or was I just a glutton for punishment? My daughters did not see this as superhuman but as super-stupid. As I carried the bags inside my darlings barely batted an eyelid. They were far too engrossed in something on the television.

As the minister for everything outside the house walls, taking out the rubbish bins was my domain. This meant that if the kitchen bin was full, my daughters would rather spend ten minutes squashing its contents to a pulp to make more room than take two minutes to carry the full bag outside—the dreaded wilderness where they would be attacked by killer spiders!

'Dad, do you seriously want me to ruin my back and carry something heavy?' quizzed Michelle, as if this were not about her gender but about me being a gentleman. She had been a tomboy until she was about thirteen, but she now drew the line at physical work.

'Look at my bones and look at your bones!' she would protest.

'But, Michelle, I do men's *and* women's work so—'

'You can't compare. You're a parent!'

We soon grew to detest the tasteless supermarket specials and to pine for homegrown organics from my father's farm, especially the *jiddo* (grandfather) salad. We named it after my father, who made it by mixing fresh green herbs such as thyme, mint and oregano with a pinch of salt, pomegranate syrup and a drizzle of olive oil. The salad looked plain but the taste lingered all day. What a contrast it presented to the picture-perfect strawberries that looked juicy-red but tasted like cardboard.

I struggled to remember the seeds my father had sown in us about planting trees, then how to prune them and when to fertilise. It must be there somewhere in my memory vault, even if I had not been listening consciously. I hungered to learn about harnessing nature. My beloved Bible was rich in garden metaphors about vine branches, mustard seeds, olive trees and fig trees, but it was not a gardening manual. Was it too little, too late? Nothing beats the tactile lessons of working with your father while he looks over your shoulder. Now I wished he had *made* me learn.

The only solution was a trip to the nursery. A lemon tree was essential, especially as my children loved extra lemon on their tabouli. The olive tree, too, was important. They are sacred for Maronites. We pickle the olives, of course, but we also use the olive branches for the Palm Sunday Hosanna procession at church. Almonds, especially *lawz akhdar* (raw green almonds) are a treat in our culture. They are a family favourite, so I planted two almond trees in our Sydney garden. I whispered to them in Arabic, on behalf of my father. I love dipping green almonds in salt and washing them down with an icy-cold Corona beer. The bitter-salt-sour cocktail ignites my tastebuds. In my family of eight children, I think it was me who craved green almonds the most.

An overdose caused annual constipation, but was worth every minute, or hour. It was nothing that some pears, which were in season at the same time, could not fix. They were always on standby as the natural antidote.

During the BC era when we lived in Melbourne, I mapped out which almond trees in our multicultural neighbourhood had branches hanging over the fence. After work, in the dark, I would blitz them all, standing on front fences, ripping my trousers on thorny rose bushes, jumping to reach whole branches and escaping the jaws of barking dogs. But I stayed focused on my mission: to feed my family and secure another generation of Lebanese tastebuds.

At home, Nadia saw my pockets bulging.

'Come on, kids, check my pockets,' I said, beckoning them to me.

Grace emptied my front pocket of a dozen green almonds and squealed in pleasure.

'Well done, Goochi. Your turn, Boo-Boo.'

Michelle reached into the other pocket and extracted another dozen. Nadia's eyes lit up and she grabbed a cereal bowl.

'More pockets!' I challenged them.

Joy was still a toddler and had never seen these green treasures before. Grace and Michelle pursued the treasure hunt, ransacking every other pocket: back of pants, jacket pockets, shirt pockets. Nadia licked her lips and replaced the cereal bowl with a salad bowl. We feasted into the night on this 'forbidden fruit'.

Now, as the annual almond season arrives each October, it also marks our wedding anniversary. For me it has become a bittersweet time.

I think of almond trees as a cross-pollination of my wife's and my father's personalities. He often said, 'The more you pick its fruits, the more it feels loved, and the more generous it will be next season.' Nadia often said, 'Let's sit in the shade of the tree and invite friends over to celebrate together.'

But sometimes I sacrificed these pleasures in her honour, rather than celebrated them. If the celebration reminded me too much of her, I felt guilty enjoying it without her.

HOW TO ROCK

All this time since Nadia's death, I had been making a sacrifice to her memory. It was my daughters who pointed out that this was only hurting us, that I had sawn off a limb I needed in order to function.

As one of eight children, my immigrant parents could not afford to buy us brand-new toys. But there was one thing I craved like a missing limb: a magic wand with six strings that could make you sing, scream, cry, dance or sleep.

One Saturday morning at the age of eight, I woke up inspired by the story of Noah receiving instructions to build the ark. From our back shed, I seized a wooden fruit box. Long before massive supermarkets, my father bartered for boxes of fresh fruit for our family from Victoria Market on Saturday mornings. He carried these wooden boxes back to his station wagon on his shoulders and drove them home. He would set aside the wooden boxes as firewood for our bread-baking days in the homemade *fourn* (wood-fired oven for Lebanese bread).

Knowing my father was at the market as usual, I grabbed his hammer and his bucket of nails clinging to a large horseshoe magnet. I seized the three prized fishing rods that belonged to my big brother Bass. It was time to build my own magnet, a musical one.

Using the hammer, I carefully removed one cubit (Noah-speak for the length of a forearm) of wood for the guitar neck and the thicker headpiece of the box for the guitar body. I nailed the body and neck together neatly from behind, so that no nails could be seen from the front. For the tuning keys, I banged six flat-headed nails into the end of the neck at equal intervals, and another six on the body as the bridge.

I extracted two cubits of fishing line from each of the three reels. I cut off the hooks and sinkers but I did not know how to thread them back on. I wound these strings in order of thickness on my unfretted contraption. Of course, I was in big trouble from Bass for destroying his rods. And of course, my homemade guitar sounded ghastly.

It did, however, catch the attention of a family relative, who made me a gift of my first real guitar: a Yamaha nylon-string for beginners. I polished it and rushed to the local library to borrow books on how to play guitar. How else was I supposed to learn for free in 1970? Each day after school, I would hurry home, close the bedroom door, pull the guitar out from under my bed and unleash melodies from an unknown place within me. My guitar *did* become my magnet—for making friends.

On my first trip back to Lebanon in 1988, I heard Nadia's angelic singing voice and the rest was history. Music became an inextricable part of our lives together, and of our family life.

Music served a more medicinal purpose for Nadia after her diagnosis. After each singing session, she would sigh with a hand on her heart and say, 'Joey, when I sing, I forget that I'm sick.' When every faculty in her body eventually shut down, only her voice remained untouched. Nadia was blessed with a soprano voice that rose above all mortal pain.

But when her voice stopped singing, my guitar stopped playing. For the first four years of my widowerhood, my guitar stood in the corner of the lounge room as a relic of my past, gathering dust. It had become a silent shrine to a life gone by.

And then one day, as we were spring-cleaning, eight-year-old Joy started an interrogation through her missing front teeth: 'Dad, what's happening with this guitar? You used to play it every day, but now—'

'Now it's history for me. Did you want to learn to play it?'

'But why have you stopped?' Michelle was now twelve and squinted as she read my facial expressions.

I sighed and stared at the guitar. 'Sometimes you feel good when you make a . . . sacrifice,' I said, nodding to reassure myself.

They frowned as none of this 'survivor guilt' made sense to them. I tried to explain it by referring to one of our favourite movies. 'Remember *The Sound of Music*? Remember the dad, Captain von Trapp? Remember how he stopped everyone singing in his home because it reminded him of his wife?'

My head was spinning as I stared into the round sound hole of the guitar. As I gazed, it became a vortex, carrying me back into the past. I heard echoes of Nadia's voice singing 'I Will Survive' and realised it had all been a lie. I smelt the popcorn at the parties where I had played and she had sung. I saw her flamenco dancing as I strummed Gypsy Kings songs. All of it was captured deep inside that dark circle. Then I heard the quick clicking of fingers, but it had no rhythm.

'Dad? Hello, Dad!' Grace called, clicking her fingers to snap me out of my spell.

I peered up at her face and was reminded once more just how much she looked like her mother. At fifteen, she was even Nadia's height. 'Dad,' she asked with wisdom beyond her years, 'do you really think it makes Mum happy to make yourself unhappy?'

'What do you mean?' I felt cornered now.

'Mum was happy when you played guitar . . . and she knew it made you happy.'

Michelle planted the dusty guitar in my lap. 'Play, Dad!'

Joy coughed at the dust but Grace was determined to checkmate me: 'You've always said that our talents are God-given gifts.' Just like her mother, Grace always stayed anchored to logic, centred by her moral compass.

Like me, the strings were rusty and out of tune. It felt so familiar yet so foreign. But the wooden neck of that guitar became a bridge that helped me cross over from my past to my future.

'Pretend you'd given it up for Lent, Dad, and now Lent is over,' Michelle said, trying to unknot my guilt. When did these girls of mine get so wise?

'Look, your mum and I were a team. I'd play while she'd sing. It's not the same without her.'

'*Ya Allah* (Dear God)!' sang Grace in irritation, slamming her hand onto her forehead, imitating her teenage cousins in Lebanon, who in turn imitated their parents.

'But Michelle plays piano and *dirbakki*,' Joy reminded me. It occurred to me that Joy was now the same age as I was when I started playing guitar. There seemed to be something poetic in her egging me on to restart now.

I was pleased that they were all headstrong girls with an answer for everything, but I had never expected them to confront my own hypocrisy. We made a pact: 'I'm happy to play music again,' I conceded, 'so long as it starts with you, my family.'

Just like her mother, Michelle sang perfectly in pitch, sweetened no doubt by a honey-dipped dummy when she was a baby. She introduced me to a classmate who was an aspiring drummer. We three secretly practised a surprise song, Evermore's 'Light Surrounding You', for Joy's First Holy Communion. It had the perfect chorus for the girl with the golden halo and indeed for our family. In honour of our pact, 'Grace on bass' was next in line. I taught her from scratch and the deep instrument suited her solid personality.

'No offence,' suggested the drummer, 'but my sister is an awesome singer.'

I love how 'no offence' gives kids permission to say something offensive. I sang but I was not a singer, apparently. Our drummer's sister was a classmate of Grace's, so I figured that two sets of siblings still made us a 'family band'.

Joy was too young to join us but was dubbed our 'manager', as she decided which songs qualified for our repertoire and which clothes we wore on stage. We called our five-piece band The Heartbeats, because life is a free gift that starts and ends with a heartbeat.

The band took our family relationships in a new direction. On stage, in the garage rehearsals and in the recording studios, we were equals and all musical ideas were equally valued. Even their friends called me Joe. Only when we re-entered our home did I become the parent again.

During an ABC radio interview for *Life Matters* in November 2007, we were compared with the Partridge Family, from the television show of that name where a widow forms a family band and they go on tour in a bus. Perhaps music was a part of *their* grief, too. We launched the band at a sellout concert at Parramatta's Riverside Theatre on 16 April 2008, and produced several studio recordings of our original songs.

We were often asked how it felt to play music together. This was our answer. My daughters enjoyed engaging with me at a time when teenagers and parents often drift apart. I enjoyed having their feedback on my songs, as teenagers are the biggest consumers of music, and their responses were honest. They were excited when I played classics such as 'Stairway to Heaven' and even more excited if I could teach them a riff they could later play to their peers.

'So, Dad, what were the big hits in your day?'

'In my day?'

'Yes, when you were a teenager.'

'Let's get something straight. My day is now. Every day is my day.'

Michelle rolled her eyes, embarrassed in front of her friends. 'He's in denial,' she whispered indulgently. 'Midlife.'

'I heard that!'

Their laughter exploded. 'Well, it's true!' Michelle laughed. 'Some men buy their dream Harley Davidson. You buy your dream guitars.'

'Rubbish!' I retorted. 'I've always had them.'

Maybe I *was* in denial, though. When I first started playing again I had four guitars and now I had eight: nylon-string electric, twelve-string, bass, semi-acoustic, and a wallet full of plectrums! *Vroom, vroom*, squealed the guitar through a raunchy valve amplifier.

They were embarrassed when I 'moved too much' on stage, so I asked them to move much more, but of course teenagers are too cool for that. I admit that it must have looked weird, though—a father in his forties 'rocking' on stage with his teenage daughters.

Sadly, our family pact could not last forever. As Grace approached Year 11, her school workload became too demanding for her to spend time rehearsing and playing with the band. My parental voice trumped my musical passion—I did not want her to feel guilty about leaving the band.

In the lead-up to the Year 10 school talent quest, Michelle auditioned with a group of *dirbakki* players as a high-energy percussion ensemble. A week before the contest, an older student remarked that it was 'weird' for a girl to play *dirbakki*. Michelle came home and put away that drum. Forever. Just like that.

I was furious. 'Who cares about her opinion, Michelle? Since when were you affected by peer pressure?'

She stared at me, offended. 'Me? Peer pressure?'

'Michelle, you're so talented. You've been playing since you were three. It's natural. It's God-given. It's . . .'

She raised the palm of her hand, looked down at the floor, and did not want to discuss it. Apart from her school uniform, I could not recall ever seeing Michelle in anything other than jeans. From that day on, though, the jeans were replaced by dresses. Did the caterpillar really have to die so tragically for this butterfly to emerge from the chrysalis?

Once my daughters were too busy to take part, the 'family' band evolved. As young friends who loved the music stepped in, the mirror told me to step out. My daughters never lost their love of listening to music. When Michelle sings, we sometimes think it is the radio—singing in tune is her effortless inheritance. We secretly recorded Grace singing 'My Heart Will Go On' in the shower, where she sings her best. We played it back as blackmail—until she realised she sounded 'damn good' and it became a hollow threat. When I reminded her that this was her mother's favourite shower song, Grace was gobsmacked. Joy refuses to shower without her iPhone blaring her favourite songs, although she does not sing along. When the three sing together, it is a sight to behold. They are so animated that they don't need to use hairbrushes as microphones. They even videoed their teddy bears singing and dancing to their favourite Beyoncé songs.

My daughters honoured their side of our musical pact and we have permanent recordings that prove this was not a dream. They taught me that a sacrifice is not necessarily what you forsake, but what you offer in an act of love.

HOW TO DO THE MORNING SCRAMBLE

Sick days? Mondayitis? Sleep-ins? Not me. Not in my home. How would the children get to school without Dad the driver?

There was no school bus from our area to their school, as most of the students lived south of Kissing Point Road, not in our leafy Hills Shire. The families we befriended through the school were parochial. When we invited them to our house, they insisted that we lived 'too far away', so we went to their house instead.

It was Nadia who insisted on our children attending the mono-cultural Maronite College to round out their education with a good grounding in their faith and the Arabic language. She believed they would appreciate other cultures and faiths when they had a solid understanding of their own.

For me, the radio switching on as the 6.20 alarm went off sounded like the starting pistol for a race. With one bloodshot eye wedged open and one ear tuned to ABC Radio National to hear about the latest score in some war or the latest drive-by shooting in Sydney, I would sit up and start the day. I had to listen to the radio first thing—I had no time for reading newspapers or watching television.

On your mark—get set—go! On autopilot I would stagger to the girls' three beds to wake them up. Yes, I was their personal alarm clock. I would try to sound firmer than a snooze button but gentler than a news bulletin.

'Joy, Joy, time to wake up, darling,' I would whisper close to her ear. If she squinted, that was a good enough sign for me.

Knowing it would take an hour for a full laundry cycle, I would load the washing machine with darks or lights and hope there were no 'hand wash only' garments tangled up in the mix. As the motor ran, so did mine. Time for a shave, shower and sh—. I would quickly lather the shaving cream over my face and apply the razor blades against the grain. If there were no footsteps coming from the bedrooms by this stage, it was time for level two.

I would return to my sleeping beauties, stamping my feet and toughening my tone. 'Wake up *now* or we'll be late.' If that didn't work, the sight of me probably did the trick: a hairy man, standing in his underwear, with shaving cream on one side of his face. I should have uttered 'Ho, ho, hurry up!'

With this daily ritual of running back and forth to the shower, I sometimes did not finish shaving but would not realise this until I was halfway to work. I would spend the rest of the day hoping no one noticed but unable to stop rubbing that annoying rough patch. In the spin, I sometimes started to brush my teeth a second time and only realised it when I noticed the brush felt wet. For me the mirror was something I passed by, not a picture frame in which to pose.

If, after my shower, anyone was still snoring, it was time for the military level three: lights on, doona lifted, voice raised: 'Seven o'clock, breakfast bench!' I almost expected to hear a 'Sir, yes, sir!' I certainly expected to hear marching feet.

I had worked out that we could only make it to school by 8.20 if they were seated for breakfast by seven. The breakfast bench was indeed my mission control, with me standing to serve on the drawer side, and the three students sitting on stools in height order on the other. I dished out their needs like an athlete on steroids to ensure the pace did not slacken.

'Spoon please, Dad.'

I obliged instantly.

'Not that spoon, the smaller one.'

I rolled my eyes, snatched the wrong spoon and slammed down the right one with a sigh.

Cereals were easy, but Grace preferred *za'atar* (a herbal mixture of oregano, thyme, sumac, sesame seeds and olive oil) on toast and as a topping in her *'aaroos* (Lebanese bread wrap). I passed on the Lebanese folklore my father had imparted when I was a child: '*Za'atar* zaps your brain and boosts your intelligence.'

'We know, you've told us a hundred times,' they muttered.

But I persisted. 'Always have some for breakfast before a—'

'Maths test, we know.'

Their monotone contrasted with my melody. Was it just that I am a morning person, or was I the rooster crowing to wake up the chicks? Their brains seemed to wake up two hours after their bodies. Once one yawned, it was contagious. They would stretch their clenched fists and nearly knock each other off their perches.

'You can't wake up any later, so you should get to bed earlier,' I counselled.

'What's the point of going to bed if I can't sleep, just staring into—' they began.

'Wrong answer!' I interrupted. 'The correct answer is "Yes, Dad".'

They rolled their eyes and sighed. 'Wrong answer?' laughed Michelle. 'Is this a game show?' She stretched again and cracked her joints to wake herself up.

'Snap, crackle, pop!' I teased her. 'It'll give you arthritis.'

'No, Dad, I researched it,' she rebutted. 'Like most of what you say, it's an old wives' tale.'

Old wives' tale? Did I *look* like a housewife to them?

To their credit, my daughters learnt early on to make their own school sandwiches. Joy was so addicted to a Nutella *'aaroos* that I invested in a 5-kilogram jar. When she reached the bottom, she emerged with chocolate elbows.

Michelle teased her: 'If I squeezed you, Nutella would ooze out of your ears!'

While they rushed off to do their hair, I would do the dishes. By then, the washing machine would beep, the starting pistol for sprinting outside with a laundry basket. It would usually become a pegging relay—invariably, one of the girls would take over so I could clean up inside.

That was unless, of course, they were having a bad hair day, a concept I never understood. Two strokes of the brush through my hair was enough for me to look neat—if I remembered to brush it at all. They talked about it as if hair wakes up and announces with an evil laugh, 'Today, I'm going to be *bad*!' I would hear their irritation as I sprinted past their bathroom. 'Grrrr! I *hate* my hair!'

Michelle sometimes tamed her wild fuzzy curls with her favourite navy headband.

I made sure we left the kitchen spotless, every inch wiped clean, each morning. Michelle would mutter as we finished, 'I'm already exhausted before I even get to school. Some of my friends live on the same street as the school, and they literally wake up five minutes before the bell.'

She was right, it was unfair. It was cruel that they were so exhausted, but even though I felt so sorry for them, I never wanted them to feel sorry for themselves. Sometimes, when I had no consoling words, it was better to remain silent. But other times, I could not resist gleefully invoking the threat of the creepy-crawlies they so abominated: 'If we don't clean up, cockroaches will come!'

As they loaded the car with their brick-heavy schoolbags, I checked that all the lights were out and the windows locked. I was always more worried about burning down our home than someone breaking in, as we did not have much to steal.

'Did you turn off the hair straightener?'

'Yes, Dad. And it's safe anyway.'

'Are you sure?'

'Yes.'

'What about the iron?'

'I think so.'

'Are you sure?'

No answer. I would turn back at the roundabout and return home to double-check.

Whoever was having a bad hair day would fight for the front passenger seat so they could use the mirrors—and leave hairpins in my car for the next victim.

We worked out that the trip to school was exactly long enough to recite the five decades of the rosary. We did this especially in October, the month of the rosary on our Catholic calendar. If the traffic was slow, we would add our personal prayers at the end, using our 'Thanks . . . Sorry . . . Please . . .' formula. If the traffic was fast, we never left the car until the rosary was complete.

In the other months, my daughters would flick through the radio stations to hear the latest popular music. It would have been hypocritical of me to criticise this, because 'back in my day' I did the same thing to listen to the top 40 hits. Perhaps I had been naïve, but I did not recall the radio presenters having R-rated chats between songs back then. Now the hosts would laugh about nude photos of celebrities, starfish lovers, swingers, adultery, genitals, Viagra and condoms so often that my children became desensitised to radio pornography.

Marriage and fidelity were not sacred for some announcers. Weddings were all about show. The amoral messages pumping out of my speakers and into my children's ears clashed with the moral messages being instilled in them by our church, their school and me.

Soon my left hand was poised to change radio stations, like the beep button for censorship. 'If you don't like it, change channels!' the radio hosts laughed. The problem is that all the hit songs target teenage consumers but the radio programs playing them target adult commuters.

When I was exposed to the same songs over and over again, I soon discovered that the lyrics were as pornographic as the radio announcers, but hidden behind metaphors such as 'blow my whistle'. I will refrain from giving you any more examples.

'The lyrics are disgusting!' I cried, switching channels.

'Dad, we're not even listening to the words. I love the beat.'

The beat? Did they mean *doof doof*? Perhaps it was a way to wake their bodies up. Give me Pink Floyd, U2 or Coldplay any day. At least their songs have melody and meaning—and real guitars, not some 'DJ X FT (featuring) rapper Y'. I glanced at my angry face in the rear-view mirror: was this ageing rock guitarist becoming conservative? My daughters even talked slang like the rappers. They murdered the letter 'T', saying wha' instead of what and go' instead of got. I offered five cents for each time they pronounced the endangered letter 'T'.

As the front-seat passenger kept changing radio stations, searching for songs instead of chatter, all I could hear was non-stop dirty talk, even though the radio promo promised non-stop music. 'Do you go for bums or boobs?' one announcer asked. 'What are you like in bed?' Charming!

The girls kept changing stations. Beep . . . beep . . . beep . . . As the radio frequency increased from 96.1 to 106.5, so did the temperature on my mood thermometer. In frustration, I turned the radio off and offered age-appropriate games instead.

'Make up a three-word sentence with the letters on the number plate in front of us . . . now!'

'You mean SKM?'

'Exactly. It's an acronym for?'

'Small . . . kittens . . . meow?'

'Perfect! That's another five cents.'

CDs and iPods rescued me from the radio porn. Their mobile phones plugged into the sound system and 'DJ Joy' finally delivered 'non-stop music'. I reminded my daughters that 'back in my day', I made mix tapes of my greatest hits collection by taping them onto cassette from the radio.

What I really craved with my captive audience was conversation, but they were never in the mood that early in the morning. For them the music probably numbed the pain of waking up so much earlier and working so much harder than their peers.

They soon outgrew the kiss goodbye.

'Bye!' Slam.

'I love you too!' I would call out after them, laughing because I wanted to cry.

I watched from the car as their friends saw them coming and waited for them. I watched as they were embraced. I watched them behave as if they were normal, to hide their abnormality.

'Hands up those who have washed dishes, hung clothes and wiped benches before leaving home this morning,' I imagined their teacher saying to the class.

To add to the cruelty, I discouraged sick days unless my children were bedridden. There was no one home while we were all out, and

I did not want to lean on anyone. Besides, I wanted to prepare them with good habits for the real world, where reliability and punctuality matter.

By the time I reached my office, I had completed a two and a half hour marathon. I probably clocked up 400 metres just sprinting between the rooms of the house and the backyard. I know many working mothers will smirk and say, 'Welcome to my life!' but it came as a surprise to me.

Nadia's sister Lola graciously picked up my children after school and drove them back to her place for the afternoon. They were usually chirpier once the school had shrunk in the rear-view mirror. By the time I picked them up at 7 p.m. and asked about their day, they had already changed gear and were ready to relax rather than relive the past.

HOW TO COME CLEAN

One day, they came home and handed me a 'Dear parents' letter:

> Next week we will be teaching your child about the changes during puberty in a Christian context . . . There will be some co-ed sessions and some segregated sessions . . . Please confirm . . .

Even if I did feel comfortable discussing this with them, did they feel comfortable discussing it with me?

'Don't worry, Dad,' Michelle reassured me. 'I already know this stuff.'

'Worry? Who said I was worried?'

'Your face. You're trying to act calm.'

'I *am* calm,' I said, raising my voice. 'Now *how* do you know this stuff?'

She rolled her eyes.

'From me,' smiled Grace. 'Obviously.'

I squinted. 'And you learnt it all from school?'

'The basics,' nodded Grace. 'I had the same newsletter, remember?'

'So you know how you were born and . . .'

'Yes, Dad!' they sang out in harmony, avoiding eye contact with me.

'Will you come to me if you ever have any questions?'

They glanced at each other. 'Why?' asked Michelle. 'We already know from TV, from friends, from—'

'That's exactly why,' I said, pointing to our television. 'I don't want you to learn from TV. I want you to learn from me. Your body is so . . . sacred.'

'The temple of the Holy Spirit, they taught us,' Grace reassured me.

'And I've seen people . . . kids . . . use their body for . . . selling it for money . . . as something cheap.'

They frowned. 'And what does your work with street kids have to do with us?'

I shook my head, remembering those poor unloved children with no respect for their own bodies. 'All I'm saying is don't be embarrassed to ask me anything about . . . having babies. I have a wife . . . had a wife . . . Don't let TV teach you.'

'Don't worry,' laughed Grace. 'I get grossed out by any scenes of birth and blood.'

'*I* don't!' bleated Joy.

'That's *all* I need!' I cried, slapping my forehead.

'I'd love to be a nurse when I grow up,' Joy continued. 'I love seeing babies being born.'

'You've gotta watch her,' Michelle waved her finger at Joy. 'They start younger and younger. She's only eight and probably learns from friends with big sisters.'

'*I've* got big sisters,' Joy lisped through her missing teeth.

'When I had these . . . talks at school,' I began, 'it was a shock.

My parents never told me. And I never asked anyone. I just thought babies were a miracle . . . from God.'

'Like a stork brings them to your front door?' laughed Grace. 'You're so cute!'

'As a kid, I couldn't connect something that seemed so disgusting with something as beautiful as a baby.'

'So what happened?' Michelle was poised to mock me with her cheeky grin.

'I told the teacher he was lying and that none of it was true.' As my daughters laughed, I heard echoes of the other boys laughing at me in the classroom. 'Then one summer morning, I woke up and a forest had grown on my legs, just like that.'

'Yeah, sure!'

'I was wearing shorts and my father noticed. I'll never forget how he asked me in English, "What happen?"'

My daughters went quiet, curious about my answer.

'I looked at his smile and said, "You're asking *me*? I should be asking *you*!"'

'Were you angry with him?'

'No, not angry, because his father probably never told him either, but I just promised myself that it would be my children asking me, not me asking them. Which means I have to make sure you feel comfortable and I never embarrass you, no matter what questions you ask.'

'O-kay,' they said slowly, as if I was being very weird and making a big deal about nothing.

'And I didn't like wearing shorts for a long time after that.'

'Ohh!' they moaned in sympathy.

It might have ended in them pitying me, but at least this talk opened the door, unconditionally, and they cannot say otherwise.

They never asked me detailed questions about the birds and the bees, but they never shied away from talking about girly things in front of me either. It was a privilege to be trusted, and I learnt so much about how they feel and express their feelings. We men are missing out on so much. Girls don't bottle things up and they feel so good when they find the right word to express how they feel. 'Exactly!' they say with excitement. The truth sets them free. Yet we men are prisoners, bottling up our truth, as if suppression is a sign of strength. How can fear of letting go be a strength? All we do is make ourselves sick.

Sometime in her mid-high school years, when the novelty of secondary school had worn off but the finish line was too far away, Grace had a testing time. Having witnessed a friend scrawl obscene graffiti in the girls' toilets, she was called into the principal's office and treated as guilty by association. Why had she not stopped the offenders, the principal wanted to know. Why did she just stand there? Was loyalty more important to her than morality?

I did not find out about this incident from my daughter, but from my nephew, many days later. Then I found a crumpled letter at the bottom of Grace's bag that she never handed to me. The offender was suspended. The witnesses and accomplices would be given a formal warning (first level). When I broached the subject with her and her sniffles had subsided, we huddled up and hugged. I know now from my adult daughters what I did not know then: teenagers are often angry at themselves, and only need their parents to 'bed down' the lesson they have already learnt.

'Dad, I was so scared you'd be so angry . . .'

'I promise that if ever you need to tell me anything, no matter how bad it is, whether it was your fault or not, I'll stay calm. I won't lose my temper. I'll talk to you like we're talking right now.'

It must have sounded like a wedding vow to all three of my attentive daughters.

'But in return,' I raised my finger and looked each of them in the eye. 'I must never find out anything second-hand.'

'Second-hand?' asked Joy.

'From anyone else,' explained Michelle.

'No nasty surprises,' I shook my head. 'Fair enough?'

They nodded.

'Your mum had a nasty surprise. She felt a lump, here,' I pointed to my chest, 'but she was scared and didn't tell anyone. We went to so many doctors who tested her for so many other things instead—blood, bones, viruses. She kept telling herself that the lump came from breastfeeding. But it was the beginning of something nasty. Something that could have been removed straight away. God knows she could have been like all those mums who are still here today because they did not delay.'

'What's that got to do with anything?'

'No secrets. No fear. If you feel a lump anywhere, see a doctor straight away. If anything's worrying you, please don't bottle it up. Talk to me. There's no problem so big that we can't fix it . . . together. We've been through the biggest of them all and we're never alone. We have God and we have your mum as a guardian angel.'

'Amen.' Joy fluttered her eyelashes. 'Dad, you're so dramatic!'

'Badly!' laughed Michelle.

It was comforting that they could laugh now, but it had been an awful time. Once we knew Nadia had secondary cancer, her death was more or less certain. Our nightmare started with her unplanned hysterectomy.

It was 10 January 2001.

Our obstetrician needed to see what was causing Nadia's abdominal fluid to build up. For months she had been suffering from flu-like symptoms and chronic fatigue, but at the time we (or at least I) did not think the two were related. The doctor had delivered both Michelle and Joy as caesarean babies and we trusted him, but this was different. This was not about the beginning of life.

'The laparoscopy gives us a chance to look inside and see what's going on,' he explained calmly. 'If it's a cyst on the ovary, we may be able to remove it using medication, but in case it's something nasty, I need you to sign here so we can take it out.'

My hand trembled as I signed the form in the file. Behind that form, I caught a glimpse of the original referral letter from our local GP. I remembered the day I brought that letter home with a shaken Nadia. She had visited the doctor about her anaemia and fatigue, but as soon as the GP saw the results of her blood test, she wrote that referral letter to a specialist, requesting further tests to rule out cancer. When we returned home, shell-shocked, I found an envelope in our letterbox marked with the words 'Personal—In Confidence'. Inside, it read:

Dear Mr Wakim,

I am writing on behalf of the Governor General to inform you that you are being considered for the award of the Medal of the Order of Australia . . . The citation proposed for the honour is 'For service to the Arab community and to multiculturalism, particularly through the Australian Arabic Council, and to youth' . . . The proposal should remain strictly confidential.

On any other day, this humbling announcement would have called for wholehearted celebration. But receiving it on the same day as the doctor's referral made it seem like a cruel joke. I looked up at the sky with the cancer letter in one hand and the confidential letter in the other and asked, silently, 'Why? Why us? Why now?'

And now here was Nadia being wheeled away to the operating theatre. As I waited for our obstetrician to re-emerge and tell me the news, I was suddenly overcome with the feeling that I was suffocating and found myself gasping for oxygen. The laparoscopy was taking too long. I rushed outside for a glimpse of some semblance of the mundane on Grattan Street, Carlton. What I saw was patients wheeling saline bags on mobile stands while puffing away on cigarettes. Among these signs of sanity and insanity, I found myself hugging a metal streetlight pole to hide my face. It was perhaps the next best thing to a human embrace.

The pole felt so cold that my body became numb. I did not care how it looked: a grown man weeping on an unfeeling pillar of strength. People walked past on the footpath, going about their daily cosmopolitan life in fast motion, as if they were immortal. But I was facing mortality—not my own, but my beloved wife's. Through rolling tears and gritted teeth, I exhaled from my soul, 'Please.'

Back upstairs in that familiar hospital corridor, nothing had changed. 'You win!' I screamed silently to the cancer posters around me and the 'thank you' plaques from the families of the deceased. 'Thanks for giving us so much hope! What about some plaques from those who beat this bastard and survived? Or don't they exist?'

All the time I waited, I fielded many phone messages and offers to hold my hand from family and friends. 'Just pray,' I responded. I was already holding hands with the rose-scented rosary. Whenever I felt palpitations again or felt that I was going to pass out, I inhaled the rosary's sweet fragrance. I had been waiting for five long hours.

And then it happened.

In the distance, two automatic sliding doors opened, silently. My vision was blurred. It looked like a black-and-white movie about someone else, playing in slow motion. I sat up and inhaled the rosary, praying the Hail Mary in fast motion.

It may still have been light outside the hospital, but inside it felt overwhelmingly dark. The silhouette of our family obstetrician looked different. He walked with slow, heavy steps. He was probably exhausted, but I read his gait as meaning he had life-changing news to impart.

He paused to whisper to a nurse to accompany him. Never had I felt so vulnerable. My heart pounded in my chest and I felt the arteries in my neck throbbing. I tightened my grip on the rosary. As the doctor and nurse reached me, I rose to shaky feet.

'P-please, doctor, how is she?' I panted.

'Let's sit in here.' He ushered me into a smaller room with white walls where the nurse sat next to me. His face was ashen and I braced myself for the worst.

'So, how is she, doctor?' I pleaded.

Thankfully, he came straight to the point. 'It was a very long operation, as you know,' he said. 'When we looked inside with the laparoscope, we found a very dark mass. We had to remove it, so we performed a hysterectomy. We removed her uterus and both her ovaries because they were all . . . black.'

Suddenly even the clinical white walls and white ceiling looked dark. Everything around me changed colour as the blood rushed to my organs, and my limbs felt limp.

'So we can't have any more children?'

'Well, no. Not any more than your three.'

'But how is Nadia?'

'Well, she will be very drowsy when you see her. And then she'll want to know what happened. So I'll arrange for an oncologist to speak to you as soon as possible. Nadia will need immediate treatment. We'll take it one day at a time.' He leant forward to explain the situation using a familiar metaphor. 'You see, the cancer is like a dropped bag of rice that has fallen. We mopped up the mess as best we could, but there'll be other grains we couldn't see and so couldn't remove.'

'So . . . my wife has . . . cancer?'

The doctor gave the nurse a glance and that was her cue to catch me if I fell. She gently squeezed my arm.

'Yes, we found a tumour and removed most of it.'

'So will she live . . . the rest of her life?' I might as well have asked how long she had to live.

'Well, she won't live to be an old lady, but you should make the most of what you do have.'

∾

When Nadia finally opened her eyes, she murmured, 'Did they find something bad?'

Had she suspected it or was my face so revealing? 'Well, *habibti*', I said, holding her hand, 'whatever they find, we'll face it together, and we'll deal with it together, one day at a time.' I tried to sound as calm as the obstetrician, but Nadia saw right through me.

'So they *did* find something bad.' This time it was a statement, not a question.

Later, after she fell asleep, I drove to my parents' house. When my big sister Eva opened the front door, I shuffled in, just as the surgeon had shuffled through those sliding doors. I could not muster the strength to tell my family the news, so I detoured to Eva's room and collapsed on her big bed, sobbing.

'Nadia will never see our children married.' This was the first image that pierced my heart. 'My children won't have their mum at their weddings.' I buried my head in her pillow and could not hear Eva's consoling words.

At our next hospital visit, the doctor told us the biopsies had revealed that Nadia had breast cancer, not ovarian cancer. The cancer primaries were in her breast and it had then spread to form secondaries in her ovaries and beyond. Suddenly, Nadia's chronic fatigue and flu made sense, as did her recent prudish behaviour in bed. She had not wanted me to notice any lumps.

'But, *habibti*,' I protested, 'if you noticed them, why didn't you say something or do something?'

'Because I kept telling myself that they came from breastfeeding.'

'Breastfeeding lumps? A year after you stopped breastfeeding?'

'I was scared . . .'

And I knew the rest of that sentence. In our culture, cancer cannot be named for fear of invoking it in our life. Instead, it is referred to as *hedaak al marad* (that other disease). We want it to stay out and far away. Why disturb this sleeping monster? Nadia's cancer-phobia had become a self-fulfilling prophecy.

When it raised its ugly head, her only defence was denial. And the more she delayed, the more it grew.

But that other disease has a name. We need to look it in the eye and shout out its name without fearing we will be cursed. Cancer! You have a name. Cancer! You do not scare me. Cancer! You are but a hard crab with claws. You try to wedge yourself in my valleys of fear, but my mountains of faith will banish you. Cancer! Cancer! Cancer!

Everything changed. Our normal family life was disrupted, and soon we moved to Sydney, so that Nadia could be close to Lola. It was a boon to have Lola nearby, especially to support Nadia when I was at work and the children were at school, but it was no longer the life we had hoped for, or dreamt of, on our wedding day.

HOW TO DO THEIR ASSIGNMENTS

'Grace, why don't you study in the study room?'

She was sitting at the dining-room table with her schoolwork scattered around her and her head down typing. She could not hear me over the music pumping through her headphones. I waved my hand in front of her eyes.

'Sorry?' she yelled over the music.

I unplugged one ear so she could hear me. 'If you're studying, go to the study room.'

'It's too quiet. And I can spread my work out here.'

'But now we can't watch TV and make noise,' Michelle protested, coming to my rescue. 'And this is the living room.'

'Exactly,' smiled Grace, 'and that other room is the dying room! I get claustrophobic squashed in there by myself.' She was so much like her mum—always wanting well-lit, wide-open spaces with people around.

'When I was a student,' I reminisced, 'I needed silence to study.'

'Well, girls know how to multitask,' was Grace's riposte.

If I let her stay, it would set a bad precedent for her younger siblings, who were looking to me to set benchmarks. The eldest child is often used to set the example, becoming a principle as much as a person. The eldest child in many families ends up complaining that the youngest child has it easy because the parents have relaxed the rules.

'Grace,' I said now, 'remember what they said to us at the parent–teacher meeting?'

She rolled her eyes and muttered, 'Probably the same thing they told everyone else.'

'That parents need to check their children's homework every night and sign their diary. We need to give you parental guidance.'

'Parental guidance?' she laughed. 'Sounds like a TV show. I'll tell you if I need parental guidance.'

'Can I see the assignment task?'

Grace handed me the paper. It was a religion assignment, and the task was to present Saul's conversion to Paul on the road to Damascus as a newspaper article. I just loved how the guidelines gave students a table matching criteria to marks. To achieve more than 90 per cent, students had to demonstrate a comprehensive understanding of the scripture reading, using appropriate language, adhere to the word limit and present their work creatively. To achieve 80–90 per cent, students had to demonstrate a competent understanding. To achieve 70–80 per cent, students had to demonstrate a sound understanding. A mark any lower would indicate underdeveloped skills. As if a student would say: 'Umm, I think I'll go for 65 per cent. Never had that mark before. So what exactly do I have to do?'

'Why would anyone not aim for full marks?' I asked Grace.

'If they weren't going to continue with the subject?' she suggested.

'When is this due?'

'Next week, I think. They've smashed us with three assignments at once.'

'Yet nothing for the last three weeks?' Then I looked at the due date and panicked. 'Grace, this is due tomorrow!'

'Oh, is it?' She froze.

'What are the other assignments?' By now I felt guilty for not checking on my children daily. Grace was right. She did have three assignments due in the one week. 'This is ridiculous,' I said. 'I'll raise it with the school tomorrow.'

'Please don't,' begged Grace. She did not want me to use my position as chairperson of the Parents' Association to raise personal matters, and she did not want to draw any attention to herself.

'Trust me, has it ever backfired on you when I've complained before?'

'But the teachers aren't stupid. They'll work out which one of their students—'

'Well, if you won't let me complain, then at least let me help you.'

We shifted to the study room, with no headphones.

'Now, Grace, what are the five steps for every assignment?' I asked, extending the fingers on my right hand.

'What's the question,' she recited. 'Subheadings . . . I forgot the third one.'

'Research.'

'Writing. And format last.'

'Exactly,' I nodded. 'Don't be like those girls who waste time formatting before they know what will fit.'

'Anyway, Dad, I'm tired, so can we get to the point?'

'The point is that you can use these five steps for every assignment, every subject, every year.'

As we worked through her assignment, I suggested many edits, and poor Grace soon saw it rewritten from her style to mine.

'Dad,' she yawned, 'this is about converting Saul, not converting *me*!'

'But why go for 70 per cent if you can score 100 per cent?' I asked to justify my intervention. 'The other students might have their big sisters to help them, or their parents or a tutor . . .'

'No, Dad. Some are lucky if their parents read and write English and very lucky if they take an interest.'

As I continued with my edits, Grace shook her head. 'No, Dad. Miss knows I'd never use that word.'

'Evangelise?'

'Yes, Dad. Just leave it as it was.'

'As it was? "Get up and go into the city?" "Get" is a baby word.'

'It's a quote from the Bible.'

I paused, embarrassed for not knowing this. 'Then you shouldn't plagiarise,' I said. 'Better to paraphrase.'

It was late but it was due tomorrow. I could have written a note to the school, but I insisted that Grace must set a good example, even if it meant we would be grumpy with each other. Now I wonder what I was scared of. Poor marks being seen to reflect poor parenting or a neglectful father? Proving that 'the girls' needed a mother to be home early enough to help with homework at godly hours?

Grace shifted from typing to taking dictation. By 10 p.m., we had swapped seats.

'Watch and learn,' was my excuse for reducing her to a passive spectator. These were desperate measures and not at all what the school meant by 'parental guidance'. As I worked, I was plagued by thoughts of what the nagging naysayers would say. 'I told you so,' they would crow. 'He can't do it on his own. He's torturing his children just to prove himself.'

I flicked my head as if repelling a mosquito, and answered their imagined criticisms in my mind: 'I'm not proving anything to anyone, just being myself. What do *you* know about parenting and love?'

'Love? Ha! Look at her. This is sleep deprivation. Love is letting her sleep.'

By 11 p.m., Grace was curling up in her seat, struggling to keep her eyes open. Her feet were cold, so I tucked them under my thighs.

What was I thinking? Could she seriously be absorbing any useful lessons in this state? Was I punishing her for losing track of the due date or punishing myself for losing track of my parental obligations? I resolved to install a whiteboard on the study-room wall, where they could all list the due dates of their assignments for everyone to see. By the time I had the inkjet printer buzzing back and forth, line by line, Grace was in a deep sleep.

The following evening, I asked her if she had handed it in on time.

'Oh yeah, Dad. About that. Miss gave us all an extension until next week because too many students complained about being smashed with assignments.'

My jaw dropped. 'And you were worried about *me* complaining?'

'Exactly! You didn't have to.'

Night after night, I asked Grace if the teacher had marked this assignment. Was I seriously losing sleep about a teacher half my age marking my daughter who was half her age? Apparently so.

When the assignment was finally returned, I was like a panting puppy. 'How did we go?' I asked impatiently. She handed me the assignment with a deadpan face. The front page had 27/30 written in red and circled.

'Wow! That's . . . 90 per cent! That's an A!' I struggled to hide my smile. 'So how did you rank?'

'Second highest, I think.'

'So why aren't you smiling?'

Her honest brown eyes said it all.

I certainly learnt my lesson from this escapade. I learnt that no matter how high the mark, if my daughters did not feel that they genuinely deserved it, it was meaningless to them. I learnt that parental guidance is by invitation only. They would rather achieve 80 per cent in the driver's seat than 95 per cent in the passenger seat.

Unlike assignments, exams they had to face on their own. As I drove my daughters to school during exam weeks, I would nurse their study notes on my lap and ask them the questions in jumbled order. They needed to understand, not just memorise their notes.

Just before they slammed the car door, I waved my finger: 'Remember the three golden rules: keep away from nervous people, you know more than you think you know, and answer the question.' I hoped these tried and tested maxims would echo in their heads—and eventually in their children's heads. Once they were gone, I crossed myself and prayed that their knowledge would flow through their hands like rivers.

At work, I kept looking at the time. 'Right now, they would have just started,' I would tell myself. 'Right now, they'd be halfway through . . .'

After school, I could not wait to phone and check on them. 'Any surprises?' I would ask.

'There were a couple of questions from a chapter that wasn't supposed to be in it,' Grace said once. 'But Miss said she didn't set the exam.'

In general, Grace had a habit of overestimating her results. 'At least 90 per cent plus, I nailed it!' she'd say confidently. Perhaps she wanted to make me proud, even though I already was. Fast-forward two weeks: 'Aren't you proud of me?' she would ask. 'Seventy-three per cent. I got above the class average!'

Joy was the opposite. 'I don't want to have high hopes, Dad.'
'But roughly?'
'Can't say.' And then she would achieve above 80 per cent.

Michelle was annoyed by students who exaggerated. 'We walked out, and she was nearly crying and carrying on as if it's the end of the world: "Oh my God, I think I failed! I did crap!" And I tell her it wasn't that bad. I thought I did okay. Then two weeks later, she tops the class with 93 per cent and I get 79 per cent!'

While they were studying late at night, I tiptoed around the house, trying to create an ambience conducive to mental application. I needed a ready supply of fresh food at exam time as they apparently burnt more fuel. It was like tending to pregnant women, each with her own craving. Joy yearned for a garden-made *jiddo* salad to spark her tastebuds—it was her herbal equivalent of a caffeine fix. Like her mother, she also loved a foot massage at bedtime. Michelle craved celery and fennel to crunch as she worked, while Grace craved caffeine in the form of cola or hot chocolate. They were so excited by the sight of their treat on a wooden platter that they would snap a photo and share it with their friends.

When they were on a break every hour, their favourite form of relaxing was laughing out loud at the American sitcom *Will and Grace*, even if they had seen the episode before. Perhaps this was when the lessons sank in, subconsciously. While they were being productive, they preferred the sound of me being productive in the kitchen to complete silence. Perhaps it made them feel less alone.

Their study methods varied. Grace was visual and preferred to hang notes on doors, walls, windows and mirrors around the house. Michelle was more aural and preferred to read her notes aloud in the study room. Sometimes she paced back and forth as if she were shaking a censer, so that all the good bits would sink in. Joy studied by teaching the lesson to an imaginary class, closing the study-room door to prevent any embarrassing interruptions. We sometimes even heard her raising her voice at mischievous students, threatening them with detention or sending them out of her class. Imparting what she knew to others (even imaginary ones) helped the knowledge sink in and gave her the best results.

Throughout their studies, it was critical for me to be at home, on standby, in case they were stuck. If I heard footsteps after one in the morning, I would treat it as a cry for help and drag myself out of bed, if only to keep them company or make them a hot drink. Until they all slept, I could not fall into a deep sleep.

We celebrated when exams were over.

'You did your best. Now the exam is history.'

'No, it was maths.' This showed how tired they were.

'It's in the past. Worrying won't change anything.'

'But are you proud of me?'

For my daughters, the opinion of their exam results that mattered most was not their teachers', not their peers' and not even their own. It was me, their parent, who wielded the most power. Perhaps sometimes it was too much power. I remember once hearing an adult friend say that they felt damaged by their parent because nothing they did was ever good enough: 'I felt that my parents were ashamed of me, and I've even seen a psychologist about it.' I made sure that my children grew up feeling loved unconditionally, and not that my esteem for them was conditional on their test scores.

HOW TO BE A 'DANCE MOM'

Like many mothers, Nadia dreamt of one of her daughters becoming a prima ballerina.

Grace had the requisite petite frame and graceful looks, so we enrolled her in a dance school at the age of three. She would practise and perform her dance routines on our shiny timber floor back in Melbourne.

When we invited friends to dinner in our home in the BC era, dessert was always a live floorshow by Grace, followed by a duet with Michelle on *dirbakki* and me on guitar. Baby Joy would skate around them in her ballet shoes, waiting for her time to shine. Like Grace, she started dance classes at the age of three.

These became after-school activities and an integral part of my daughters' identities. 'How's Grace? How's her dancing? How's Michelle? How's her drumming?' But dancing was much more than an activity and an identity. It was an industry. From one night a week and Saturdays, it soon evolved into two or three nights a week. Later, when it was just me, this meant racing from work to rush Grace and Joy to the dance studio. Michelle had *dirbakki* lessons, piano lessons and tennis coaching. Depending on the traffic and timing, their homework was sometimes completed in a hurry in the car, as was their dinner. We would ascend the studio stairs, puffing and pretending to smile to the 'dance moms' in the foyer.

'I hate being late, Dad,' Grace would mumble with her mouth full of sandwich as she tied her shoes for the first class. The teachers did not dare chastise the parents to their face, so they sent the message through their children.

'The warm-ups start at 6.15. Why are you late?'

Just once I wished a student, rather than blushing, would dare to respond: 'Well, you see, miss, I drove as fast as I could in the peak-hour traffic, then I got pulled over for speeding and driving under-age, without a licence. So I explained that I was late to a dance class where students are expected to take responsibility for their punctuality. The police officer then asked about my parents and I explained that I was fed up with being a passive passenger at the mercy of my father, who is at the mercy of his work and then at the mercy of the traffic. So that's why I'm late, miss.'

Part of this satire was sadly true. While we watched our angels dance, the dance moms and I would compare our speeding fines and demerit points, all in the name of punctuality and love. How I wished that punctuality worked both ways! The finish time was nominally 8 p.m., but when they actually finished depended on how well prepared the students were and how well they had rehearsed during the lesson. So it was their fault if the class ran until 8.30 p.m.

When Grace had 'extra' classes on weeknights, Michelle and Joy would wait in the car with me, as leaving them at home alone at night was inconceivable. They would try to complete their homework in the car, with limited lighting, no desk and no internet access. Some of these extra classes ran for no more than an hour, so it was not worth the round trip back home.

I became time poor. Every minute was precious and patience was no longer one of my virtues. I saw every minute wasted in the car park as time I could have spent ironing, washing or cooking. When all the dishes and domestics were done at the end of the evening, I did not crash on the couch and watch a movie, nor did I crawl into bed and read a book. I collapsed. Many mothers will find this familiar, but I doubt many fathers will.

'Don't you find this exhausting?' I asked a dance mom while we panted up the stairs together.

'Depends how much you love your child,' she smiled.

Since when was my love of my daughters in question? How could anyone use this sacred word as emotional blackmail? Easy.

While shuttling my daughters back and forth from home to the studio, there were inevitable spats.

'Michelle, why are you sitting in the front?' protested Grace. 'You know I need the mirror.'

'You always sit in the front,' insisted Michelle, 'and it saves me jumping in the front after we drop you off.'

'Stop arguing!' cried Joy.

These squabbles were distracting and dangerous while I was driving. But the girls were tired, hungry and irritable.

'Enough!' I intervened. 'Grace, you look left out your window. Michelle, you look right out your window. Silence until we get there!'

'What about me?' asked Joy innocently.

'You look . . . straight ahead,' I watched her obey through my rear-view mirror. 'And you look . . . beautiful.'

'Dad,' she began with her cutest voice, fluttering her eyelashes, 'Can I sit in the front because . . .'

'No!' I insisted. 'Not until you're seven.'

'I'm seven next month,' she replied with a lisp.

'Great!' I exclaimed, nodding. 'Then I'll have *three* kids competing for the front seat.'

But I knew that this wouldn't be happening if Nadia were still here, sitting in the front.

When eisteddfods, competitions, holiday workshops (now that's an oxymoron!) and 'extra' classes were offered for an extra fee, the heartstrings were again tugged.

'Oh, hi, Joe, just checking if Grace is attending and if you want to secure her a *limited* place,' asked a dance mom volunteer on behalf of the studio. 'So far, they're all coming along and we just don't want her to be the *only* one to miss out.'

We? The only one? Miss out? Really? As if anyone could care about my daughter more than I! A few car-park conversations through wound-down windows soon confirmed that the other dance moms had received the same phone call. Was this dance mom peer pressure?

The first time I did not fall for these tactics, but I was heartbroken to see Grace sit it out while the rest of her peers performed a troupe dance in fancy costumes. Because I had not enrolled her in those extra classes, she was relegated to the role of helper. She showed true team spirit, but I'm not so sure the organisers did. The dancers under the stage lights were spectacular, but my gaze was transfixed by the little girl dancing alone, in the dark wing, mirroring their every step in perfect unison. She was happy for them, but surely she belonged with them on the illuminated stage. Was this her fair 'punishment' for not enrolling in the extra classes, on an extra night per week? As I watched, I ground my teeth, my fists clenched, and my gaze blurred. What on earth has love got to do with it? This was child cruelty!

I capitulated. Grace joined the A team and smiled from her heart. I tried not to dwell on the invoices, the elephant in the room that shoved family holidays out of the budget. Instead, attending the dance competitions became our family weekend *mishwar*. While Grace and Joy made us proud, I felt guilty that Michelle's weekends were sacrificed to support her sisters.

When I dropped Grace off backstage, it reeked of hairspray. Tiaras and tutus hung from costume racks. Tinsel and glitter sparkled in their hair and on their faces. Anonymous plastic bottles of water lined the walls.

'No food or drink when you're in cos-tume!' sang out one of the volunteer dance moms, the two-note melody reminding me of my paperboy days at railway stations: '*He-rald*! Read all a-bout it!'

There were dancers stretching, dancers shaking on the spot, dancers rehearsing, dancers rotating in front of the mirror, dancers on pointe shoes. The nervous energy was palpable.

Then came the magical moment when the dance moms could see themselves reflected on stage. The footlights magnified our babies and our hearts fluttered. Dance moms sighed and even cried as their darlings took centre stage. Some girls wore a plastic smile as if they had been injected with botox. I would watch their mothers in the audience, exaggerating their own smiles, encouraging their little stars to shine. Some of the girls were tarted up, with fishnet stockings and caked-on make-up. Some dance moms even paid for professional photos of their 'cute' daughters. It was an obsession and an industry. Was I the only dance mom who saw this as sexploitation of our children for the sake of a take-home trophy?

During the intermissions, I was one of those embarrassing dance moms who bought a souvenir trophy just in case my child returned home empty-handed. It was worth it to me, even if all I had to engrave on it was, 'You are always a star in my eyes.'

At the end-of-year concerts, dance moms bought extra tickets to win over those relatives who had shaken their heads and discouraged dancing as a waste of time and money throughout the year. In the car park, I would see these relatives nodding their heads with approval, suddenly proud.

'See, I told you!' the dance moms would exclaim in vindication.

'It was all worth it in the end, hey, Joe?' said one dance mom as she nudged me at the car-park 'after party'. 'I was gonna pull him out, but now I'm gonna enrol him in extra classes.'

'What about all the stress?' I asked.

'Oh, that's nothing,' she said, waving her hand at me and counting on her fingers. 'I drive him to tutoring on Monday, dancing on Tuesday, karate on Wednesday, piano lessons on Thursday and dancing on Friday night and Saturday. He might as well sleep there!'

I stared at this proud mum until she stopped laughing, then shook my head.

'What's wrong?' she asked, nudging me again, as if I were part of her sorority. 'The stress? I love it.'

'I wasn't asking about you.'

'Him?' another elbow to my ribs. 'It'll keep him off the streets.'

There was no point trying to continue the conversation. I realised we were singing from different hymnbooks. For her it was a simple choice between two paths: enrol your child in every club, or lose him as he loiters. Was there no middle path that cost no money, such as creating your own family fun at home?

What is this obsession with busy-ness? I asked myself, not for the first time. When we first moved to Sydney, I tried many times to make friends and invite other families on a *mishwar* with us.

'Oh, hi, it's Joe, how are you?'

'Is everything okay?' What they really meant was 'What do you want?'

'Yes, fine. Look, my kids really enjoyed the company of your kids the other day, and we thought we'd invite you over and . . .' I was simply asking 'Can we be friends?'

'Well, let's see [sound of footsteps then the pages of a calendar turning] . . . the next two weeks are a write-off, then the first week of next month, we have a birthday party on Friday, a christening on Saturday and not sure about Sunday . . .'

I sighed. Does a christening take all 24 hours of the day? Were they 'not sure' about Sunday in case they received better offers? All the while, my children would be looking up at me with pleading eyes and holding their breath. This was humiliating, waiting for the verdict as if we were booking an audience with the Pope.

'Okay, let's pencil it in . . .'

Pencil, not pen? Were we not worthy? Ironically, we bumped into each other at a shopping centre the following weekend. While our shopping trolleys stopped to graze, our children, who were similar ages and had similar interests, played. We chatted for nearly an hour, in transit. We could not have done it if we had planned it.

'Dad, can we invite them over?' pleaded Grace as we stood there.

I looked at the blank-faced, trolley-pushing mum.

'My husband is waiting in the car,' she said. 'After half an hour in this place, he felt claustrophobic.'

'I used to be like that,' I laughed. 'For me, retail is the opposite of therapy.'

My children kept nagging me to invite the family over, and I kept widening my eyes as my mother's code for 'Stop now, I'll explain later'. But my children remained oblivious to my signals. When our trolleys finally parted company and rolled in opposite directions, I had to explain the code to my children.

'Sometimes you just need to trust me when I say stop.'

'But you didn't—'

'I did . . . with my *eyes*. Like this . . .' I widened my eyes again.

They imitated me and I realised how silly I looked. We giggled together.

'But why?' persisted Grace.

'Sometimes parents see things you can't see,' I explained. 'Sometimes I can't tell you the reason on the spot. But if you push your friendship, you might push people away.'

'But why?'

How I loved those two words. I had hung them on my bedroom wall during Year 12 to inspire critical thinking. 'Sometimes people are too embarrassed to tell you the truth, so you need to respect them.'

'What truth?'

I knelt down, even as other shoppers and trolleys were passing. 'When I was young, my friend kept inviting me to sleep over and I always told him that my parents didn't let me.'

'Was that the truth?'

I shook my head. 'I had bed-wetting problems, but I didn't want anyone to know.'

'So you lied?'

'Not really. My parents wouldn't have let me go anyway, for the same reason—to protect me . . . from embarrassment.'

Joy looked confused. 'So does that mum wet the bed?'

Lucky for me, none of my children had this problem. Otherwise, we would have struggled with those dance events that required sleeping away from home.

Eventually, the elephant in the room loomed larger and could no longer be ignored. The dance-class fees added up to electricity plus gas plus water plus school fees. The dancers needed different shoes for different dances—ballet, tap, jazz, pointe. Sometimes they left the studio at nine o'clock on a Friday night and needed a pair of shoes repainted in a different colour by nine o'clock Saturday morning. How? The dance shops are closed at 5 p.m. Unlike soccer players, who need only one pair of boots, dancers need an entire wardrobe. Being children, they sometimes lost a shoe—and a new pair cost triple digits.

As the studio expanded its classes beyond dancing to singing, I mentioned Michelle's ability to sing perfectly in pitch. When we persuaded her to enrol in a singing class, Grace was thrilled. They were given an apt song, The Carpenters' 'Close to You', to perform together. When this duet harmonised, I had goosebumps, but each time I tried to capture it on video, they dissolved into giggles.

During this short spell when all three girls attended the dance studio on Saturday mornings, I was left at home alone to dust, vacuum, mop and cook. Michelle soon lost interest, while Joy struggled with the early starts on Saturday mornings and wanted to sleep in, but Grace thrived and would come home starving.

'Oh, Dad, it was such hard work today!'

'Yet *we* pay *them*,' I vented. I felt guilty for making her feel guilty about missing the Saturday chores.

'Do you want me to stop going?' She was not sarcastic and had never asked this question before.

Grace without dancing was unimaginable for me but imaginable for her. I realised that she had never taken my support for granted. 'No,' I replied, 'but the studio sucks up all our money and there's nothing left for your sisters.'

Grace looked at her sisters through maternal eyes. 'Maybe I can help by . . . teaching there?' she suggested.

I was inspired by her creative problem-solving. Why didn't *I* think of that? 'Will they let you teach and . . . pay you?'

'Well, I've been dancing for ten years,' she shrugged. 'If I continue my classical ballet RAD exam classes, I'll be qualified to teach it.'

Miss Grace was offered the beginner's class. Some of the toddlers were still in nappies and others were being toilet-trained. In performances they would freeze on stage, squinting at the lights before waving to the audience, forgetting all the dance moves Miss Grace had taught them.

She kept up her dancing and teaching until she reached senior high school, when it became a struggle to juggle it all with her schoolwork and, of course, The Heartbeats. She left dancing of her own volition, 'to take a break', but we all knew that this chapter had ended. I grieved for the end of Nadia's dream—that Amazing Grace would be a prima ballerina.

Her dancing was her identity and our investment. Now it was her history, and a treasure trove of trophies, photos and videos. Just as I never gave away my guitars, in case the flame was reignited, Grace never gave away her dancing shoes. I hoped that they would be dusted off one day, just like my guitars. Her dancing had helped her rise above her grief and enter a zone where dance was the opposite of death. It released endorphins, kept her fit and gave her a multicultural social group to complement her monocultural schooling.

HOW TO SMASH STEREOTYPES

'*Abou meen* (Father of who)?' asked a Lebanese elder. Our cultural tradition was to name parents after their eldest son.

'*Abou banaati* (Father of my daughters),' I replied, grinning.

He frowned. '*Lakan ibin meen* (Therefore, son of who)? *Shoo ismu abouk* (What's your father's name)?'

'Jalil.'

'*Lakan min sammeek abou Jalil* (Therefore we'll call you father of Jalil).' The innocuous logic was that if I had a son, he would be named after my father. This patriarchal lineage of fathers and sons was so engrained that variations of these words had become Arabic surnames, such as Bou (father of) and Bin (son of).

Even in my childhood, I found it odd that my parents were named after my eldest brother, James, rather than their firstborn child, Eva.

After the birth of Michelle, a handful of men presumed I was secretly disappointed. 'A girl? That's all right,' they consoled me. 'Maybe next time.'

Nadia overheard one such whisper and fired back. 'Will a boy hoist us to heaven?'

After the birth of Joy, one aunt tried to explain to me that this attitude was practical, not cultural. 'In the old village, the son was a farm hand and helped his father. Like your father Jalil helped his father and became so skilled in the garden.'

'But it wasn't just the muscles, aunty. The son carried the family name . . .'

'Listen to me, aunty,' she replied (it is a form of endearment for her to call me what I would call her), 'my daughters are closer to the family and they visit me more than my sons.'

The theme of sons and daughters continued at the Sunday gospel reading. It was the opening chapter of Matthew, the genealogy of Jesus: fourteen generations from Abraham to David, fourteen generations from David to the exile to Babylon, and fourteen generations from the exile to Jesus. Every father had a son and only four notable mothers are mentioned, culminating in Mary, mother of Jesus. So would they have struck me from that genealogy and chosen one of my brothers instead because I fathered no sons and therefore don't count?

Whenever my parents were disappointed with human nature, they mentioned *Banni Adam*. I thought it was a swear word until I realised what it meant—children of Adam. Why were we not all children of Eve? To counter the patronising platitudes about not having sons, I turned the tables.

'What kids do you have, Joe?'

'Two girls and a girl,' I would say with a casual nod, then watch while the penny dropped.

'Oh . . . oh . . . oooh!' They finally registered, embarrassed. It was not my problem but I preferred to make a pre-emptive strike. Or was I just making assumptions about their assumptions?

Even if my cultural traditions were patriarchal, my family history was more matriarchal. Our men did not marry subservient women. Our women did not marry domineering men. During my 'pilgrimage' to Lebanon in 1988, I researched our family tree and found that women were our heroines. One great-grandmother on my father's side fought fearlessly on the front line against the French when they came to her village to 'take' the wheat during their Mandate over Lebanon between 1923 and 1946. She amassed a local 'army' of women to defend her village, waving her flag, embellished with the cedar of Lebanon. She figured, correctly, that the French army would not dare attack women and she succeeded in protecting her village. My other paternal great-grandmother was an audacious trader who sold her produce from village to village on the back of a donkey. She died trying to cross a flooded river to reach the next village. On my mother's side, women lived a long life and remained sharp, with their humour and wit intact. The men may have worn the pants, but the women chose them.

My daughters inherited these assertive genes. It was strange to hear them tell each other to 'man up'.

When Nadia's mother, Georgette, visited us from Lebanon, BC of course, she saw a domesticated man, ironing. 'It's good that you help your wife at home,' she remarked.

I shook my head. 'How am I helping my wife? It's not her job. It's *our* job. We both work full time. I see *aammi* work inside the house.' I was referring to Boutros, my father-in-law.

'It's all good,' she nodded and we grinned at each other.

'And Nadia mows the lawn.'

'Oh . . . that's no good,' she laughed.

Nadia widened her eyes and gave me the hand signal that meant 'I'll fix you later'. It was the forefinger circled onto the thumb with the three other fingers pointed straight. It looked like an axe with a round handle. Nadia did not want her mother to worry.

Nadia and I spoke to our children only in Arabic during their preschool years, to bed it in. According to an ancient Arabic proverb, learning in the early years is akin to etching in stone. But as our children grew up, they responded only in English.

After Nadia passed away, the only time I ever spoke Arabic was when I was angry. It is blessed with some coarse, guttural sounds that dramatised my growling more effectively than English. If some of these expletives were put into practice, a number of us would be in jail. Take 'I will extract your intestines from your mouth', for example. My father passed down some confusing curses such as 'You son of a dog' or 'Curse your father'. I deleted them from my repertoire. It is probably a blessing that I was never angry enough for my daughters to learn these Arabic phrases, but I must confess that the Arabic 'poetry' still echoes in my head whenever I bite my tongue.

When we took our daughters to Lebanon in 1995, 2002 and 2006, they loved the village life. They absorbed their ancestry and their identity. Back in Australia, though, our identities were frequently questioned because our appearance mismatched the media stereo-types. Apparently, we had the wrong colour eyes, wrong colour skin and wrong colour hair.

'But you don't look Lebanese . . .' people would say.

'Get used to it,' I shrugged. 'Plenty more like me where I come from.'

'But you know the typical Lebanese look that you see in the—'

'Media?' I raised my brow. 'That's not typical. That's *stereo*typical.'

'But you don't even have an accent. You must have been born here.'

'Wrong again.'

Other times, they would say, 'I thought your culture was mainly interested in preparing daughters to be good mums and good wives.'

'Well, you thought wrong,' I would respond. 'We want our daughters to be good people.'

The assumptions did not stop there. When people realised we were Lebanese, they would reassure us politely that the food was halal.

'Who said we're Muslim?'

In my father's twilight years, we attended a Christmas pageant for senior citizens. As the nativity play began, the staff whispered to each other, panic-stricken, then rushed to our family.

'So sorry,' they said. 'Is this okay?'

'Is what okay?' I asked.

'The Christmas theme . . . your dad isn't offended, is he?'

'Why would he be?'

'Aren't you Lebanese?'

'Yes. Lebanese Christian.' I pointed to the crucifix hanging from my father's neck.

'Oh . . . oh . . . are there Christians in Lebanon?'

I pointed to the characters in costume. 'Where was Jesus born?'

'Bethlehem?'

'Down the road from where we were born.'

'Oh . . . true! But I didn't know there were Christian Lebanese.'

'They've been living in Australia for more than 150 years.'

'Oh, really?'

'And by the way, Muslims also believe in the virgin birth.' I winked.

When I told my daughters these stories to prepare them for the inevitable questions, their responses surprised me.

'Dad, get over it,' shrugged Michelle.

'It's not their fault that they don't know,' added Grace.

'Yes, it is,' I insisted. 'Ignorance is no excuse.'

'Have they committed a crime?' laughed Michelle, 'just by watching TV and reading the papers?'

'Don't worry, Dad,' Joy said, putting her hand on my shoulder, 'we're proud of being Lebanese. We know who we are. We don't need to prove who we are.'

This stopped me in my tracks and sent chills down my spine. Could Joy have remembered her mother saying those words? When I was writing opinion columns about reversing stereotypes, Nadia would nudge me: 'Stop trying to prove yourself. Just be yourself.'

The Wakim family at Clifton Hill, Melbourne, 1970. Back row, from left: me, Eva, Jalil, Souad, James and Bass. Front row, from left: Georgina, George, Joan and Peter.

A family *mishwar* to the Lerderderg River, Bacchus Marsh, Victoria, 1971. I'm in shorts, third from the left.

With Nadia at Our Lady of Lebanon in the mountain village of Harissa, Lebanon, April 1988.

Serenading Nadia (third from left) in North Lebanon, April 1988.

Nadia and I were married on 22 October 1988, in Carlton, Melbourne.

Nadia and Grace, Coburg Lake Reserve, Melbourne, in the autumn of 1992.

Playing guitar to three-year-old 'Michelle, Ma Belle', 1996.

New Year's Eve, Melbourne,
ushering in 2000.

Palm Sunday, Melbourne, 1999.

Grace's First Communion, Melbourne, 4 November 2000.

Michelle, Joy and Grace on Palm Sunday, Melbourne, 2000.

My daughters on a family outing in 2000.

Grace performing a split jump at a dance competition in 2002.

My parents, Jalil and Souad, tell their granddaughters some family stories in 2002.

This photo was taken only months after Nadia's passing in 2003.

The children in uniform on school photo day in the winter of 2003.

Rowing on the Yarra River, Melbourne, 2009.

In front of Our Lady of Lebanon Church in Melbourne, 2011.

On our way to a Father's Day lunch, 2014.

Joy, Michelle, me and Grace stepping out in Sydney, 2013.

Grace with Aunt Lola, at her
21st masquerade party, 2012.

In 2014, dressed by my three personal stylists, of course.

Cycling in North Carlton, Melbourne, January 2015.

Michelle's 21st, March 2015.

HOW TO WEAVE MAGIC

'And that's . . . the end . . . of the . . .'

'No!' Young Michelle kicked her legs under the blanket. 'More!'

'But it's late and Joy's asleep.'

'Please . . . one more!'

For as long as they could remember, story time had been a bedtime ritual for my daughters. For me it was a scary but magical moment, watching them drift from this world into their dream world, watching them sleep with their lips apart and their ears receptive like antennas to whatever voices they heard.

After prayers, it was time for intimacy, for reflecting on the day, for sowing seeds in their fertile imaginations. I felt privileged that mine was the last voice they would hear each night. I looked forward to it as much as they did. Michelle and Joy shared a bedroom, so Grace would snuggle up next to Michelle and I would do the same with Joy.

First up, I would ask them to select a book from the shelf and we would take turns reading. If they read well, they earned a bonus story.

'But with the lights out,' I insisted.

'Why?'

'So you can fall asleep.'

If they earned a bonus story, they had two options: 'from your head' or 'from your childhood'. Over time, the line became blurred. Fiction became infused with fact, and fact was narrated as fiction. The stories should have been calming, but I challenged myself to make each night's story more exciting than the last. 'How much out of ten?' I would ask them if they were still awake at the end of the story.

I would hear Nadia's voice in my head whenever they laughed. 'Are you stirring them up or putting them to bed?'

One rainy night, as I conjured a story from my head, I noticed an intricate motif etched into Joy's bedhead. I suspected that my children had probably never noticed it before.

'Once upon a time, there was a family of fairies. A father and three children.'

My children wriggled in excitement under the blankets.

'Where was the mum?' asked Joy.

'Shh!' replied Michelle. 'It's just a story.'

'They loved each other very much and danced and sang in the breeze. The father told his children, "If ever you are lost, look for the family motif, the circle with the three triangles inside. I have drawn it in three places near here." And he showed them where the family motif was drawn in the neighbourhood. "If ever we are separated, wait for me near one of these and you'll be safe because they're in the homes of good families, like ours. I'll keep flying between them until I find you and we'll be together again."

'Many weeks later, there was thunder and lightning.' The rain intensified outside our bedroom windows, right on cue. I saw them curl up into foetal positions under the blankets.

'The fairy family hung on to each other but the wind was too wild. They were thrown in different directions and yelled out for their dad. They heard his voice, reminding them to meet him at the motifs, but when they searched, they found that two of the motifs had been destroyed by the storm. The fairies finally found the third motif and waited for their father, but he did not come. "Shall we look for him?" asked one fairy. "No, he told us to wait here," answered another fairy. "If he said he'll find us, then he'll find us." The third fairy was worried. "What if he never comes back and we're alone with no parents?" They closed their eyes and imagined that he was nearby. "Come on, if we really believe it, it will be real," said the oldest fairy.'

Grace snorted to indicate that this represented her. By now my children were mesmerised. I saw the whites of their eyes as they blinked in the twilight.

'To be continued . . .' I teased, 'tomorrow.'

'No!' they squealed, kicking their legs.

'You finish it off, Grace,' I suggested.

'No!' insisted Michelle, convulsing. 'Just hurry up!'

They lifted the blankets to their noses and clung on tight as if they were going on a ride.

'Well, close your eyes tight, just like them. This is what they heard: "I'm so proud of you. You trusted me." When they heard their father's voice, they opened their eyes, just like you, and flew into his arms. He had one broken wing but fairy wings grow back when there's a rainbow. And they danced around the circle that saved their life. And that circle . . . is . . .'

'Come on, Dad!' they were all holding their breath.

'Just above Joy's head on her bed.'

'What!' Michelle kicked off her blankets and rushed to the light switch. When they looked at the bedhead and saw the circle with three triangles staring back at them, their eyes nearly popped out of their sockets. They were speechless.

'So we should always trust our father in heaven, even in a storm. Goodnight.'

Of course, I was thinking of the biblical story of Jesus calming the storm when the apostles panicked about their boat sinking.

'Oh, why do you love such dramatic endings?' Michelle asked, adding 'Goodnight!' in a fair imitation of my deep voice.

I turned off their light and let them sleep on it. Wishful thinking. The real rain became so torrential that one by one, they crawled into my bed. Having Joy in my bed in emergencies was uncomfortable enough for a light sleeper, but four sardines squashed into one can? Someone broke wind and no one owned up. I kicked off the doona for ventilation.

'That's not very ladylike!' I complained.

'Who said it was us?' asked Grace.

'Yeah, right, it was the fat fairy!'

After trying several different geometric shapes, our sixteen limbs must have looked like two octopuses fighting. Half of me ended up outside the bed.

'Enough!' I cried eventually. 'Everybody out! Back to your own beds! *Yalla!*'

'Come on, Dad, you should be used to crowded beds from your childhood,' pleaded Grace.

'We shared bedrooms, not beds,' I insisted.

This prompted requests for stories 'from your childhood' about my overcrowded home, although I never saw it as such. It was perfect timing because now that Joy was seven, she wanted her own room rather than sharing with Michelle.

'If I took the study room,' she pleaded, 'and we all studied in our bedrooms instead, then . . .'

'No, Joy,' I interrupted, 'bedrooms should be a place of rest. Your eyes need to see the bed and think sleep zone, not see a desk and think work zone.'

'Well, Grace has her own room, and a double bed!'

After she heard the stories about my childhood, though, she saw her shared bedroom through a different lens. My sister Eva had a generous tradition of giving her nieces and nephews enough money to buy a good mattress. But the money she had recently given Joy was enough for two mattresses and my youngest lived up to her name.

After asking Michelle cryptic questions about what sort of mattress she should buy for herself with Aunty Eva's money, Joy arranged for us to buy two matching mattresses—one for her and one for Michelle. Her change of heart surprised not only Michelle but the rest of us too. Secretly, I believed that it was the magic of my bedtime stories.

In my stories 'from your childhood', I explained how we had three children to a bedroom, sometimes four. I used to write stories for my siblings to read and after my mother turned the lights out, we would continue reading and writing with a torch under the blankets.

'Three to one bedroom?' they checked.

'Yes, and one bathroom for the whole family, and one outside toilet.'

'Whoa! That's so cute,' exclaimed Joy.

'Sharing isn't always cute. But it was normal for us and for other families we knew. We even shared clothes. Most of mine were handed down from my older brothers.'

'So what happened if you were all busting to go at the same time?' asked Grace.

'After Brighton Beach, when we all needed to rinse off the sand, my mum would sometimes throw three boys in the bathtub at once and hose us down to save time. What else could she do?'

'One bathroom for ten people?' Grace shook her head. 'We have two bathrooms for four people.'

'Exactly,' I nodded. 'It was annoying when someone knocked on the bathroom door and asked who was inside. I used to shout, "What difference does it make? It's occupied!" and they would yell back, "Hurry up, Occupied!"'

'Did you need a whole bus to get to the beach?' asked Joy.

'No, my father's first car was a blue Ford Falcon station wagon. Its number plate is part of our heritage: JEC058.'

'What? You still remember?' exclaimed Michelle.

'Of course! Our first family car in Australia!' I boasted. 'It took us everywhere. On Sundays, our father would drop us off for mass at the front of the church in Rathdowne Street, Carlton. Imagine the car doors opening then three people stepping out of the front seat, four stepping out of the back seat, and another three being let out at the back. And our mum made us wear matching clothes for Sunday mass.'

'Yuck!'

'Which was normal back then.'

'What about seatbelts?' asked Joy.

'None in the back of the wagon.'

'Weren't you scared?'

I shook my head.

'The olden days were so dangerous,' Joy concluded.

'You make me sound like a dinosaur!' I retorted.

'So, you were a middle child?' asked Michelle, out of personal interest.

'You think *you* have it tough,' I grinned. 'I was one of two middle children. As number five, I had to share that too!'

'Was the other middle child Uncle Peter?' asked Michelle.

'Yep. He thought he was the black sheep of the family because he was more interested in clubbing or staying out late than studying or going to sleep early.'

'How late?'

'He sometimes came home at dawn, sneaking in through the garage door. But he had to stop our dog from barking and waking up the whole family.'

'That's hilarious,' laughed Grace.

'Sometimes, he stumbled into my father at that time but pretended he had just woken up for his plumbing jobs. My father thought Peter was a bit over-dressed for work.'

'Was Uncle Peter a bit of a rebel?' Joy laughed, revelling in these childhood stories.

'Not really. But unlike me, he left school at Year 10 and had bought a house by the time he was twenty-one. He and I were very protective of each other.'

'How?'

'When I was in Year 3, I got an A on my report card for every subject, every term. This teacher was very generous with his marks. When we had visitors and my parents asked me to show them the card, I would watch Peter's face. I didn't want to hurt his feelings, so I made sure I never achieved such high marks again and never showed my marks to visitors again.'

'Yeah, sure,' laughed Grace, tilting her head and pointing her finger at me. 'So if you got lower marks later, it's because you weren't doing your best? Yeah, right!'

'Exactly,' continued Michelle. 'If you brag about how humble you were, isn't that an oxymoron? '

'You moron!' Grace sniggered.

'Okay, I'm exaggerating . . . a bit. But I'm not bragging.' My tone was defensive. 'I'm just saying that we two middle children were close.'

Soon these stories of 'when you were our age' became a soap opera, with a continuing episode each night.

'And did your mum and dad drive you to school?' asked Grace.

'Are you kidding?' I replied. 'We walked. Even to the Saturday school, we took a bus.'

'Saturday school?'

'My parents wanted us to learn Arabic so that we could talk to our grandparents *bukra* (in the future).' I rolled my eyes, remembering how I never believed we would return to live in Lebanon.

'Didn't they teach it at your school?'

'Nobody taught Arabic at school when I was your age.'

'Lucky you,' Michelle muttered.

'I hated Arabic, too. I hated Saturday school.'

'So why did you go?'

I blushed. 'It was the first time I could meet girls. Good girls from good families.'

'There were no girls at your normal school?'

I shook my head. 'I went to an all-boys school, not like you.'

'And then you finally went to school with girls . . .' smirked Michelle.

'Back to the story,' I cleared my throat. 'I hardly knew my grandparents. They were all in Lebanon.'

'Well, ours aren't exactly here,' muttered Grace.

It dawned on me that my children were growing up without the tender love of their grandparents. Like me, they were going through their childhood without sitting in their grandparents' laps and having them whisper wisdom into their ears.

I resented our migration for robbing us of this higher layer of love, but it must have been more painful for my parents to leave their families and embark on a three-week sea voyage. Now it was one of the prices my children were paying for living in Sydney, away from their grandparents in Melbourne and Lebanon. Was this why they so craved stories of our family history from me?

'So the Arabic school was a waste of time?' asked Michelle.

I remembered my mother trying to help me with my Arabic home-work, even though she had left school after a couple of years and was illiterate. 'No,' I was adamant. 'I wish my parents were pushier about more things. Like encouraging me to learn about planting trees and cooking food and buying food at the market and . . . lots of things. I walked away from all that.'

'What do you mean?'

I sighed. 'When I was your age, whatever I was feeling . . . it felt like I would feel that way forever. Every direction I looked, for as far as I could see, was the same: Arabic is useless, gardening is useless. To me, it wasn't a phase, it was forever. To me, the earth was flat.'

They frowned and I continued reconciling myself with myself, talking at them rather than to them. 'Parents see the curve of the horizon, like they're looking out an aeroplane window. They see over the hills and far away.'

Joy smiled, aware that I was referring to the 'Three Little Ducks' nursery song. 'Mother duck said quack, quack, quack, quack?' she giggled.

'No, but I wish I could go back and listen and learn about life. Parents see what's over the horizon. They're . . . taller. They can see what you can't see . . . yet.'

Michelle saw my eyes turn glassy. 'So what does this have to do with the Arabic school?'

'My parents wanted us to have what they didn't have: educa-tion. Thanks to them, my Saturday Arabic helped me study Arabic at university and also helped me score my second job, as a social worker with Arabic-speaking people.'

⟍෧

Sometimes, the bedtime conversations felt like procrastinations to delay sleep.

'As soon as someone yawns,' I would threaten, 'we stop the stories.'

At the mere mention of the word, they would start fighting back yawns. I saw them leak out as tears. I saw the yawns suffocated with puckering lips. It was contagious. It was precious.

It could be emotionally exhausting to tell these stories from my heart, so I wove this story from my head in the twilight. It was the story of a man with ginger hair and a matching moustache. He was proud of his huge moustache. He combed it every night and told his daughter that a man without a moustache was not a man: the bigger the moustache, the greater his honour and the more he deserved respect. My children giggled at this foreign currency, even though it was part of their heritage.

The man had one big moustache but also one big problem. He could not pay the rent on his house because he was struggling to sell the eggs from his chickens in the local village. People had their own chickens and their own eggs.

So he walked up the stairs of the biggest house in the village where the *mukhtar* (village head) lived. The moustache man told the *mukhtar* the truth: I cannot pay the rent this week because I have no money to feed my own family. He clicked his thumbnail behind his front teeth, as this was the gesture for being penniless.

I demonstrated this to my children and they giggled.

'What if he had dirty fingernails?' asked Michelle, shuddering.

'No, you're thinking of the pinkie shovel, you fool,' Grace reminded her.

I continued my story. 'The moustache man begged for another week's grace to pay the rent on his house. He was not accustomed to begging because he had so much pride, but he was desperate and he loved his wife and daughter. He promised to take his chicken eggs to the nearest town, where he hoped to sell them and bring back the money.

'The *mukhtar* squinted. "But what guarantee can you give me? Do you have a gold watch or something?"

'The poor man did have a gold watch at home, but it was a sentimental gift from his grandfather, and he was keeping it in case he needed money for his daughter's wedding. "I swear by my moustache," he promised, twirling the ends of his whiskers between his thumb and forefinger. "I will shave it and live in shame if I break my promise."'

I imitated the twirling gesture so my children could visualise it. 'The moustache symbolised much more than a caterpillar growing between this man's upper lip and his nose. It was a signature on a contract. It was the mark of a man's honour. Without a moustache, villagers would know that the man had been dishonourable and might as well be untouchable. The *mukhtar* knew what shame was at stake and gave the moustache man one week to pay the rent. The moustache man knelt and kissed the *mukhtar's* hand in gratitude.

'He collected his chicken eggs, carefully loaded them into cane baskets and strapped them to the side of his donkey's saddle. He kissed his wife and daughter then headed to the nearest town. But on the way, he passed some robbers who had their eye on his donkey.

'To be continued, tomorrow night.'

Okay, stop carrying on like a child! I am not Sheherazade and this is not *1001 Arabian Nights*. It's just a story. I wanted to show you that we are all wide-eyed children at heart, with an inbuilt sense of wonder for questions and imagination for answers, at least until this wow factor is drummed out of us with comments like 'Grow up', 'Act your age' and 'You're so immature'. I heard those words many times during my teenage years, but I always brushed them off. Storytelling is not something you outgrow. It is as old as *Banni Adam* itself.

So this is how the story continued. 'The moustache man was robbed of his donkey. He begged the thieves to stop, as the donkey had been part of his family for many years. As the donkey tried to free itself and kick the robbers, the eggs fell out of the cane baskets and cracked as they hit the ground.'

My children gasped.

'The moustache man gasped just like that. He had lost his donkey and his eggs. Now he would lose his house and his honour. He raised his hand to his moustache—it was all he had left.

'As he sobbed by the side of the road, he looked like so many beggars. Passers-by crossed the road to avoid him. Even pigs came to eat the remains of the broken eggs. The moustache man cried out, "Woe is me! I have been robbed and have lost everything. How can I be a father and feed my family?"

'"Liar!" yelled some passers-by. "You're just a beggar, just like the rest."

'From a distance, a young *ameer* (prince) had seen everything and knew that this man was honest. The *ameer* was dressed in pauper's clothes so that no one recognised him. "I believe you," whispered the *ameer*. "And you have something that I don't."

'"Please don't mock me," sobbed the moustache man, without looking up. "Leave this wretched place before they rob you too."

'"They already mock me. My face refuses to grow hair. They think I'm a boy, not a man."

'The moustache man looked up at the *ameer* and saw that it was true. He was a grown man with reddish hair and the face of a boy. "Who is 'they'?" he asked.

'"Everyone. There's a girl I love. How can her parents give her hand in marriage to a man without a moustache, a man who's not a real man?"

'"Begone. You've come to the wrong person . . ."

'"I've come to the perfect person. Look at my hair colour and look at yours. If I can have your red moustache, you can always grow it back, but I'll be the happiest man in the world."

'The moustache man knew he had to shave it anyway, as part of the promise to the *mukhtar*, so he agreed. He walked back home empty-handed and clean-shaven. Passers-by spat at him when they saw that he had no moustache and no honour.

'When he told his family of his misfortune, they knew they would be homeless. He took the gold watch his grandfather had given him and that he had set aside to pay for his daughter's wedding. He decided to offer it to the *mukhtar* to buy one more week of rent.

'But as he opened his front door, a well-dressed *ameer* stood before him, wearing his own ginger moustache.

'"You, the man who took my moustache!"

'"You, the man who gave me his moustache, and will now, I pray, give me the hand of your daughter!"'

'Wow!' exclaimed Joy. 'So did they get married?'

'They did, but only when the father's moustache grew back. He would not have it any other way. As for the *ameer*, he not only paid the rent, he bought them the house from the *mukhtar* and told them to keep the gold watch as a family jewel. In later years, he and his wife would bring their children to the house to be with their grand-parents and enjoy village life.'

'All because of a moustache?' asked Joy.

'As if facial hair makes you a man . . . or a woman!' added Grace. 'I've seen women who have beards.'

'Did you meet beggars when you were working with street kids?' asked Michelle, wondering whether the story was based on someone I had met.

'Of course, but many street kids come from rich families and should have had no reason to beg. They weren't rich in the most important thing. They may have lived in a mansion but *you* have something they wish they had.'

'A bigger house?' asked Joy.

'A mansion *is* a bigger house, you fool!' snapped Michelle.

'They wanted a *home*, not a house,' I explained. 'And they treated the other street kids as their family. They ran away because they had many sad secrets but no one to talk to. They didn't feel loved. And then they began to believe that they didn't deserve love, so they treated their body . . . badly.'

My children were too young for the tragic details.

When they reached the teen years, the bedtime stories morphed into birthday stories about them. Instead of lamplit stories in bedrooms, they were candlelit stories in restaurants. I recounted magical moments, such as a preschool Grace and Michelle chatting casually while sitting on our toilet seat at the same time.

As the child in each of my girls was dying and the adult blossoming, I hoped that the sacred storytelling would survive. I never wanted them to hear the words 'Grow up!'

For me, it was already happening too fast. For the children, it was not fast enough. Nothing could buffer me from the thunderstorms on the horizon, when my three fairies wore different . . . wings.

HOW TO BUY PADS

'When she saw the blood dripping down her thighs, she thought she was dying,' explained Grace about a guest speaker at school, 'so she used bandaids and hid in her cupboard until her mum finally found her.'

'That's sad,' I frowned while washing dishes in the kitchen sink. 'Didn't her mother . . . warn her?'

This is why the school arranged a guest speaker to give 'the talk' in Year 6, separating the girls from the boys to have honest conversations about what to expect as the child's body becomes an adult's body. Grace also had private talks with Lola, and with Rita, who had been like a sister to Nadia in Melbourne. Rita prepared a kit that included tables to note the date of the period. Grace innocently invented the term 'front bum' for such conversations, and her sisters followed suit.

In anticipation, every time Grace had any sign, I rushed her to the doctor.

'Joe, you're carrying on like you're expecting a baby,' smiled our family doctor. 'Just relax. Everyone is different. The first few will all be different.'

The birth of Grace's womanhood reminded me of her actual birth. As soon as Nadia felt the slightest twinge I rushed her to hospital, but they turned out to be Braxton Hicks contractions.

By the time Grace's head emerged, I had not eaten or drunk for twelve hours and fell to the floor. When I came around, I was slumped on a couch surrounded by pillows, with my feet up and doctors fussing over me. They even offered me Nadia's oxygen mask!

'Hey!' moaned Nadia from her bed, '*I'm* the patient here, not him!'

I rose to my feet in time to witness the miraculous moment of a human emerging from within a human. Tears streaked down both our faces. A baby girl in my arms gave me permission to be soft and delicate. She melted into my muscles and my heart melted in my chest. Baby girls unleash a side of us men that might otherwise have remained dormant.

There is a wise Arabic proverb: '*Kil walad bi jeeb rizoqtu ma'oo* (All newborns bring their good fortunes along with them).' Sure enough, the next day I received notification that I had been appointed multicultural affairs commissioner for Victoria.

'Dad, are you listening?' Grace nudged me and I realised that the kitchen tap had been running water over my hands. 'You need to sign this form for school so I can see that video.'

'Oh . . . oh. Didn't I already sign the form?'

'This is different because it was added on.'

'Hang on, my hands are all wet. Wait till I finish.'

I trusted the school and knew that their view of menstruation would be the same as the church's and our family's. 'Grace,' I explained, 'this is God's way of giving you a regular clean. Your womb of human life must be in pristine condition.' I turned to face her and raised a squeaky-clean glass, surprised that the perfect metaphor for this milestone moment was immediately to hand.

When her first period finally landed, Grace was ready. We fussed, we announced, we celebrated. I knew that Nadia always bought Stayfree Regular with Wings, and assumed that Grace had inherited the same anatomy and preferences. The brand name was deceptive, though. It sounded like a free-flying bird, but the marketers must have been sarcastic men. I soon learnt that at this time of month, many girls cannot run, cannot swim, cannot dance, cannot bend. Some even throw up and are bedridden for days. Perhaps they should have a more honest brand name, like Stay Put or Not Bloody Going Anywhere.

Like Grace, Michelle's first period arrived when she was thirteen. But unlike Grace, she experienced cramps and headaches as early warning signs. There was a song and dance, reminding me of her arrival as a baby.

After some 'distress' in her heartbeat due to the umbilical cord being wrapped around her elbow, Michelle was delivered by emergency caesarean. The speed of the surgery was surreal, and then the newborn was swiftly transferred to a humidicrib. For countless hours, my eyes were fixated on this glowing creation in her incubator. Not having been pushed through the birth canal, Michelle had no bruises and was beyond beautiful.

By the time Joy's first period arrived, she had two veteran sisters as 'padding'. I arrived home from work to find Grace and Michelle doing *dabke* (folk dancing) in the bathroom, stomping their feet in unison and twirling their hands in the air as if they were changing light globes.

'It finally happened!' they sang out over their revelry.

'What happened?' I panicked, guessing that Joy was behind the closed toilet door.

'Her *period*, of course! You're gonna be a grandpa, *mabrouk* (congratulations)!' laughed Michelle. 'Come on, join in!'

She took my hand and I joined the party while waiting for our butterfly to emerge from her cocoon.

'We-le-le-le-le,' we celebrated with a *zalghouta*, the falsetto ululation that is reserved in our culture for joyful occasions. This revelry from the bathroom must have sounded strange to our neighbours.

Soon the bathroom became the busiest room of our home, as my daughters conducted their hourly checks.

As the Minister of Foreign Affairs, it was my responsibility to bring home a sufficient supply of sanitary pads.

'Quick, Dad, it's an emergency.'

How was I supposed to know when stocks were running low? I needed a flashing red light and a siren on my car for these mercy dashes: make way for menopausal man on a menstrual mission—coming through! I mapped out the nearest all-night chemists, and learnt which brands had 'night and day' pads for those heavy nights.

'Someone get me a pad!' became both an SOS from the bathroom and a celebration. I was happy to be called 'someone', that hairy hand that reached inside the door carrying the sanitary pads and the sanity handshake.

'Thanks, Dad.'

'No, thank *you*!' They had no idea how relieved I was.

Once, in a rush, I bought pads without wings. It was a bad time to make such a bad move.

'What do you *mean* you didn't notice? I've told you a hundred times! These are useless!' they cried, throwing the 'useless' pack at me.

'Dad, you're so smart yet so dumb!'

Just down the aisle from the pads were the baby nappies, my old haunt. Further up the same aisle were the incontinence pads. Now that *did* haunt me. This entire aisle became a metaphor for our life cycle. I was initially very coy in this aisle. If someone was

154

in the pad section, I would park my trolley near the men's toiletries and pretend to be browsing at the razors. When the coast was clear, I would pounce and exit. I had no time to ask questions and no patience to receive sympathy. I would bury the pads in the trolley so that they could be scanned then quickly buried in a bag. Why the secrecy?

I was eight when my elder sister Eva gave me clear instructions: 'Here's the money. Now go to the shop across the road. Wait until the man behind the counter is by himself, then whisper to him that you need Modess in a brown paper bag.'

'Thank you.' Strange how I thanked her, when I was the one saving her the embarrassment of a girl asking a man for pads.

'Oh, and you can spend the change on lollies,' she would add, smiling in gratitude.

The shopkeeper figured me out and realised I had no idea what I was buying. On subsequent trips, whenever I loitered between his aisles and peered at him between the shelves, he smiled and put me out of my misery.

Times have changed. Now I am a familiar face in the sanitary napkins aisle. I spin the pads into the trolley from a distance and wave to the security cameras in case anyone watching wants a laugh. Sometimes I almost expect to hear an announcement over the PA: 'Security to aisle seven.'

Now the table has turned. Women needing access to the aisle keep their distance from *me*. Are *they* embarrassed? One lady picked up a regular Stayfree pack and I noticed that it was without wings. As she was reading the pack, I felt in all conscience that I had to help.

'Wings are better,' I advised, holding up my pack.

'I beg your pardon?' she asked, frowning.

'They're useless. They leak,' I explained. 'I tried. Never again.'

She blushed and took a step back. 'They're not for me.'

'Neither are mine,' I shrugged, 'but that's what they all tell me.'

'What?' she laughed.

'Trust me,' I laughed back. 'I should know.'

I really should have flown away at that instant like a comic super-hero, dressed as a pad with a large S for Stayfree on my chest and a Superman cape. They could have paid me to fly around the aisles as their mobile advertisement.

I had barely noticed any premenstrual tension with Nadia. Her natural temperament was calm and I was blessed. When three women live in the same house, though, their cycles apparently talk to each other and synchronise. It was like three planets orbiting the sun deciding to eclipse all at once, rubbing their hands and counting down: three, two, one—let's have a blast!

Everything about my daughters seemed sharper during these times—their words, their mood swings, their fingernails, even their teeth. There was nowhere for me to hide. Understanding the plumbing chart was one thing, but understanding the mood chart was another. As the time of month arrived, they became more peckish, so I stocked up the pantry with snacks. But I felt like I was walking on eggshells, no matter where I turned.

I learned that pimples were 'breaking out' when their periods were approaching. Back in 'my day', Clearasil cream was the standard solution, but we had to rub it in to hide the evidence. My daughters craved a faster solution and I remembered something that seemed to work in Lebanon: the panacea for all ailments—'aaraq, a clear, aniseed-sweetened, distilled spirit.

Upon my arrival in Lebanon in 1988, my uncle 'baptised' me with this drink by pouring it over my head. Apparently, this pure spirit would ward off any nasty germs and boost my immunity. It was about 70 per cent alcohol and soon evaporated from my hair, although the aroma lingered. Hours later, I would encounter my future wife for the first time, reeking of alcohol!

This bacteria-killing spirit was also drunk before eating any uncooked meat. My youngest sister Georgina was staying in Lebanon at the time and she explained how 'aaraq can be wiped on foreheads as an instant acne-killing antiseptic.

Now I was concocting my own brew by mixing 'aaraq with drops of methylated spirits and water. I poured the mixture into a Pop Tops popper, a 250 ml plastic bottle with a pop-up lid, intended for children's fruit juices. My children dabbed it with cotton balls and it cleared their pimples overnight. When their school friends noticed the results, they asked my daughters for the 'secret recipe'. I donned my apron and rubber gloves like a scientist and was filling poppers of this potion for their friends, for free. My daughters kept taking orders and I could barely keep up with the demand.

But the potion was so potent that some girls complained about dry, flaky skin. What did they want for nothing? Did I need to add a warning label: Please rehydrate your skin with moisturiser after use? My dream of becoming the acne-buster evaporated.

After witnessing many cycles, I plotted the pattern: my daughters would be at their most irritable about three days before the due date, compounded by 'breaking out'. When the period arrived, there was some relief, but on the second day, the flow was so heavy that they could not, or would not, hear me. That is almost one week per month when girls are uncomfortable. That is a quarter of their childbearing life! I could not imagine such discomfort, 24 hours a day, a week per month.

It takes a lot to make my daughters cry, but when we watched the movie *To Sir, With Love*, I saw Grace's eyes turn red.

'Are you all right?' I asked tenderly.

The floodgates opened and she bawled her eyes out. 'I don't know why I'm crying!' she wailed. She headed for her bed and sobbed and sobbed. Any attempts to console her were met with a snappy 'Leave me alone!' Michelle and Joy cast sideways glances and knew exactly what was going on. They had instant empathy and knew when to let it go.

When it was her turn, Michelle would storm into the house with barely a hello. Her hunger pains would send her straight to the pantry, where she'd swing the pantry doors open and stand there staring. We'd see her hands on the handles and hold our breath for her verdict.

'There's no food!' she'd cry, slamming the pantry doors. 'I'm going to McDonald's!'

'But Michelle, we could cook up something for you . . .'

Exit and slam again.

She ticked like a hand grenade and it was unwise to mess with her. Apparently, we were all 'annoying' and if I tried to have the last word, this was 'aggravating'.

'Joy, why are you eating off my plate?' exploded Michelle.

'It's mine. Yours is still in the microwave.'

'No, I know exactly what my plate looks like, and that's my plate!'

Joy opened the microwave door to prove her point, but Michelle simply gave a sarcastic smile and wobbled her head.

'No sorry, no nothing?' huffed Joy, her mouth agape and daggers in her eyes.

'Get over it,' retorted Michelle in a monotone.

Joy once phoned me, sobbing, while I was still at work.

I panicked and thought the worst. 'What is it, darling?'

'When are you coming home? They're screaming at me!'

'Hand the phone to Grace, please.'

'No! I'm not talking to her! Or Michelle! They were just attacking me!'

I called the house phone to play long-distance mediator, even though they were all just metres apart.

'Dad,' explained Grace, 'it's the other way round. Joy was attacking us, using language she should never use, then using her period as her excuse.'

'All over what?'

'Because Joy didn't put her cup in the sink.'

'Are you serious?'

'Well, that's how it started, then they started competing as to who does more work around the house, who takes the clothes off the line—'

'Stop, Grace. Couldn't that chat wait until Joy settles down? You know nothing sinks in when our gills are red.'

'Don't tell me, tell Michelle!'

I wished I could practise what I preached. It was wise to pick my fights and let some go until the temperature dropped. Otherwise, our family could descend into one big catfight until I barked.

When the due date had passed without a result, they would look up and plead: 'Just hurry up!'

'Who are you talking to?' I asked.

'He who controls this!' they explained, pointing to their bellies.

They'd become angrier by the day, and I soon signed their petition to 'He who controls this'.

I once walked into a yelling match between all three of my daughters.

'Michelle, you're a hypocrite. When you come home late, you turn on the bedroom light and stamp your feet as if I don't exist, and I'm asleep . . . *asleep!*' Joy clapped her hands to emphasise the point.

'Not like *you* in the morning!' Michelle snapped back. 'You never, *ever* shut the bedroom door, and you know I just need ten more minutes' sleep, I'm not asking for much!'

'Why don't you prepare your clothes the night before?' Grace suggested to Joy.

'Well, that's easy for you, princess with her own room. And you still barge into my room and take my clothes without asking. What did I do to deserve this?' Michelle asked, tilting her head back.

'Excuse me, but some of them are hand-me-downs. They were originally mine!'

Michelle gave her sister a death stare then uttered one of my scornful sayings. 'Try and make sense! If you gave them to me, how are they your clothes?' Michelle was the spitting image of me when she was sarcastic. She had picked up my exact phrases and even my facial expressions. Is that how I looked and sounded in an argument? Ouch! It had to stop immediately. By now the pitch was so shrill that I half-expected a glass to break.

'Okay, Michelle,' sighed Joy, rolling her eyes. 'I'll try and be quieter in the morning.'

'Wrong answer!' It was another one of my stock sayings that had rubbed off. 'The right answer is: "*Sorry*, Michelle, I *will* be quiet in the morning while you're still asleep."'

'So *I* should say sorry? What about *you*?'

Michelle sighed and placed her hand on her heart. 'You're giving me anxiety. You know what anxiety is?'

'I know, Michelle,' Joy stared at her without blinking.

'It's when your heart is beating fast as if you're running, but you're actually not moving.'

This was spiralling out of control and I had to step in.

'Enough! The neighbours can hear you screaming. There's a simple solution.' The three of them slowly turned their heads to face me as if something had suddenly possessed them.

'You're the worst!' Michelle's voice was now so high-pitched that I was expecting dogs to start barking. 'You yell to Joy from the kitchen *all* the way to the bedroom, when I'm in a deep sleep!' She drew an arch in the air with her finger to dramatise the distance.

'Yeah, Dad, why do you do that?' added Joy. '*And* you talk non-stop first thing in the morning. Sometimes I just want you to shut up!'

I chose to pick my fights and bite my tongue, but Michelle lit up. 'See, Dad, you let her get away with blue murder. I was *never* allowed to talk to you like that!'

'And the dishes, Dad, while we're at it!' added Grace. 'Do you *have* to pack them away first thing in the morning and wake up the whole house!'

'But I'm making room for the next batch of dishes,' I said, defending myself but sounding pathetic.

'It's the male mind,' concluded Michelle. 'Are the stupid dishes more important than your daughters' health? Do you need to announce that you're working while we're sleeping?'

Of course, no one was interested in my 'simple solution', but I will tell you, just for the record. Joy could use Nadia's half of my wardrobe to hang her school clothes and get dressed in my room rather than wake up Michelle. There. Done. But instead of hearing me out, all three just joined ranks and ganged up on me.

While I understood the need for womb-cleansing in preparation for human life, I could not work out the divine logic behind the emotional roller-coaster that rattled my children and rattled me. Was it to toughen them up for the reality of motherhood and the demands of babies?

When the 'great flood' finally arrived, there was relief in the air. The exorcism was over and they were exhausted. I wanted to hug them, but they said they felt 'icky' and disgusting. To make up for the absence of maternal affection and understanding, I offered foot massages with soothing aloe vera cream. Joy never said no to a massage, but Michelle was ticklish and Grace was grossed out by feet, even her own.

By day two, they felt heavy and the car trip to school was silent. They needed rehydration, not conversation. Out of ignorance, I used to make many attempts to chat, as this was supposed to be our quality time.

'So, are you looking forward to the weekend?'

They gave me monosyllabic answers, or noises that sounded like words but meant 'Shoosh up, I can't be bothered answering your stupid questions'. Indeed, this was the age when the two most over-used words were 'bothered' and 'annoying'.

I once found myself wishing they had a dot on their forehead that changed colour to indicate what stage they were at in the cycle. Like a mood ring! Blue for PMS so I would know to offer snacks, prefer-ably fatty foods, and stand back. Red for arrival, so I would know to offer them drinks and remain silent. And a green light for the end of the cycle, so I would know I could talk again. Of course, the dot would only be visible to me, so I knew when to enter, exit, tiptoe or run. But perhaps this just meant that I was the one going dotty.

There was a simpler solution staring at me every day: the kitchen calendar. It marked all our social commitments so we did not double book. Perfect! I added blue and red dots as my secret code to control my social calendar.

The blue dot denoted days when I should consider working back late at the office. At home, only speak when I was spoken to. Cook a meal the night before. Offer a tray of nibbles, in silence. Not buy into any arguments. Not hire emotional movies. Expect to do extra housework. Not plan any dinners or social events. And remember that it was *all my fault*. After all, as one flustered woman once reminded me while fanning herself, *men*struation and *men*opause both start with 'men'.

The red dot would denote those days I should come home earlier in case I was needed to drive somewhere. Not plan any physical activities. Hire a comedy movie and make popcorn. Expect more laundry and not complain because . . .? It's all my fault. See, I was a quick learner. At the end of the red dot 'period', I could take them out to dinner and hug them heaps.

Of course, in the real world, the cycles do not always synchronise.

'Dad, why are there so many dots on the calendar?'

Busted. 'What do you think?'

'Oh . . . oh! That's not funny,' frowned Grace. 'That's disgusting, actually.'

'Imagine if visitors see!' Michelle ripped off the page. 'Did you want the whole world to know?'

'How would *you* like it?' added Joy. 'Men never understand these things!'

It was a bad idea. I should have used the calendar on my phone instead. But Joy was right. How would I react if my children labelled their calendar G for grumpy as I went through male menopause? Or if my friends avoided me every April in the lead-up to Nadia's anniversary, as if I were a leper?

Throughout it all, I would talk to Nadia in my head. 'Oh, Nadia, I wish you were here at these milestone moments. I love them so much. I try to feel their pain, but I'm so out of my depth. I don't have a mother's intuition. I want to hug them and cuddle them in my lap, even if it looks stupid. It hurts so much when I drive home so late from work and find them asleep. I confess, it's pure selfishness to avoid their pain, but then I can't sleep all night for the pain of my own guilt.

'Where was I when they were doubling over in pain? Was I holding their hand and telling them that everything would be all right? Where was I, knowing that you weren't there either? Well, of course you were there in spirit and you see everything, but you know what I mean. Where was I? I was giving them space. Like that man at the church who wanted to give me some time to be alone!'

Suddenly, I was overcome with melancholy, even though I was making light of the situation. Is this what mood swings feel like?

When I heard other men make derogatory comments about their wife 'on the rags' and how she needed to 'get over it', I would grit my teeth. When it comes to our own daughters, our own flesh and blood, we are so protective, but why would we treat our wives differently?

While psychotherapy costs time and retail therapy costs money, I often proclaimed that hugs are free. But not all teenagers are huggers. And if they have already outgrown hugs or they have been phased out over childhood, it becomes awkward to suddenly exchange affection. I found myself feeling pangs of jealousy if my daughters expressed more affection to another relative or sat on their lap. Strange how my protective feelings could morph so quickly into possessive feelings.

With the ebb and flow of their lunar cycles, their oceans oscillated between calm and stormy. The last thing they needed was a parent acting the same way. They needed me to be an open hand, reaching out and ever-ready, not a clenched fist, shaking. What they needed most was a lighthouse that stayed solid and in their sights, that did not crumble in the wild waves, that kept signalling its presence with a steady rhythm.

I thought of that famous 1989 photo by French photographer Jean Guichard, of wild ocean waves encircling a lighthouse. I wanted to be that lighthouse, and I wanted my teenage daughters to find shelter whenever they needed to rest in the bosom of the family.

HOW TO COMPETE WITH A SCREEN

'There's nothing on,' sighed Michelle after flicking through dozens of television channels on the remote control.

'Of *course* there's something on,' I retorted. 'When I was your age, we only had five channels and there was always something on.'

Michelle rolled her eyes. 'Well, that was back in your dark ages.'

'And we had to get up to change channels, not use the . . .'

I had a mental blank and waved my hand, '. . . thing.'

'What thing?'

Was she mocking me? 'The stupid thing in your hand . . . You know *exactly* what I mean.'

'Oh, the remote control,' she smiled.

'Yeah, that thing,' I vented. 'And I didn't flick back and forth to see what's on. I bought the *Green Guide* every Thursday and circled what I wanted to watch in advance. There was always something interesting on.'

'But your interesting and my interesting are different.'

I sighed. 'Why are we paying for all these extra channels if there's nothing on?'

Michelle checkmated me. 'You know *exactly* what I mean.'

I had patented that expression and now she was throwing it right back at me. Was she mirroring me deliberately?

What hung like a magic mirror on the main wall of our living room was the large flat-screen television. It occupied centre stage and the lounge may as well have been the front row of an auditorium. Everything faced His Majesty, the television screen. Fortunately for me, my three had similar tastes in television, so one screen was enough.

When Nadia and I had designed this layout, we were celebrating the new home-theatre technology and wanted it to be enticing and exciting, but it turned out to be too much so. His Majesty morphed into my worst enemy.

His Majesty's voice was always occupying my home. He became a magnet, a fireplace, a companion, an entertainer, a therapist. He became a real man and I felt threatened. What did he have that I lacked?

'Listen here,' I would tell him, 'I hung you up and I can bring you down.' I clenched my fist at him when the two of us had a man-to-man moment alone. 'I plugged you in and I can unplug you . . . any time. This is *my* family, you hear me! You should get back in your box and stop looking down on us as if you're . . .' He had been hanging around with us long enough to know *exactly* what I meant.

But as he felt at home, he became ever more charismatic, more colourful, more charming. When I arrived home from work and longed to have a conversation with my teenage children, there he was again, seducing them with the latest fashions, wedding dresses, home improvements, Kardashians. He was filling their heads with things that we could not afford. He even gave them late nights with a *Big Brother*! It felt strange to arrive home to a man's voice. His Majesty had invaded my kingdom!

'So, how was your day, gals?'

'Good,' they hummed in monotone while their eyes remained glued to his shiny façade. What they really meant was, 'Shoosh, Dad, can't you see we're watching . . . him.'

I would grit my teeth and try again. 'Shall I make pasta that you can take for lunch tomorrow?'

Silence again.

'Did anyone hear me?'

'Whatever!'

Is that it? That does it! I thought. *Enough is enough.* I marched in front of the large screen and exclaimed, 'I'm competing with a screen!'

They did not notice my rage. The flat-faced bastard had them under his spell. They merely moved their heads so they could still see as much of him as possible. They wanted me to be invisible. And silent. And so did he.

There was only one thing left to do to release them from his evil spell. His Majesty, unplugged! *Take that!* His blank face turned black.

'Hey! We were watching that!' they protested.

'When that . . . thing is switched on, you're switched off. It's a family-destroyer.'

They marched off to their rooms, stomping their feet. When I checked on them later, guess what my teenagers were doing? Yep, watching television programs on their laptops, their Mini-Majesties.

'Seriously,' I shook my head. 'This is an addictive drug. Why don't you read a book?'

'I am!' Joy turned her screen around and, sure enough, she was reading a book online.

But at other times, the 'book' was Facebook.

'Very funny,' I would snigger. Another addictive drug. 'Put your real face into a real book!'

'Very funny,' they echoed.

Another night of grocery shopping after work. Another night where my hands ached from the plastic bags that cut into my palms. I had them in perfect balance and could not reach the doorbell. I kicked the door. No answer. I heard that bastard's voice inside, making my children laugh, making them love him, making them listen, making them obey: stay tuned, don't go away!

I yelled out like Fred Flintstone crying 'Wilma!' at the front door. No response. That bastard drowned me out, locked me out of my own home, my own family. Was this really happening? Were my children possessed by this demonic force? I waved my shopping bags, but despite all this commotion, the sensor light did not even register my arrival. Was it colluding with His Majesty? I was an invisible man, dancing in the dark.

I kicked the door again and yelled out, 'Can someone open the door please!' Finally, our hall light came on and Grace opened the door. By then, my blood was boiling. 'About time!' I panted.

'Let me take some—' Grace reached out.

'Too late! I've been standing here screaming for half an hour!' I exaggerated.

'Why didn't you just ring the doorbell?'

I couldn't be bothered explaining. 'Why didn't you hear me?'

'We were just watching—'

'TV, I know. The family-destroyer. Again!'

'— our favourite show.'

'And I just bought your favourite food. But who cares!' I shoved past and headed for the kitchen where I swung the loaded bags and landed them on the bench with a satisfying bang. 'Why am I yelling over the top of that *akhu sharmouta* (brother of a whore)?' Only Arabic could hit the spot when I was in this mood. 'Turn that thing down before I cut its cables and *shillo masareeno* (remove his intestines)!'

I wanted to cut off this artificial intelligence. I empathised with Dave who disconnected the computer named HAL in *2001: A Space Odyssey*. Dave had to destroy the monster as it was destroying his crew. I had to do the same to this oddity that was destroying my family.

My daughters exchanged sidelong glances and read each other. On cue, they unpacked all the bags into the fridge, pantry and bathrooms. Then, like robots, they returned to the same sofa positions they had occupied before they were rudely interrupted.

'Maybe we should have had a pet dog!' I remarked. 'At least he would wag his tail and jump on me and make me feel welcome every time he saw me.'

'So you're comparing us with a dog?' Michelle asked, raising her head and her left eyebrow.

'No, I'm comparing *myself* with a dog. I fetch the bones and bring them home.' I made my dramatic exit to leave that thought hanging.

In my bedroom, I changed out of my work clothes into shorts and a T-shirt so I could cool down and calm down. Inner voices spoke. *Breathe. Pick your fights. Don't scratch them with your words or you'll bleed of guilt and lie awake all night.*

I re-entered the living room. Take two. They were now watching their favourite series, *One Tree Hill*. Don't ask me which of the nine seasons, I wasn't paying attention. But they certainly were. As they watched the screen, I watched their faces. What had His Majesty done to my daughters? They were sitting forward, frozen, expressionless. I had flashbacks of the street kids who sat stoned on heroin, motionless and unblinking.

I had brought home the ingredients for one of their favourite Lebanese meals, *kousa mahshi*, zucchini stuffed with lamb, rice, tomato, onion, parsley, mint and spices, then boiled in a tomato sauce. It was all from my Aunt Abla's cookbook, of course.

As I hollowed out the zucchini, I hoped they would notice and offer to help, but there was no contest between their favourite meal and their favourite television program. They happened to be watching a scene where the characters were in the kitchen, cooking.

'Hey, instead of watching Americans pretend to cook, why don't you really cook?' I asked.

No answer. My corer went right through the zucchini and nearly through my palm. No one noticed. They would not have noticed if I had drawn blood. I became steadily more passive aggressive. I chopped the white onion as loudly as possible, in the hope they would notice and help. They simply turned up the volume, without even looking at me.

Tears rolled down my cheeks. Was that the chopped onion or me feeling sorry for myself? I knew it was not their fault. I blamed His Majesty, the drug dealer. Their faces told the story—they were zoned out and I was a shadow in the background, an annoying mosquito that buzzed and sometimes stung and did not know when to buzz off.

Now they were watching a scene of a family playing Pictionary together. We had that exact game in a box in the console beneath the television.

'Oh, we should play that game after dinner!' I exclaimed, deliberately walking back and forth past the screen, pretending to look for the Pictionary box. Their heads bobbed left and right.

'Instead of watching Americans pretending to play board games, why don't we really play?' I stood before the screen and extended my arms. 'I'm 3D, this is 2D. Why are you watching them pretend to have a life when you can have a real life yourselves?'

My venting was contagious, so they vented on each other.

'Put your legs together! Sit like a lady.'

'Well, you're not exactly crossing your legs.'

'Look, it's hot and we're home, so who cares?'

'*I* care. Look how you're all slouched,' I interjected. 'I care about your posture.'

When the tomato sauce boiled around the *kousa mahshi*, they inhaled the aroma.

'Mmm, smells amazing.'

'Reminds me of Mum's cooking.'

Why do we inhale those we love? Why does their scent—their clothes, their food, their perfume—linger in our memory long after their voices and faces fade?

When I filled the first plate, their favourite meal finally trumped their favourite program, and they were poised at the bench. I wanted to tell the story of the *Little Red Hen* that I had read as a child—the hen received no help from the other farm animals to prepare the bread, but plenty of help to eat it—but I bit my lip. I was not a hen. I was a rooster, and I was determined to rule the roost.

Just for one night, I told myself, *don't let them feel guilty. Just for one night, don't go to bed feeling guilty.* Was that Nadia speaking again?

One evening, I returned from work to find His Majesty muted, their laptops on and their mobile phones on. His big screen was flashing music videos on the MTV channel, presumably to illuminate the room like a nightclub. The laptops were presumably being used to do their homework. Their mobile phones were either playing their favourite songs or for messaging or both.

I counted seven screens switched on for only three people. They were not teenagers, they were screenagers. And they, apparently, were normal, while I, apparently, was . . . old.

'Gals, one screen at a time! Pick one. Either the TV, the laptop or the phone.'

'Dad, we're multitasking,' replied Grace on their behalf. 'We're used to it.'

'Well, you need to get used to mono-tasking,' I replied. 'And concentrate on your schoolwork.'

'The male mind can't handle it,' mocked Michelle, 'but we can juggle.'

A bell rang, alerting Grace to a text message. I did not mean to pry, but it was in my face and seeking attention. 'Umm . . . I'm not sure,' it said.

I laughed.

'What's so funny?' asked Grace.

'Do your friends actually write the word "umm"?'

She smiled and shrugged. 'Yeah, it just means they're thinking and that's why their message was delayed.'

'But their message came through in one hit, so you don't know that while you're waiting, they're umming, right, so what's the point?'

Michelle jumped in. 'Dad, you're overanalysing as usual. It's just how we text.'

'So if I yawn, do I add that as a text? Imagine—"Hi Michelle (yawn), what time r u cuming home 2nite (ah-choo!) . . . excuse me . . . and can u buy me some . . . umm . . . Panadol (cough cough) . . . coz I feel sick (burp) . . . oh soz about that."'

There was a pause before Michelle applauded slowly. 'Are you trying to be funny?'

'I don't think it's funny. I think it's hilarious! Just pick up the phone and talk instead of spelling out every sound that comes out of your mouth!'

'It's free text and we're saving you money,' concluded Michelle, raising her left eyebrow.

Should I have taken that as *my* cue to applaud slowly?

When they were asleep, His Majesty and I had to have another man-to-man chat. I sat down, but instead of venting, I felt tempted. My hand reached for that thing, the remote control, and I found myself navigating my way through his visual smorgasbord. I could escape to another part of the planet on World Movies. I could escape to the animal kingdom on Discovery. I could escape back in time on the History Channel. I could escape.

As I sat alone, mesmerised, I remembered that this was how Nadia loved to wind down before sleeping. Unlike me, who stays in overdrive then suddenly sleeps, Nadia needed to change gears gently, from standing to the couch to the bed—from vertical to oblique to horizontal. So why was I so critical of my children following in her footsteps, and sofa steps?

After indulging in my own screen time, I turned it off and figured out the solution.

'Thanks, Your Majesty,' I said to the blank screen. 'I must admit, that was . . . relaxing. But I need you to foster my family, not destroy it.'

And so I took the initiative. 'Gals, let's have a movie night and watch something together.'

'Dad? Watching TV?' They cheered.

'No, I'm not a convert,' I waved my finger. 'I just want to make the most of it.'

One film we watched, *The Help*, is a powerful portrait of the racism experienced by black maids during the civil rights movement in America. I was inspired by the female lead character, who used her pen to expose the truth. It encouraged me to sharpen my own pen and expose racism against Lebanese in Australia.

As my children 'relaxed' with His Majesty, I typed away with two fingers, hoping my opinion columns would be published. Suddenly, I was as addicted to my screen as they were to theirs, as if two antisocial wrongs somehow made a right.

Like my children, I blinked once and lost track of time. Night after night, I researched and wrote and vented. The more my pieces were published, the more addicted I became. The Middle East was almost always making front-page news, so there was never any shortage of 'hooks', nor any shortage of fire in my belly.

But too much exposure to that rectangular screen dried out my eyeballs. The bags sagged under my eyes then seemed to turn upwards, curve around my nose and extend over my eyes. Who had ever seen bags circumnavigate the eyes? The dark circles around my eyes in the morning looked like bicycle tyres.

During the night, I had been disturbed from my deep sleep by the sound of a wild animal snorting just outside my bedroom window. Or so I thought. After a couple of disturbances and after checking outside, I discovered something most embarrassing. Those wild noises were coming from me. Who ever heard of being so tired that you wake yourself up with your own snoring? I imagined being remarried and evicted to sleep in a separate room. 'Don't leave me alone with that noise,' I would plead. 'I'm coming too!'

One Saturday morning, His Majesty dealt me a treat that was too close to home. I woke up to Nadia laughing. Was this a dream? Impossible! It was uncanny. I heard it again. What were they watching on that screen?

I stumbled out of bed and headed for the living room. It turned out that they had woken up in the mood to have a laugh at old family videos from the BC era. There was Nadia, in her radiant glory days, the way I preferred to remember her, laughing.

There were no tears in our living room. I had heard of other families who could never watch videos featuring someone they missed, but my three accepted this as a part of life, not its opposite. I snuggled up next to them, and we all laughed together—me, Nadia and our three girls.

I take it back, Your Majesty, I thought. *You brought Nadia into our living room. You brought smiles to our faces. You brought our family closer together. Sorry about cursing you, especially in Arabic.*

HOW TO SATISFY THE STYLE POLICE

'A widowed father with three daughters? Bet they pamper you!'

I heard this comment so many times during social introductions when someone mentioned my 'status' as if it were a badge of honour. I would look down at the floor and shuffle my feet, as I knew exactly what would follow.

'You're so lucky,' they would add, patronising me, nodding as if they knew exactly what it was like. 'Bet they cook and clean for you, especially in your culture.'

I turned the stereotype on its head and pretended to be bourgeois. 'Oh no, my daughters are too good for that. They're too busy with the *sèche-cheveux* (hair dryer), *bronzage* (suntan) and *chauffeur*. They might wreck their nails. I have my house maid to cook and clean, like we do back in my country.'

'Wow, you speak French?'

'And we have electricity, too.'

I admit it, that last comment was uncalled for, but the stereotypes were so far from the truth that they deserved to be shaken and stirred.

In one department of my life, though, my daughters did take a keen interest. I had graduated from a free university degree to a career on the streets, so you can probably imagine my op-shop taste in clothes. No, an op-shop was upmarket. I had no taste. I would throw on the same jeans, whatever shoes and a loud top, all with no sense of colour coordination. My sisters used to frown at my mismatched clothes but my response remained, 'I care not!'

Perhaps opposites attract, given Nadia graduated from university as a designer! In time, she taught me about the correct length of a tie, how belts should match shoes and which colours clash.

While my daughters did not 'pamper' me, they did protect me. They did not want me to be embarrassed or criticised. They did not want to hear any bad words said about their dad. And so they became my self-appointed style police.

They had an innate sense of 'this goes with that' and I became their apprentice. Perhaps it was the fashion parades screened by His Majesty. Perhaps it was inherited from their mother. I wanted to take my hat off to them, but they wouldn't even let me wear a hat!

'Hats make you look too young, or too old,' insisted Grace.

'Besides, all the friction makes you go bald,' warned Michelle, enlarging her blue eyes.

'Correction, bald-er!' giggled Joy, patting my head.

'Not funny.' I covered my bald patch with my palm. A *yamaka* would have concealed it perfectly. 'My lunar panel absorbs my lunacy.'

As the style police came to life, our spontaneous outings died. My daughters needed notice to check all their angles in front of the mirror. I realised that a house without a mirror would be torture for a teenager. Even when His Majesty was switched off, he still served as a mirror for my daughters.

Our hall became a catwalk.

'Do these look all right together?' they would ask each other.

'Hmm, the white pants make your hips look big. Haven't you got black ones?'

I was intrigued by their sharp lens and their prompt responses. Their sense of style was so strong that both Grace and Michelle were later offered weekend work at a menswear store.

'Your sunglasses are growing on me,' I once heard Grace say to Michelle.

'I told you,' replied Michelle. 'It always takes you a bit longer to like what I like. But once you like it, you love it.'

My benchmarks must have been low, because I could not understand the fuss. I stood at the crossroads with two options: be a passive recipient of their verdicts or be an active player and learn! Why some men walk away from the latter opportunity is beyond me. The creator mixed and matched certain colours in birds. Who would have thought that bright pink, pale pink and grey feathers would look so perfect on a galah and inspire artists? So of course my daughters, His mini-creators, could be a reflection of this natural beauty. And so could I.

They taught me some basic rules: vertical stripes on a shirt make you look thinner; black shoes go with almost everything; a white shirt goes with almost everything; pants should be a darker colour than the top; checks clash with stripes. And the most important rule: obtain their stamp of approval. At least while I was their apprentice.

On one occasion, they conducted an audit of my wardrobe. They were no longer the style police, arresting and prosecuting me for crimes against fashion. They had become the juvenile judiciary, judging me. They sat on the edge of my bed with their arms and legs crossed.

'Next!' they demanded.

As I exhibited each item, they declared their verdict: yes, no or *hell* no. I reserved the right to appeal some no verdicts with a fourth category: sentimental, for those clothes that were a special gift from a special person. The juvenile judiciary was ruthless and gutted my wardrobe. The mountain of preloved rejects became bags of unloved offerings to the charity bins.

'But now I have hardly anything left,' I protested. 'My wardrobe is bare.' That was not strictly true. Some of Nadia's clothes still hung in the central section of the wardrobe. Memories of her affinity with earthy colours flooded back.

'Are you gonna cry?' laughed Michelle, noticing my melancholy face and raising her left eyebrow. 'Over clothes?'

I had to snap out of it.

'Don't worry,' consoled Grace. 'We'll go to DFO together on Saturday and get you a whole new wardrobe. You're way overdue.'

It was a privilege to have three in-house stylists who cared so much.

As the gap between their heights decreased, their sharing of clothes increased. This solved one practical problem.

'Did you wear that top last week?' asked Michelle.

'I think I did,' replied Grace.

'Then you can't wear it tonight.'

'Why not?' I intervened.

Michelle rolled her eyes. 'Do you want people to think your daughter has no other clothes?'

'I don't care what people think . . .'

'What?' frowned Michelle. 'So *you* don't care what people say about us?'

'You know exactly what I mean.' Wrong way! Go back! 'I thought *you* didn't care about peer pressure.'

I was really pressing their buttons. 'Dad, you're insulting us,' squinted Michelle. 'Since when were we followers?'

I was not concerned about wearing the same set of clothes in front of the same group of people on a different occasion. I was not concerned if anyone thought or said, 'Oh, how cheap! He's been wearing them since last week. They must be stuck to his skin. Doesn't he have any other clothes? Doesn't he have daughters who care?' Maybe men have it easy. We can wear out the same jeans and sneakers as our every-weekend clothes.

But I wondered and worried about my daughters. How much of this pressure to avoid a repeat performance was self-inflicted? Their creativity in mixing and matching each other's clothes was a sight to behold, but when they accepted invitations to attend three parties in one night, did they really need costume changes in case someone somewhere recognised a dress from a previous party last week or last month? I never understood how appearance could trump comfort, or how the pain of swollen feet or the freezing cold was worth the pleasure of looking stunning.

'Dad, I need to buy a skirt for the party,' Joy would explain. 'I have no clothes.'

No clothes? It was just like them complaining that there was nothing on any of the pay-TV channels or that there was no food in the house, in spite of a full pantry. In the corner of Joy's room was a bag of clothes she had 'outgrown'.

'Of course you have clothes,' I said, pointing to the bag.

'Yuck, they're old and ugly.'

'And the new clothes will be the same one day . . . Is that what you'll do when *I'm* old and ugly?'

Joy rolled her eyes, pursed her lips, put her hands on her hips and tapped her foot, refusing to respond to my comparison.

'What do you want, exactly?' No, I didn't surrender to Joy's request. I was just asking.

'Skirts, Dad,' she explained. 'My hips are wider and . . .'

'Borrow something from your sisters.'

'They're too big. And have you *tried* borrowing their clothes?'

'Not lately. Their skirts don't suit me.'

She gave a sarcastic grin.

At this point, Grace walked in. 'Dad, can I borrow your scarf?'

Joy and I looked at each other. 'Only if Joy can borrow a skirt,' I said.

Grace gave Joy a stern gaze. 'Are you sulking to Dad now? Joy, I already told you, it's too cold for a skirt. It's winter!'

'But you and Michelle wear skirts in winter!' Joy retorted.

On cue, Michelle entered the fray. 'Did someone use my name in vain?'

The bedroom was getting crowded. 'Follow me, gals, I have an idea.'

They sat on my bed and crossed their arms.

'Hurry, Dad, we're already late.'

I slid open the middle door of my wardrobe to reveal some of Nadia's clothes. My daughters froze.

'Why not wear your mum's clothes? They're all yours and they . . .'

'Not now, Dad,' replied Grace, closing her eyes.

I thought it would be an honour with a personal connection, like wearing someone's jewellery. Perhaps they did not want to be compromised and forced to reject anything sacred belonging to their mum.

'Look, I just need some new clothes, not hand-me-downs,' Joy reminded me.

'Most of my clothes were hand-me-downs,' I reminded her.

Grace and Michelle resented these comparisons from last century and crossed the floor in Joy's defence. 'Dad, she can't keep waiting for us to outgrow our clothes,' Grace offered. 'She needs her own.'

'Needs?' I sniggered. 'These are wants, not needs.'

'Here we go,' Michelle rolled her eyes. 'I can feel a lecture coming on.'

'You bet,' I raised my voice.

'What's your point, Dad?' asked Joy.

'My point is that "I want" is selfish. "We need" is considerate. I want to hear more of "we need".'

'You do realise how funny you sound?' asked Michelle. 'You just said "I want"!'

'You know exactly what I mean,' I snapped.

'All right, *we need* to buy Joy some new clothes,' nodded Grace.

'And *we need* Joy to look good and feel good,' shrugged Michelle.

I stared at Nadia's clothes, hanging around, for what? I remembered the sleeves being animated when she was alive. As I gazed at them, I could almost see them swaying. I remembered that when she looked good, she felt good. I remembered how important it was to keep telling her how good she looked, so my words could challenge what she saw in the mirror.

My voice said, 'Nadia, you are glowing today. That dress really brings out your eyes. And your hair really completes your face.'

But her mirror said, 'Nadia, you look paler than yesterday. That dress looks like it's hanging on a skeleton. Your eyes look sunken. And your hair is moulting; there are strands on your shoulders.'

I would grit my teeth and clench my fists. Sometimes, I hated the mirror and wanted to grab Nadia's bright-red lipstick and scrawl all over it: 'Today you look better than yesterday and tomorrow you will look even better than today.'

Joy's voice rescued me from the dark days. 'So . . . why are we just sitting here?'

'Of *course* I want you to look good, Joy.'

'*I want*?' mocked Michelle. 'What happened to *we need*?'

Over time, their definition of what looks good rubbed off on me. It seeped under my bedroom door, stained my mirror and coloured my lens. In any case, I knew that once I stepped outside my door, the juvenile judiciary would deliberate and consider their verdict.

Once I tried to circumvent them altogether. It was only two steps to escape from my bedroom door to the front door. As I turned my door handle and stepped out, Joy was running between bedrooms and stopped in her tracks. She looked me up and down.

'You're joking, right?' She may as well have blown a whistle to her sisters. Busted!

Grace's head appeared from her bedroom and Michelle's head from the bathroom.

'*Hell* no!'

'What's wrong?' I pleaded innocent.

'You can't wear that classy Tommy Hilfiger shirt with those boring blue jeans,' Michelle shrieked, as if I had committed a crime. *Who's Tommy . . . whatever anyway?* I thought. *Never heard of him.*

'Why not?' I asked, pretending to know what I was talking about. 'They're both blue. They match!'

'They *don't* match,' Michelle replied, clapping with each syllable as if talking to a toddler. 'They're a different shade of blue. They clash. Do you *want* people to laugh at you?'

'And the runners, Dad,' Grace looked down and shook her head. 'They make you look like you've run straight from the gym. They're too loud and they're a different shade of blue again!'

'Are you trying to look young and cool?' added Joy in a pitying tone. They might as well have screamed 'Guilty!' and slammed down the gavel in court.

'I'm not trying to look . . . anything.' I clenched my fists. 'I'm not even trying and I *hope* no one looks.'

They exchanged glances and read each other like a book. They realised it was time to tone down.

'Look, Dad.' Grace held out her palms in conciliation. 'You can't wear checks with stripes. It has to be busy with plain.'

I frowned, confused.

Michelle took up the baton. 'Let me explain, Grace, so that even Dad can understand.'

'Oh, thanks. Charming,' I muttered.

'Look, Dad, that Hilfiger shirt with its patterns and lines. That's called busy. The jeans with one block colour. That's called plain. The runners are two colours, blue and white, so they are . . .?'

'Derr!' I wobbled my head. 'I'm not stupid!'

'So why are we having this conversation?'

'Look, I used to design clothes, believe it or not . . .'

'Not!' exclaimed Joy.

'Seriously. I designed a label called Egg Shells when I used to work in a children's clothing company.'

'Egg Shells?' repeated Joy.

'Yep, clothes for pregnant mothers before they hatch. Egg Shells. Get it?'

They tried not to laugh and Grace played polite. 'Oh, I didn't know that.'

'How come I never heard of . . . Egg Shells?' sniggered Michelle, not believing my true story.

'Well, the idea never really . . .'

'Hatched?' Michelle could not resist the pun. Her wit was frightfully familiar.

The 'busy' shirt was allowed to remain, but the blue jeans had to be replaced with camel trousers, and the 'cool' runners with plain black shoes.

'Yep,' nodded the juvenile judiciary. 'That works.'

And I was only going to a friend's backyard barbecue. When I arrived, my friend and his other guests widened their eyes and commented on how smart I looked. I wished I could take credit but I had to be honest.

'Nadia used to help pick my clothes. Then I let it go, you know.' I rubbed my chin to indicate not shaving on weekends. They nodded. 'But now, it's my three daughters. They . . . pamper me.'

'They have good taste!'

'Put it this way: I wear the pants, but they choose them.'

With each subsequent outing, I knew that the style police were now targeting bad taste. I knew that the bad-taste detector would either trigger an alarm or I would be arrested.

'Stop. Arms folded. Turn around . . . nice and slow. Hmm. Nope. Back inside. That doesn't work.' The judiciary had spoken and I was under house arrest, pending their approval.

There were some exception clauses, such as walking to the corner shop or walking for exercise, but even then, they demanded that I wear the right runners, a bright-white top and lose the hood.

'But it's night-time! No one can see me!'

'That's the problem,' insisted Joy. 'Cars need to see you. And it's dangerous on your own this late.'

I returned the hood to my head. 'That's why I want to look dangerous. Who's going to dare come near a jogger in trackies and a hoodie in the dark?'

Really, they were not pampering me. They were parenting me.

Summer was a time to be hairless, apparently. My daughters prepped themselves well in advance with laser hair removal. In my childhood, Lebanese women used caramel to wax their legs or whatever other body parts. Now the pressure was on men to do the same, but I actively resisted.

'Dad, it's better than always wearing a rash vest at the beach,' suggested Grace.

'I don't just wear the top to cover my hair,' I pretended. 'It saves on sunscreen.'

'We know lots of men who use laser,' consoled Michelle, 'and the hair is gone forever. Imagine never needing to worry about things like—'

'Who said I'm worried? Look, if you'll be embarrassed standing next to a gorilla-gram, I'll keep away.'

'Oh, shall we get out the violin?' asked Joy, pretending to play a tiny violin.

'Look, why are you girls always so . . . mean to me? What have I done?' Alarm bells were ringing and so was that voice in my head: 'Warning, don't say anything now that you'll regret tonight.'

'We're not picking on you,' Grace shook her head. 'We're just very . . . protective.'

'Yeah, and we don't want anyone saying anything behind your back,' added Joy.

'My hairy back, right?'

'Are you hearing us?' laughed Michelle. 'Are you hearing yourself?'

I sighed. 'One day I'll evolve, monkey.' I grabbed Joy and she screamed as I threw her on my bed.

HOW TO WEAR A FORMAL DRESS

'Have you found your formal dress?' I overheard Grace asking this question before she continued the phone call in her bedroom. 'Oh really? . . . How much? . . . No way!' The rest was muffled as she swung the door closed.

I wanted to hear the answer to that question: 'How much?' When she emerged from her private chambers, it was time for interrogation.

'Grace, what's the point of a Year 10 formal? Can't it wait till Year 12?'

'No, Dad,' she insisted. 'Some students are leaving school and it will be the last time we're all together.'

'So why isn't the school organising it instead of a few students?'

'I don't know,' she shrugged. 'I think some kids mucked up in previous years or something.'

This was a crash course in event management for the sixteen-year-olds. They did everything from collecting deposits to selecting menus, printing tickets, arranging security and booking DJs. In the lead-up to the big day, I saw some of Grace's classmates experience so much stress that I started to wonder if it was worth it. The workload seemed to fall on the shoulders of a few, who were only criticised by the others.

'Grace,' I suggested, 'if you really wanted to catch up with the students who are leaving, you'd all make an effort.'

'But it's not the same.'

I soon discovered that the emotional 'last time we're all together' scenario was an elaborate excuse for an extravagant dress-up. For the boys it was simply tuxedo time but for the 'sweet sixteens' who were emerging from their acne age and stepping out as ladies, it was a major source of excitement. It was also, like the machine that catered to the dancing dreams of young girls, an industry: ka-ching! Unlike the First Holy Communion, where all the girls looked identical in their white dresses and crowns, the formal dress had to be unique, an expression of individuality—and everything had to match: dress, shoes, hair, make-up, bag, nail polish, even the false eyelashes. Their bodies had to be adorned like a work of art.

The grand entrance, aimed to turn heads, was also reason for excitement. Many planned to 'rock up in a Hummer', while some boys preferred to arrive in a hotted-up car, culminating in a 'burnout', and emerge from the smoke like gangsters.

Given the Year 10 formal was so close to all the sweet-sixteen birthday parties, I rationalised, why not wear the same clothes?

Grace was horrified. 'No one *ever* does that, except—'

'Smart people who don't want to waste money?' I suggested with a smirk and crossed arms.

'Tight people, Dad.'

While girls who wore the same dress were cheap, apparently boys who wore the same suit were cool. I found it all completely mystifying. I overheard one conversation about two girls who happened to have chosen the same dress: 'No, you shouldn't change at the last minute . . . But you chose it first! . . . And what about your deposit?'

When Grace 'stepped out' of her bedroom, it was as if a butterfly had stepped out of a cocoon. This was not a kid. My baby was a lady, wearing stilettos. I had to look up to her.

'Wow,' my jaw dropped. 'You look so—'

'Come on, Dad, I'm running late.'

'—much like your mum.'

It was cruel that Nadia could not witness this magical meta-morphosis—but maybe she did. It was cruel that Grace could not have the blessing of a mother's finishing touch before she graced the world stage. We stared at each other and there was nothing more to say. I wanted to hug her but did not want to smudge her make-up. I extended my elbow and Grace hooked on as I walked her to my car. This formal walking arm in arm gave me butterflies. It was like a rehearsal for her wedding day.

I was to drop her off at the waiting Hummer, where her fellow 'formalites' had congregated. Parents hovered around the Hummer, watching their princes and princesses, fantasising that they were royalty or celebrities for one night only, embark for the ball.

Yes, it was very exciting and the photos soon flooded Facebook, but the grand entrance back home after midnight was a ceremony in itself.

'Oh, my feet,' Grace moaned. Her 10-centimetre stilettoes were moulded to her feet and she could not unbuckle them.

'Dad, sorry, but can you help?' She sat down with her feet extended.

'I remember doing this for my father after work . . . and you did the same for me, remember? Now we have gone full circle!'

Grace gestured with her hand that it was in the past. She was in too much pain in the present.

It took me about three attempts over three minutes to peel the shoes off her feet. 'Was it worth it?' I asked.

'Definitely,' she replied. 'We danced nonstop. It was a blast!'

Michelle was much fussier when it was her turn to choose a formal dress. I saw that it was stressing her out, so I was relieved she had Grace to help her. Michelle's childhood tomboy looks were well and truly dead and buried. These days her blue eyes illuminated her face, even without make-up.

By the time Joy had her Year 10 formal, no one even bothered pretending that it was the last time they would all be together. Her December formal was a welcome relief and celebration after her November exams.

Joy emerged from the reception centre wearing a black sash. As she approached, I saw that it was emblazoned, in golden letters, with the word 'Princess'. How I wished Nadia was there to crown her!

'Wow, Joy, why did you win that?'

'Oh, we all voted but I had no idea!'

It turned out I had no idea. I was horrified when the other 'royalty' emerged, their sashes labelling them Prince, King, Queen, Hottest Body, Best Dressed, Best Eyes and Model Material. This was the epitome of vanity.

'Joy, is this all about looks?' I asked while we walked to my car.

'No, Dad, it's all about fun!'

One waiting mother overheard us. 'Your kids are lucky,' she nodded. 'They never see you arguing with your wife.' She must have known about Nadia.

'Lucky?' I frowned, offended. Was she mocking me? I had never thought anyone would think we were lucky because of what we *don't* have.

'Yes,' she continued. 'They know that your word is first and final. You wouldn't believe how many arguments my husband and I have had over this formal.'

Perhaps this eavesdropper did have a point. My daughters will not remember witnessing how their parents settled disagreements—the beginning, middle and end of an argument, the tension, silence, stares. But if, in the future, my daughters quarrelled with their husbands, what would be their reference point? I selfishly wanted it to be me, but how? Did I need to quarrel with myself? Out loud? I needed them to learn how to listen without interrupting and how to compromise without being stubborn.

Sometimes I would hear whispering and whimpers from their visiting friends.

'Dad, some parents have full-on fights in front of their kids,' my daughters explained. 'If they come here for some time out, please don't say anything.'

I shrugged. 'Why would I?'

'And don't ask any questions, cos they don't want to think about their problems.'

I rolled my eyes. 'Since when did I pry? I always give you space and I tiptoe away.' My daughters cherished the trust their friends bestowed upon them, and I never betrayed this trust by anything I said. I played dumb. 'You know,' I said, 'I pick up all these . . . things . . . without you telling me.'

'Eavesdropping?' they snarled.

'No,' I smiled. 'Parenting.'

Their sweet-sixteen birthday parties were also a time to puff out my chest as the protective rooster. I stood at the door of the chosen venue, frisking the teenagers and checking the guest list. It was at times like these that I missed Nadia the most, not because I needed her to help me organise or run the parties but because she deserved to feast on the fruit of her labour by seeing her children grow and celebrate.

191

With each milestone party, the expectations were higher—and as the bar was raised, so was the budget. They needed theme colours, a photo booth and a personalised banner as a backdrop to their celebrity-style poses and 'selfies' with the birthday princess. I ended up with Excel spreadsheets listing who was doing what, for how much and by when. It included the DJ, audiovisuals, security, catering, decoration, photo collage, salads, drinks, cakes and a bar that groaned under the weight of glass lolly jars.

On another spreadsheet was the running sheet for the day, including make-up appointment, when to pick up the hall key, when to pick up the cake and when to inflate the helium balloons. And there was a budget spreadsheet that kept inflating and inflating. Now I could see why those kids organising the formal were so stressed!

I seemed to be succumbing to the immoral formula that equated love for my children with size of the budget. When I spoke to a father who took out a bank loan for his daughter's sweet-sixteen birthday party, he shrugged and gave me the old 'dance mom' line: 'It depends how much you love your daughter.'

I frowned. 'What's love got to do with it?'

'Well, you know, nothing personal, but I've met some parents who are tight with their money, and use all these moral arguments as excuses. How much is your daughter's happiness worth? Do you want her to step out ashamed and feeling inferior?'

I clenched my fists and resisted thumping him. How dare anyone be so judgemental!

For Grace's sixteenth, I went to pick up the 30 pizzas we had ordered. No one warned me that the steam from the pizzas would fog up my car on a winter's night to the point that I was struggling to see through the windscreen. No one warned me that girls barely eat at these parties. Why not? Does food smudge their lipstick? Instead of lolly bags, I handed out unopened pizza boxes to the departing teenagers. And still there were pizzas left over. We were forced to eat them for the next week.

Instead of boxed gifts, my daughters preferred cash so they could save up for one major gift they really wanted. In this way, for example, Joy put together the budget for her MacBook Air.

They certainly put in what they got back. It was an expensive time. I could never understand sixteenths held at a restaurant where my children had to pay their own way plus pay for a gift. Even my wallet flinched! It seemed to me that all the host family had left to pay for was the cake.

It was not too long before we moved on to the 21sts. Grace's was a masquerade party. I used the sweet-sixteenth spreadsheet but added an alcohol bar. This, of course, meant the flow of more emotions and fewer inhibitions. There was also the flow of relentless rain. It did not dampen our mood but it did slow down our driving to and from the venue as we put the finishing touches in place.

Despite all the party-planning chores, there was something I had to do in the pouring rain to clear the lump in my throat. I deviated to the cemetery and knelt by Nadia's headstone, my tears washed away by the rain.

'Thank you for the gift of Grace,' I told my wife. 'I'm so proud of her. You should be so proud of her . . . I miss you so much.'

I knew Grace was busy at her hairdresser's appointment, but I sent her a text message: 'Today, I visited your mum to thank her for bringing you into this world. We are so blessed and so proud to see you blossom. Love you always xo.'

When surprise guests arrived from Melbourne and removed their masks, there were screams and hugs—and then more tears. When the time came for the speeches, I offered a few words: 'This is the closest thing our family has ever had to a wedding. Similar emotions just sneak up on you . . . Grace is all those virtues that her name stands for—elegant, decent, prayerful, merciful, calm . . . Little things like your presence are actually the biggest present . . . Grace, Mum would be so proud . . . you are already a mother figure to your sisters . . .'

Michelle delivered her speech through tears and sobs. It was painful, but it all had to be said—the pain of who was absent, the guardian angel watching over them. Masks were removed, physically and emotionally. The dimly lit hall fell silent, except for the sniffles and nose-blowing that ricocheted around the venue.

Grace herself spoke calmly and looked like royalty in her silver and blue sequinned dress. Rather than wear a mask, she had sequins glued to her face.

As we packed up in the pouring rain, we realised that more than 40 helium balloons would now go to waste. I put the weights in the boot of my car and closed it so that the balloons and their ribbons flew freely behind us. As we drove home in the pouring rain after midnight, passing motorists laughed at the spectacle, reminiscent of that long silver train trailing behind the bus in *The Adventures of Priscilla, Queen of the Desert*.

As if farewelling their childhoods were not emotional enough, soon I was farewelling the girls themselves at airports. It was a heart-stopping experience. When Grace went to Madrid for World Youth Day (WYD) in 2011, and then when she and Michelle went to Lebanon in 2012, I felt that a part of my own flesh had been ripped off my body, leaving me bleeding. They counted down the sleeps until their D-day (departure). I counted down the same sleeps until my D-day (depressed).

When I farewelled Grace with the WYD pilgrims, I knew that a one-day stopover in Paris en route to Lourdes was part of their itinerary.

'You'll be fulfilling your mother's dream, through your eyes,' I whispered. 'She dreamt of going to Paris but never made it. Don't be surprised if you feel her presence there.'

Grace smiled and knew exactly what I was talking about. 'Don't worry,' she whispered back. 'I'll take plenty of photos.'

I hung on to her hand until the last set of security doors opened at the international airport. When the doors closed and there was silence, I had flashbacks of the doors closing as Nadia was wheeled away to surgery. I tried to be strong but the wailing in the departure lounge was ringing in my ears. It could have been a funeral scene, yet my daughter would be back in less than a month.

When Grace and Michelle departed to Lebanon together a year later, the emptiness they left in our home was palpable. I pitied those who lost a child forever, knowing they would never return. I pitied widowed parents with no children, who would have experienced this emptiness every night. Missing people is a selfish emotion and probably guilts us into not wholeheartedly enjoying ourselves when they're away. A part of me was jealous that I had never been to Europe. It was a little like 'our' school assignments, but instead of 'How did we go?' I asked 'Where did we go?' They were already planning their next overseas trip, to Europe. I wanted them to spread their wings and be happy. I wished we could travel together, but I could never afford it on one income.

Before they returned, I behaved like an expectant father, again. I washed their cars, changed their bed linen and ensured that a homemade meal would be ready and waiting. It was exhausting but exciting. It was not that I was insecure and wanted them to miss home; I merely imagined that they would feel weary, hungry and homesick after a long trip.

As I waited at the international arrivals terminal for Grace to return from her WYD pilgrimage, I watched the parade of fatigued faces wheeling their baggage trolleys down the ramp. I held a bouquet for Grace, exactly as I had when Nadia returned from her last 'pilgrimage' to Lebanon in 2002.

Nadia had gone there hoping to break the news of her cancer diagnosis, but then she changed her mind. She loved her parents too much and could not bear the thought of sharing her cross with them. During the trip, she tried to hide her loss of hair and her real reason for wanting to visit all the holy places that were renowned for miracles. Fortunately, her sister Lola was by her side the whole time, buffering her from interrogation.

I was so glad not to have gone with her, as I was afraid of telling the truth if they cornered me about Nadia's symptoms of ill health. I sent her many prayers and poems, which I ensured were cryptic in case they landed in the wrong hands and created suspicion. She had developed malignant lumps on her neck and we were praying for a miracle if she drank holy water from the sacred sites of the saints. 'Dear Nadia,' I wrote, 'I pray that you quench your thirst and clear any bumps along the way.'

When Nadia finally staggered onto the exit ramp after four weeks away, I rushed to her with my bouquet. She looked pale and her hair had thinned, as had her legs, which could barely carry her. Her eyes were deep-set and her eyebrows were the colour of her skin. The cancer had spread to her liver but we did not know this yet. She clung to me and sobbed. She knew this was her last trip, ever, and that she would probably never see her parents again. I was glad that I could catch her when she fell into my arms, exhausted.

Our children remained oblivious to the seriousness of the situation. Nadia could not handle worried faces around her; she wanted to be surrounded by hope. She needed me to be her warrior to protect her, not her worrier to upset her. We both prayed fervently for the intercession of the saints, yet the test results this time were a step backwards. The local priest allocated to visiting the sick once told me that Our Father does not deliver what we want at our time, but what we *need* in *God's* time.

At these words, I pondered my own father and our faith in him. As a child, we would often ask him for a small sum and hope to receive it the next day. When nothing arrived, it was tempting to lose faith in him and feel forgotten. But the following week, we would receive much more than we asked for and it was well worth the wait. We learnt to ask once, then trust that he knew what was best. Usually, he knew what we wanted before we even asked for it. I was honoured to have inherited this generosity from my father. I gave my daughters more than they asked for but not always when they asked for it.

'Joey,' Nadia asked me on her last day, looking into my eyes, 'am I going home today?'

Between her gurgling and moaning, she had bursts of lucidity, but I did wonder if this was the morphine speaking. As she drifted in and out of consciousness, Nadia recalled that this day, 19 April 2003, was the day we were to move in to our newly renovated home.

How I wished I could tell her we would be there soon, but when I arrived on my visit that morning, the nurses had whispered to me about 'being prepared'. The acetone odour and rasping sound of her laboured breaths heralded the beginning of the end. I imagined her body as an illuminated home where the lights were being switched off, one by one.

'Today, *habibti*,' I said in answer to her question, 'you'll be in the most beautiful white house, and it will be the best homecoming party.' It was a paraphrase of what the crucified Jesus said to the good thief: 'Today, you will be with me in paradise.'

My voice was calm, but my lips trembled and I turned my head so she could not see my tormented face. I gently squeezed her hands, which were softened by the massages I gave her each day with lanolin. Touch is perhaps the first and last of the senses we use in this life. Not far from this room, in the maternity wing, a mother's touch pacified a newborn baby after their first breath. And here I was, a father pacifying a mother, my wife, before her final breath.

As I fought back my tears to keep her spirits up, I glimpsed the glorious autumnal sunset from her window in Westmead Hospital. It was the day we call in Arabic *Sabat el nour*, the Saturday of light on the eve of Easter Sunday. As if basking in her own miraculous light, Nadia leant forward with the most beatific smile and reached out to the picture of Jesus mounted on the shelf facing her. Was her soul already floating between both worlds? Perhaps the 'hour of our death' mentioned in the Hail Mary prayer is more truthful than our idea that leaving this life is like a candle being blown out.

As the gaps between Nadia's last gasps became longer, I kept kissing her hands. And then I could hear Celine Dion's classic song about a sinking ship: 'My Heart Will Go On'. Except it was my wife's voice singing in my head.

When Nadia exhaled her last breath, I inhaled a gasp of strength and hope. While my tears of farewell rolled down my cheeks and onto her hospital bed, I saw Nadia approaching a heavenly welcoming party that applauded her and threw flowers as she headed for the loving light.

This vision was dissolved by the physical contact of my friend Scott's embrace. He whispered, 'You've just lost your soul mate. I'm so sorry.' It was the only thing to say. It was the perfect thing to say.

Scott had flown up from country Victoria to stand by my side. Even though he is an Irish McFadden and I am a Lebanese Wakim, he could be my twin brother. He is himself a father of four, but Joy called him the 'boy with the earring'. He was a fun-loving dad who changed nappies, baked bread and nourished his children with no hang-ups about gender roles. My own daughters were very fond him, although they often found him just as embarrassing as they found me. To me, he has always been 'Great Scott', the man who listens with his heart.

During my last moment alone with Nadia, I kissed her feet over and over again. I had also massaged them each day, so they were as soft as her hands. I tasted the exfoliating cream on my lips and remembered how she smiled each time I 'embalmed' her feet. The last time I did not hold back my tears, and I knew that she knew.

Now that Nadia's candle had flickered and faded, it was time for me to face the new normal: 'You are the lone candle now. Shine.' Nadia and I were both aged forty.

'Scott, I need to see my children straight away. Please. Before anyone else tells them anything.'

Even though he was unfamiliar with Sydney's roads, Scott drove me to Lola's house in my car as if it were an ambulance on a rescue mission. Upstairs, my children and I huddled on a rug together, cross-legged. In this private moment, I clasped my wooden rosary and inhaled its rose scent. How on earth would I tell them about their mother?

'Now,' I asked my precious darlings, 'you know how all our life we pray the rosary?'

They nodded, but they knew from my overly calm voice that something was amiss.

'And we pray that we'll always be ready to see Jesus and Mary face to face?' I continued.

By now they were squinting with suspicion, but my words kept rolling out as if I were telling them a bedtime story.

'And you know how Mummy has been very sick and everyone has been praying for her? Well, today, while we're waiting for Easter

Sunday and for Jesus to rise from the dead, Mummy has gone to meet him.'

They blinked and opened their lips as if this would help them absorb the gravity of the moment. They shifted their gaze to the rosary chain I was rotating between my thumb and forefinger. Far too soon, my daughters experienced the sudden revelation that death was *not* the opposite of life but a *part* of life, part of the same cycle. Rather than 'died', we inscribed 'born into eternal life' on Nadia's headstone.

I gripped the wooden crucifix of the rosary and laid it on the rug in front of them. 'Mummy has crossed that bridge from this life to the next life in heaven,' I said. 'So now your mummy is an angel.'

They stared at each other, intrigued.

'So she died?' asked Grace in plain English.

I nodded and mouthed the word 'yes', but it would not come out.

'I *knew* something happened!' exclaimed Michelle, sitting up straight.

'But where is she now? Can we see her?' asked four-year-old Joy, struggling to make sense of this.

'We can't see her from here, but she can see us,' I said, reassuring myself more than them. I picked up the rosary and clasped it to my heart. 'We can't see her but we can talk to her through this. The rosary will be our mobile phone to heaven, our hotline to Mummy.' This made them smile, but they could not know that I was consoling myself.

As I choked up, I had to hide the rising pitch of my voice, so I whispered, 'We used to pray for *her*, but now she can pray for *us*, with the angels. We'll need that *so* much. And we'll miss her *so* much.' I embraced them and buried my emotions in their shoulders.

My tears welled up but none of them cried. It was too much for them to take in all at once. My only comfort was that they saw a grown man cry, expressing his raw emotions rather than suppressing them. I hoped they would learn to associate tears with strength. Tears do not mean that solid ice has melted to mush but that dark clouds have unloaded and passed—and it feels good when the patch of blue shines through once more.

While we sat together on the rug, I hoped that my tears would sow seeds of honesty in our family garden, that it would become a garden where tears could fall like leaves, not choke like weeds, where the only forbidden fruit would be bottling up our tears. It would be a garden that transcended genders and generations. I mustered a smile between my tears and hoped that this would give them permission to open their own floodgates. But they would grieve in their own way and in their own time.

Mahadda bi rooh illa bi wa'tou. Nadia often recited this maxim with serenity to those who lost sleep over mortality. In plain English, it means: 'Stop fretting as if you can change the hour of our death: it is already written.' Perhaps she knew just how much my daughters would teach me, once she was gone.

When Grace finally appeared at the same international arrivals ramp nearly ten years after her mother had done, my flashbacks were immediately resurrected. Although she bore an uncanny resemblance to her mother, she was a healthy young lady with a beaming face returning from her pilgrimage.

My only pilgrimage was within. After all, as Mother Teresa once said, 'The longest journey a man must take is the eighteen inches between his head to his heart.' Yes, it was a long journey, trying to make sense of the senseless and solve the insolvable.

When Grace collapsed on her bed, glad to be home, I reminded her: 'When you book your wedding car, remember to book an ambulance and a stretcher for me.'

HOW TO SAY GOODBYE

'Dad has been taken to hospital due to breathing problems last night. Could be pneumonia. Don't panic. He seems more settled now. Will keep you updated xo.' It was surreal to be awoken by this SMS message from my sister Joan one week before Christmas 2011.

Our father Jalil's mental age had been regressing since his diagnosis of Alzheimer's disease ten years earlier. Some suspected that it was triggered by the head injuries he had sustained in the roadside accident in 1966. Others thought it was hereditary—his mother suffered from dementia after she was knocked over by a cow on a narrow path terraced into a hill. Apart from this debilitating disease, our father was physically healthy. Our 'iron man' had built up a lifetime reserve of strong muscles.

I did not dare to compare the prospect of losing my father with my children losing their mother. I was an adult and my father was more than double Nadia's age. As the Alzheimer's progressed, we experienced many false alarms. Our father had repeatedly been rushed to hospital and blessed with the last rites, then bounced back and returned home, resiliently and triumphantly. Were these our dress rehearsals? Were they intended to bring on the anticipatory grief that I experienced with Nadia?

But it was difficult not to panic when I received another SMS message from Melbourne an hour later and I was nearly 1000 kilometres away in Sydney. I gathered my children and we huddled around a candle. As we lit the flame, I had flashbacks to gathering my children after their mother's death.

'*Jiddo* is in hospital,' I told them. 'He's struggling to breathe. The doctors are trying to keep him alive, but we're not sure what will happen. There isn't much we can do from here except pray. But we can offer a lot of support to everyone there.'

'Should we leave now?' asked Joy.

We had already planned to drive to Melbourne and celebrate Christmas with my parents and siblings, as was our ritual each year. But we usually arrived on Christmas Eve after I finished my work year, not the week before.

'Yes. And pack extra clothes in case something happens to *Jiddo*.' They knew that 'extra clothes' meant funeral clothes.

Within hours, we had packed and locked up the house.

Joan's update SMS confirmed that we had not rushed in vain: 'Dad staring at Mum. Doctors say not improving but making him comfortable, and we should be prepared. Priest on his way xo.'

In this last stage of his regression, he called my mother 'Mum'. Was he a frightened child, staring down a tunnel into the afterlife where his real mother Hawa (Eva) was waiting with open arms with his father, Yousef? Perhaps he could see Nadia there, embracing him upon his arrival in heaven, just as he had once embraced Nadia upon her arrival in Australia. His blue eyes were always a reminder of her father's blue eyes, so she said, and this helped her homesickness.

I remembered how Nadia, in her final hour, reached forward. Could she see angels welcoming her to that room upstairs? I will never forget how her face lit up, as if she were radiating a bright light. And then the lights in the rooms of her body were switched off, one by one, before she locked up and was lifted away.

We all knew that 'prepared' included the last anointing, the last communion, the last confession. Special oils, prayers and hymns were reserved for these last rites. Our resilient father had received them so many times before that I wondered if he held the record. I also wondered how much more prepared and how much purer this made his soul. He seemed to cling to the love in this life, especially from my mother, who refused to consider a nursing home, and my eldest sibling, Eva, who cared for him with the patience of an angel.

'Dad, did you blow out the candle?' asked Joy, as I buckled my seatbelt for the ten-hour drive to Melbourne.

Too many memories were flashing through my mind, but my youngest grounded me in the here and now. I unbuckled the seatbelt and dashed inside. Yes, the candle was extinguished, perhaps on autopilot, but beneath the candle was a drawer full of DVDs. Family videos of my father! Of course! They could come in handy if my extended family needed 'therapy'. My own immediate family had experienced death and grief, and the happy videos had been helpful for us to remember Nadia in full flight. I grabbed the DVDs with their memories from more than ten years ago. It was like raiding a cellar for vintage wines to celebrate his life, not just mourn his death.

We crossed ourselves and headed south. We chanted the rosary as we went and took turns driving—we had no time for stops except to refuel and use the bathroom. As we approached the Victorian border, we were treated with the most spectacular sunset, painted in glorious colours and patterns by the divine hand.

'Wow, heaven!' remarked Joy.

Who was I to correct her? Perhaps it was a blessing that my children visualised their mother's dwelling place and my father's destination like this. Perhaps this last gasp of the sun on the horizon was a metaphor for his last gasp on the horizon of his earthly life, reflecting a glimpse of the next.

I resorted to my storytelling tone in the hope of lulling them into a familiar space, but perhaps I was just lulling myself out of my anxiety that I would arrive too late for my father.

'When I was a child,' I told them, 'I thought it took 40 days to travel to that beautiful place in the sky, and that's why we had the 40-day memorial mass after someone died.'

Through the rear-view mirror, I could see them staring at the sunset, which illuminated their faces, but they did not respond. At that moment, the text arrived. The phone beeped twice, like a final heartbeat. 'We have just lost Dad,' it said. 'May he rest in peace.'

We stared intently at the fading sunset and remained silent. Finally, I said, 'My father is now with your mother,' and kept staring at the road ahead. 'And they are with their heavenly father and mother.'

'We are so sorry, Dad. You should stop driving,' Grace said, resting her hand on my shoulder. 'I could take over now.' She had already driven half the journey and reached for her P plates in anticipation.

'I'm okay so far . . . I'll let you know as soon as my eyes get tired.'

My eyes shed no tears. Was this because I had said goodbye so many times before and already grieved, or because I was trying to mentor my daughters in the traditional men's mould? Did I want them to be dry-eyed when I died? I shuddered at the thought of leaving them. 'We all cry in different ways and at different times,' I said, reminding them that men should shed tears.

There was much going on in my head that I kept to myself. Would we have reached the hospital on time if we had flown instead of driven? Did I want my daughters to witness my father gasping for air?

My heart went out to my mother, now widowed, like me. After many attempts to phone her but having insufficient reception, we finally reached a point where the signal bars increased to a useful level. She tried to sound calm, worried about the dangers of our long drive, especially in the state we would be in now.

I tried to sound calm too and reached deep within for words of comfort, in Arabic. 'He has arrived,' I said. 'He is with his father, his mother, his brother, his sister, and my wife. He has no pain. I'm coming to help you with yours.' I remembered how much Scott had helped me with my pain.

'I've never seen this in my life before,' she responded like a bewildered child. 'He changed colour and went . . . still. Just like that.'

I took the phone off Bluetooth, as I did not want my daughters to hear and visualise his death.

'I called him and he didn't answer,' she continued. My poor mother was in shock. In all her life, she had never witnessed anyone's last breath. Both her parents died in Lebanon when she was living in Australia.

'Like a candle that had been blown out?' So it turned out that sometimes death is like that after all.

'Yes. I can't believe it. Just like that.'

'I know, Mum.'

It was so surreal for her that she then talked about the weather instead. 'I saw storms on the TV. Just stay at a motel on the way. Don't drive if it's dangerous.'

What storms? We had just witnessed a masterpiece in the sky on a clear blue canvas.

As my daughters and I chanted the rosary, the repetition made me sleepy. I was ready for Grace to take over while I napped, but dark clouds were caving in on us. The rain on our car roof was deafening. The wipers only added to the angry noise. Each time an oncoming truck passed us, our car was blown sideways and our windscreen became a waterfall. The rainfall was so heavy that my wipers could not keep up. My daughters were petrified.

Visibility was reduced to a few metres. If we slowed down or stopped during this narrow stretch, vehicles behind us might not see us, even with our hazard lights flashing. If we kept driving, we might not see if vehicles in front of us had stopped or slowed down. My grip tightened on the steering wheel and I leant forward as if I were hanging on for my life. Our prayers now had a dual purpose: that my father would arrive safely in heaven and we would arrive safely in Melbourne.

We had never seen anything like it. The rain was pelting so loudly that we were yelling to hear each other. My daughters were scared but smiling. We all stared ahead, holding our breath for the horror storm to pass.

When we finally arrived, our faces were wet with rain and my mother's face was wet with tears. Our arrival at my parents' home had always been an exciting and welcoming experience, and my sister Eva tried to ensure that this time was no different. She had prepared a homemade meal in case we were hungry, even on this fateful night.

Halfway through the night, I felt compelled to sleep in my father's bed. After all, I had not been there when my siblings were gathered around his hospital bed. I inhaled the scent of his pillow, hoping to inhale the sanctity and selflessness of our father. At first I pretended he was there, but then I sensed his presence. It was my last one-on-one time with him.

So many times, on this bed, I had kissed his unblemished forehead, his leathery hands and his swollen feet. Each time we left Melbourne, we had farewelled him as if it could be the last time. Over the years, his farewell comments regressed from a wise sentence, to an unintelligible word, to medicated silence. As his life reversed, I was transformed from his son to his brother and then his father.

I felt one last embrace from my father and buried my sobs in his pillow so as not to disturb my mother. That embrace smelt of earth and had protected me from the woes of this world. I had passed it on to my daughters, and now he had passed on to heaven.

The next night, my mother wanted to sleep in his bed and grieve in her own way. But it was a high hospital bed designed for lifting and hoisting. My mother dreamt that my father's blanket had slipped off and he was cold. In her dream, she leant over to cover him, but in reality, she slipped off the bed and landed on the timber floor.

The next day, my brothers and I replaced the bed base but kept the linen and pillow. The widow's wishes had to be respected— I remembered inhaling the scent of Nadia's socks. My daughters smiled as they watched my brothers and I work. I smiled back. They only saw me with my Melbourne siblings for a few days each year, so now I hoped to show them how brothers and sisters can love each other and help each other as adults, in midlife and beyond.

We knew other families where the siblings had cactus relationships and refused to talk to each other. The way I saw it, if God can forgive all our sins, who are we to bear a grudge against anyone? We don't choose our siblings, but we could remain lifelong best friends. I hoped my daughters would do the same.

Every one of my siblings had personal memories of our father, and we pooled them all into one eulogy. As the one with previous experience, I offered to take the task of writing the eulogy. We decided that our eldest sibling, Eva, would read it and that I would stand by as her back-up, in case she could not make it through. I locked myself away to work on it and do justice to this mountain of a man. How could I distil so much love, history and memory on a single sheet of paper? Memories of making Nadia's funeral arrangements flooded back: writing her eulogy, choosing her coffin, selecting her clothes, attending the viewing, deciding on the readers, picking the prayers.

As a father myself, my thoughts turned to my own inevitable demise. How had I made my mark in this life? What would be etched in stone by those I left behind? Would it be: 'Here lies Joseph, 8 November 1962 to . . . Beloved father of Grace, Michelle and Joy . . .' And then my favourite quote from the Bible? Or a poem? It made me shudder but we should all ponder the inescapable fact of our own death. What if how we want to be remembered and how we will be remembered are not the same?

I had heard so many eulogies that lamented, 'I never told him how much I loved him.' What had they been waiting for? Did they think he would live forever? Thanks to the many false alarms, we did not have that problem. My siblings agreed that our father was 'the man from the mountain who never saw a mountain too high to climb'. None of us could recall him doing or buying anything for himself. It was always for us, his family. We were comforted by this biblical quote: 'He who humbles himself will be exalted.' I did not inherit his hands but I hoped to inherit his heart.

When I translated the eulogy for my mother in my broken Arabic, her face lit up. The spoken words had a healing power and lifted her spirits.

'Come closer so I can kiss you,' she said, leaning forward to plant a kiss on my brow.

My neck tightened, my lips trembled and my tears welled up. We were kindred spirits, now both widowed.

After Eva and I delivered the eulogy, our parish priest gave a moving homily about the lines on my father's hands that had left their indelible mark on so many lives and so many gardens. Perhaps an image of the lines on his hand, rather than the lines on his epitaph, would most aptly tell his life story.

After the funeral, we headed to the cemetery. It would be the first time my daughters had witnessed the lowering of a coffin into the earth. We car-pooled, so I had two daughters, a nephew and a niece in my car. After a few red lights, we lost the funeral cortege, and none of the cars behind us had their headlights on either.

My father's allocated lot was in a new section of the cemetery. I literally lost the plot. We followed the signs to the main entry and followed the nearest procession. As they stepped out of their cars, we realised that none of their faces were familiar. Wrong funeral!

Eva phoned to check on us and told us the name of the new section, but there were no signposts. What sort of a cemetery has no signposts in sight? Surely visitors are emotionally disoriented enough, without adding to their confusion. The priest kept phoning us as we had a tight schedule to return to the church hall to the waiting mourners and the mercy meal. He described landmarks that meant nothing to me.

'Now, Joe, where are you? What can you see?'

'Graves. Rows of them.'

As we kept driving in circles on this hot December afternoon, I broke into a sweat. 'Oh another dead end! This is ridiculous! Give me a sign!'

The teenage passengers could no longer contain themselves after the restraint and solemnity of the morning. They broke into giggling followed by guilt then more giggling.

'Joe, we really have to start,' the priest eventually said. 'Some of the interstate guests need to make their flight back home.'

'What can I do?' I vented. 'I didn't plan to get lost at my father's funeral.'

My passengers tried to contain their giggling but it trickled out as tears instead. One of them mocked me: 'A logistics manager who's always lost!' Their shoulders were convulsing.

When we finally reached the site, our red eyes blended in with the rest. My anger and embarrassment blurred my memory of the ritual, although I do recall the ceremony of dropping sand onto the lowered coffin.

Exactly a week after we drove through the first storm, another one struck Melbourne, just after our Christmas Day lunch. Some of us spontaneously stood outside in the hail together and opened our mouths to eat this manna from heaven, fantasising that our father was watering his garden of children and grandchildren. The fact that the hail was the size of cricket balls, and cricket was our father's favourite sport, solidified our conviction that he was somehow behind, or above, all of this.

As the hail pounded on the tin roof above us, we had a collective urge to scream above its 'applause'. One of my saturated nephews opened his arms and yelled to the sky, 'Rain down on me, *Jiddo!*'

Even my mother could not resist a smile for the first time in seven days, but I could see that depression was knocking on her door. I recognised that glazed look in her eyes from when it had stared back at me from my own mirror. In a room full of visitors, she looked completely lonely. Her marriage had lasted nearly 59 years, almost four times longer than my fourteen and a half years with Nadia, and many of her peers had either died or were dying. Who was I fooling that our widowhoods were comparable? I could still do cartwheels on the beach and my mother needed a walking frame.

Joy reminded me of the 'therapy' videos we had brought. One of them featured an interview with my father from before his Alzheimer's, while I was researching our family tree. We all gravitated towards the screen with our jaws agape. It was one of those rare times when His Majesty was magnanimous. My daughters and I knew how helpful this would be.

Suddenly, there he was, the way we wanted to remember him: sharp, witty, jovial, loud and coherent, with a glint in his blue eyes. When he gave a hearty laugh, his entire torso shook like Santa's. Indeed, he wore the Santa suit for many Christmases, and it really suited his physique and his laugh. During the video interview, he was often sarcastic, which reminded me of the way I interacted with my own daughters. But of all my brothers, I was convinced that it was Peter, the other middle child, who most closely resembled my father in his mannerisms and movements.

This was the man we wanted to remember. This was how he would have wanted to be remembered. A decade with our fallen father had obscured our memories of the mountain man he truly was. As for his grandchildren, they barely recalled this *Jiddo*. Someone turned up the volume and my father's voice resonated between the walls of his home, for the first time in a long time. My mother wanted to watch the video over and again. For her, this shining memory would replace the duller ones.

'Dad, we should make everybody a copy,' whispered Joy.

'We should make everybody a coffee!' I exhaled.

We had been late to the hospital and late to the cemetery, but perhaps this was our atonement.

My 50th birthday—8 November 2012—would mark eleven months since my father passed away.

Our family home in Melbourne had become the place of grieving for my father, but traditionally it was a house of celebrations. While I respected the custom of keeping the house sombre for at least the first year, I asked my mother for her blessing to celebrate my 50th birthday there. I explained that this would be the reunion of some lifelong friends who attended my 21st birthday in exactly the same backyard. And that it would be a mature gathering with no loud music or excessive drinking.

My mother was usually very sensitive to gossip and sharp tongues, and there were some who would have been ready to shame her for holding a party just before the first anniversary of her husband's death. But my mother was bold and brave, agreeing that the sounds of happiness must return to the family home.

Some Sydney friends and relatives even flew to Melbourne to join us. Apart from reliving memories of 1983 and playing the music of that year, we even revisited the hat theme of the original party. Joy prepared a slide show of photos featuring images of my 21st hat party with the same people in the same backyard. It was a surreal blast from the past.

'The hats are a great cover,' laughed one friend. 'At least they hide our bald heads so that we look like the photos in the slide show!'

After blowing out 50 candles, I read my printed speech in a size 16 font. I of course thanked my daughters, then declared that 'I'll need an ambulance on stand-by when I become father of the bride,' trying to make light of a moment that I really dreaded.

I presented a bouquet to my mother with the message, 'There is no birthday without birth. Thank you for the free gift of life. You are the epitome of marriage vows, in sickness, in health, in good times and in bad.' I also presented a bouquet to Eva, this one with the message, 'To one person who is as selfless as our father, the foun-tain of giving. These Eva angels are rare gems. Our whole family is indebted to you for being our second mother.' Then I thanked God for 'reminding us that no matter how big or small we find the crosses we have to bear, there are always people carrying far bigger crosses, and with grace. Even when we are alone, His whispering words of wisdom never let us feel lonely.'

Just for fun, I prepared a karaoke version of the Queen classic 'Bohemian Rhapsody', in which my siblings had set lines to sing, even if they couldn't sing. I had received a guitar case for my 21st; for my 50th I was given a ukulele. It looked like a shrunken guitar with two strings missing—a metaphor, perhaps, for my shrunken eyes and hair loss. But with its higher pitch, it gave a new lease of life to old songs and became the life of the party.

Suddenly, at least half the world was younger than me.

HOW TO GET THINGS STRAIGHT

I was so disappointed with myself. Every time I took a daughter to hospital, the memories of Nadia's last days kept flooding back. My heart would race and my head would spin, but for the sake of my daughters I would fake the kind of plastic smile demanded by dance moms.

One week before Christmas 2008, seventeen-year-old Grace was rushed to triage with sharp abdominal pains. After three medical opinions, fasting for three days and a saline drip, the doctors agreed that she had appendicitis.

The sight of Grace in a hospital bed with a drip was painfully familiar. Even her tired nods were an uncanny replica of Nadia—her eyes closed, her slow swaying, her expressionless face. When I held her hand, it was Nadia's hand, with its slender fingers and the stubby fingernails. Even the veins looked the same.

'Snap out of it! This is Grace!' I kept telling myself. Why were my emotions still so raw after so many years? I thought my daughters had 'raised me better than that'.

As Grace was recuperating after her keyhole surgery, I slept on the couch in her hospital room. But she felt guilty and insisted that I go home to bed. Michelle and Joy were sleeping at Lola's house, so I ended up at home alone.

That did not mean that I slept. How could I sleep? It was two o'clock in the morning, but I got my second wind. Grace had not eaten for four days. Out of empathy, I had not been able to stomach any food. How could I? My heart bled for her and I nearly fainted for her, just as I had when she was born. What would Nadia have done? I felt an urgent itch to cook for my daughter.

I decided to surprise her with one of her favourite meals, *kibbit raahib* (monk's soup). This Christian Lebanese dish is traditionally reserved for Lent and especially Good Friday, because legend has it that it was eaten by Mary on the day Jesus died. It is free from any dairy or meat products.

It might have been Grace's favourite, but we were in the throes of preparing for Christmas, not Easter. It was the wrong meal in the wrong season. Still, I decided, it would be the most beautiful surprise for Grace in the morning when she woke up.

I illuminated the kitchen, pretended it was two o'clock in the afternoon and followed the instructions in my Aunt Abla's cook-book. In spite of the season, I had all the ingredients: lentils, garlic, lemon, pomegranate molasses, burghul, onion, mint, parsley, flour and spices. Oh, and the most delicious ingredient of all: love.

In my excitement, I forgot to create the dough-like dumplings, instead mixing all the ingredients into the one runny soup. If anyone asked, I would pretend that this was deliberate, to avoid giving Grace solids on the day after surgery.

By four in the morning I was exhausted, but I was sure that my labours would make Grace's day. Man, was I dreaming!

'Are you trying to kill her?' the nurse berated me as soon as I arrived, Tupperware in hand.

'Why?' I asked.

'Strictly juices and jelly on the first day after surgery.'

What! After all that work, my surprise had backfired.

'Oh, you're so cute, Dad,' cooed Joy.

'Thanks, Dad,' Grace said, mustering a smile and tapping my hand.

When I looked down and saw Nadia's hand, I grabbed it and kissed it.

'Oh, yuck, Dad,' laughed Michelle. 'You don't know where her hand has been.'

'It's a hospital!' I retorted. 'Everything is circum . . .'

'What?' Michelle widened her eyes, embarrassed for me.

'You know exactly what I mean,' I retorted, tired.

'No, I don't. How do you know what I know?'

'Sterilised?' offered a nurse who happened to be in the room.

'See!' I bounced back. 'Even a stranger knows what I mean.'

When Grace told our Lebanese visitors this 'cute' story, they shook their heads: who offered Lent food during Advent? When I returned home with the monk's soup, I tucked it carefully in the fridge so that it would not go to waste.

I vetted the phone calls and restricted the visits, exactly as I had for Nadia, until Grace felt ready. Then two days later, I was jubilant to see the exit sign at the hospital and drive Grace home.

Before this drama, we had planned to drive to Melbourne for Christmas. But Grace was not ready for a road trip, so we booked her and Michelle on a flight, while Joy was my front-seat passenger in the car. When she was bored, I encouraged Joy to tell me what creatures or shapes the clouds resembled. It did the trick: soon enough, she was tired and slept. My instinct guided me to pull over, recline Joy's seat and throw a blanket over her.

What I did not know was that we would be back in hospital for Joy five years later, but this time for quite a bit longer.

⟲

When Joy first complained of back pain at the age of thirteen, I suspected it was growing pains. I never saw her in the shower, so how was I supposed to know that her spine was growing faster than her body and forming an S-shaped curve?

When she tiptoed to my room at night because her back pain prevented her from sleeping, I tried to comfort her by holding her hand. My touch comforted Joy in her valley of fear.

There was once a time when schools conducted spinal tests while students touched their toes. Early intervention would mean the child could wear a brace and avoid major surgery. But Joy 'progressed' from a physiotherapist to a chiropractor to an osteopath to prevent surgery, all in vain, because her S-curve was so severe.

For many months, we sought numerous referrals and Joy was seen by three scoliosis specialists. No matter how hard I tried to suppress them, it gave me constant flashbacks to oncology consulting rooms in December 2002—the waiting rooms, the rosary in my pocket, the pretence of calm, the X-rays in my hand, the second opinion, the anxious phone calls.

There should have been two waiting rooms, I decided: one for patients, with a piano playing comforting melodies; and one for 'im-patients' like me, fitted with a punching bag and soundproof walls.

When Joy was diagnosed with scoliosis, I felt guilty for starting her at school one year early. I suspected that her 46-degree curvature could have been caused by carrying book-laden schoolbags or even by her many years of dancing. The latter fear was, of course, irrational, given Grace had danced for longer with no ill effects. But the three surgeons we consulted all reassured us that Joy's situation had nothing to do with her practices or her parentage. They took that horrible guilt off my back.

'Do you know what idiopathic means, Joy?' our surgeon asked.

'No, not really.'

She looked at me as if it were an idiotic question. I held hands with Nadia through the wooden rosary in my pocket. 'It means that the doctor is an idiot and has absolutely no idea what caused the curve,' he replied. My grip on the rosary relaxed and I winked at the doctor, glad his sense of humour had elicited a welcome giggle from Joy.

Surgery was a painful pill for us to swallow but procrastination was not an option. We made the decision when Joy was aged fourteen, in December 2012. She was adamant that she wanted the third surgeon we saw to perform the operation. We did our research together and discovered this surgeon had an impressive success rate. He also operated from Westmead Private Hospital, which was closer to our home and where I used to take Nadia for chemotherapy, so it was familiar. Joy would need to be in hospital for more than a week. I was relieved that the surgery would not take place at Westmead Public Hospital, where Nadia had taken her last breath. If I had to 'live' there for a week, the memories would have been unbearable.

The surgery was booked for 11 June 2013, just before the mid-year school holidays, to minimise disruption to Joy's schooling and to minimise her exposure to the summer sun. Five weeks of rehabilitation would follow. She would have one scar on her left side, which would be covered when her left arm was down.

When our family friend Sister Sayde heard of our anxiety leading up to the surgery, she suggested that we speak to a family she knew in Melbourne whose daughter was waiting for the same surgery. I knew this family, as they were distant relatives my father had taken in when they first migrated to Australia.

While visiting Melbourne for my father's one-year memorial mass on Saturday, 8 December 2013, I had hoped to visit this family but there was not enough time so I decided to phone them when I got home. Then, while searching for my seat number on the aeroplane back to Sydney, I found someone already sitting there.

'Excuse me,' I said, 'I think you're sitting in my . . .'

A girl turned her head and looked up with a grin.

'Joe!' her father sang out from the seat behind me.

The girl sitting in my seat was Joyce, the very girl waiting for the same surgery. Not only was she booked on the same route, at the same time, on the same plane, but in exactly the same seat! As we flew, I wondered if my wife and my father were behind (or above) this conversation above the clouds.

Through photos from my iPhone, I introduced Joyce to Joy. When they met in Melbourne later that month during our annual Christmas trip, they were instantly inseparable. They shared similar passions and became 'solid spines' for each other in a way no one else could. After their surgery, they would became the scoliosis survival sisters, and I suggested they take as their motto 'We'll straighten you out!'

When the orderly wheeled Joy into the operating theatre, I was dressed in scrubs—blue gown, cap, mask and slippers. It was a cold room with machines buzzing and beeping. I tried to avert my eyes from the sharp cutting tools on the stainless-steel benches. Pretending not to be scared, I held Joy's hand while my other hand squeezed the life out of the rosary in my pocket. I felt Joy's pulse speed up. Or was that mine?

She uttered three words that made me melt: 'Daddy, I'm scared.' Something deep within me wanted to embrace her and buffer her from any fear.

Then they gave Joy an injection to calm her before the anaesthetic and it was time for me to leave my baby in the hands of these masked men.

'Don't worry,' the anaesthetist reassured me in a muffled voice. 'I'll phone your mobile when we're halfway through and give you a progress report.'

'How long will it take?'

'About four hours, so I'll phone you in about two hours.'

When I left, I asked the surgeon, 'Doctor, you have a daughter, don't you?' He nodded and I spoke to him father to father. 'Please, doctor, treat Joy like she's your own daughter.'

His eyes smiled above his mask and he squeezed my shoulder.

I was allowed to give Joy one kiss through my mask and was glad she could not see my quivering lips.

Four hours until I could kiss her again? I knew they would feel like forty hours. I shuddered at the thought of never seeing my baby again. I could not imagine the pain of Nadia's parents after losing their daughter, their flesh and blood.

As I waited for the anaesthetist's call, I recalled my earlier wait during Nadia's surgery, with its terrible outcome. As awful as the waiting was now, I was glad that we had been decisive with Joy and opted to operate. When it came to health matters, I hated fear and procrastination more than anything. They were murderers.

As I paced back and forth in a nearby corridor, my phone rang. It was Michelle, asking me where I was. She and Grace were waiting for me downstairs in the hospital foyer. Soon other relatives arrived to keep watch with us, but I found it difficult to engage in any conversation. I was holding my breath for the phone call from the anaesthetist. As each minute passed, I panicked that something had gone wrong. Although my déjà vu of waiting for Nadia's surgery continued, I was gratefully aware that this time I had my family with me.

When the phone finally vibrated, I inhaled and my heart raced.

'We're more than halfway,' the anaesthetist said, 'and everything's going fine.'

'Thank you so much, doctor. God bless you.' I did not care if he believed in God or not. I prayed that God would guide their hands. I had permission to exhale. As the relief flooded through me, my tears welled up.

'Oh, you're making me cry now,' Grace said, smiling. I buried my head in her shoulder and imagined she was Nadia.

'Shall I buy you a drink, Dad?' offered Michelle.

'I'm okay,' I whispered. 'Thank you. I just need to . . . walk.'

I slept at the hospital in Joy's room for over a week as, one by one, the tubes were removed. Day by day, she was taught to walk again. The surgery through one rib was miraculous.

I ensured that my mattress was close enough for Joy to hold my hand. When I did, it was that sense of touch that spoke to her, with every massage of every finger, with the clasp, with the squeeze, with the release.

'Daddy's here,' I whispered to my baby. My desire to comfort her and see her safe was boundless.

As a result of the surgery, Joy gained a centimetre in height and gradually regained her agility in sport. She kept a photo of her X-rays on her iPhone, in case her titanium rod ever triggered the metal detectors at airport security.

More than a year after her surgery, my bedroom door squeaked open. I thought she had come to say goodnight, but instead she dived into my bed.

'What's wrong, Joy?' I asked.

'I'm sleeping here tonight.'

'Is that a question or a statement?'

She smiled and her eyes closed.

'What's wrong?'

'I don't know.'

And so the parental fishing expedition began. 'Are you worried about anything?'

She shook her head and kept her eyes closed.

'Joy, remember what we said about bottling up versus opening up. Nothing you tell me will make me angry.'

She opened her baby-blue eyes. 'It's not that, Dad. It's this . . . spinning thing.'

My own head started spinning but I disguised it with a casual smile and a monotone to reel in the fish. 'Yeah, go on.'

'I feel dizzy, like the room's spinning, before I go to sleep.'

'When did this start?' I asked, trying to stay calm and not get anxious.

'A couple of nights ago.'

'And what do you do when the spinning starts?'

'I hang on to my bed and wait for it to go away. Dad, what's wrong with my body?' She sounded angry, which was better than scared. 'Why can't I just have a normal year, where nothing's wrong with me?'

That was a tough question to answer. 'We've been through the worst . . . together, and we'll figure this thing out together. It's probably just a middle ear infection. Easy fix.'

She sighed and read right through me. 'I know you're trying to be positive . . . can I see a doctor tomorrow?'

I smiled. 'I'm so proud of you.'

'Why?'

'Because you don't muck around with your health. You're logical.' How I wished Nadia had seen a doctor within a couple of days rather than thinking positive and willing her monster away. Then again, had I raised my daughters to become hypochondriacs, paranoid that every ailment could morph into a terminal disease?

'Can you come with me?' She sought reassurance and I held her hand.

'Of course,' I said, clearing the lump in my throat. 'Is it happening now? This spinning thing?'

'As soon as I'm in this bed, it stops.'

'Hmm, what about if I sleep in your bed so you can have this one all to yourself and . . .'

'No, *you* have to be here.'

I kissed her petite hand and remembered how infants crave the scent of their parents.

'Dad, is it bad if I sometimes ask if there's a heaven?' she asked now.

My eyes widened at this surprising question. Was my baby worried about death? 'No,' I replied, 'it's good to question everything. When I was your age, I used to always ask, "But why? But why?"'

'Like, what if we all just die and there's no heaven. Like, how do we know for sure?'

I remembered tormenting a priest with similar questions after Nadia died. 'Well, some people believe because of their dreams,' I suggested. 'The Bible is full of stories of angels from heaven visiting people in their dreams.'

'Yeah, but people always interpret their dreams in their own way. Does that mean that if we have no visits, there is no heaven?'

Was I dreaming or was Joy really asking the big questions? 'Joy, if there was no heaven, would you live your life differently?'

She thought about it. I could almost hear her blinking in the dark. 'No. No difference.'

I was relieved that she believed we were wired to be humane, not cruel or immoral, just as I was learning that we are wired to be parents, not fathers or mothers. 'Exactly,' I agreed, 'we're born to be good. And whoever made us good also told us that there's an eternal reward for being good. Whoever made us also loves us.'

'But that's faith. That's not proof.'

'What about all the miracles by all the saints? If there was no heaven, they would never—'

'Yeah, I guess that's true.'

I heard an owl's deep hoots echo from a nearby tree. 'Hear that?' I whispered excitedly. 'When I was in Year 12, we studied a book called *I Heard the Owl Call My Name*. Some people believe that when the owl calls your name, you're called to heaven.'

No response from Joy. Why was I whispering scary thoughts instead of sweet ones?

'Darling, your questions are good. I'm so proud of you.'

Was my voice now a distant echo in her dreams?

'If you think about death sometimes, you appreciate life. But if you think about death all the time, you don't appreciate life.'

She was sound asleep, breathing through her mouth, with a blocked nose.

'Goodnight, Joy.'

As her spinning subsided, so did mine.

The next day the doctor prescribed eardrops for vertigo. Joy regained her balance and I regained my bed.

HOW TO BE BUSY

'Dad, I got the job!' Michelle seemed surprised, as her humble resumé did not list any work experience. 'We just clicked straight away,' she continued. 'She asked so many questions, I had a feeling she'd offer me the job.'

'You deserve it!' I said, smiling proudly. 'Good businesspeople can pick good businesspeople.'

Michelle always admired smart but simple ideas. She was a 'gun' at this pop-up warehouse selling Easter eggs. The owner took Michelle under her wing and taught her about greeting customers immediately, using the till, personalising the service and engaging the children. Michelle also learnt to tidy up the mess customers left behind without losing her smile.

'Dad, I could kill them,' she would say after a long day. 'They crack the eggs and dump them everywhere and the parents say nothing, as if cleaning up after them is my job!'

Michelle had a natural knack of establishing instant rapport and looking customers in the eye. Her results were rewarding and set her up for the basics of business. Yet as a child, Michelle had been most reluctant to approach a shop assistant, even if we were next in the queue, always asking me to speak on her behalf. Now she was the approachable shop assistant who knew what it was like to need a push.

As a career, Michelle was tossing up between psychology and business. Ironically, this was my first career plus my second career. I was careful not to push my unfulfilled dreams onto her. Yes, I would have loved to stay in my chosen profession of psychology, but that did not give me the right to saddle her with the burden of following in my footsteps. She had the patience and curiosity to listen to people, combined with a drive to seize lucrative opportunities. Her ultimate choice of university course was a perfect blend of the two: human resource management.

Michelle was the epitome of objective when it came to listening to people. She empathised and did not have a prejudicial bone in her body. 'But have you ever thought of it from his point of view?' she would challenge her friends as she paced back and forth with her phone glued to her ear, changing ears each time her arms got tired.

'No, don't give them the silent treatment . . . I know you're not talking to him, but he's your father, and he'll be your children's grandfather, so you have to find a way to communicate . . . Why don't you offer to have a coffee away from home, and when he talks, just listen, without interrupting . . .' She sounded so much like me, but how did she know all this stuff? Had she been eavesdropping on my phone conversations all these years?

Just as Michelle was an evolution of my interests, Grace was an evolution of her mother's. Nadia's first career was as a designer, working with textiles and graphics. Then she studied to become a teacher. When threaded together, the result was a teacher of technology, which included textiles and design. Like her mother, Grace was always firm but fair.

Part of her double degree in teaching included food technology, so she became our resident master chef.

'Dad, don't waste olive oil on frying. It burns. Use canola,' she instructed.

'The Lord works in mysterious ways!' I cheered. 'Finally, a real chef in the family.'

While Grace and Michelle were university students, they both worked as casuals at a menswear store. It was confusing for customers when they both worked the same shift because they looked so similar, apparently. How lucky was I that they became master stylists, specialising in middle-aged men! The style police had become professionals, with strangers seeking their opinion. My wardrobe soon looked like one of their store racks, with the same brand-name logo on virtually all my clothes. I became their walking, talking mannequin.

I was intrigued by how my daughters knew which clothes suited which man, someone else's father. Was it their inheritance from their designer mother or had they simply graduated from practising on their argumentative father? I once visited them at the menswear store as a fly on the wall to find out.

'Dad, no offence, but compared to our regulars, you'd be the customer from hell,' warned Michelle. 'They don't argue with us, they don't umm. They're in a hurry and decide: bang, bang, bang.'

Like me, she was impatient. Yet I somehow expected her to be patient when I weighed decisions by drawing up a list of pros and cons.

'Yeah,' I protested, 'but I don't like clothes that make me look—'

'Fat, I know,' she nodded. 'But you overanalyse and—'

'Well, there's no point buying something I'll never wear.'

'It's just clothes, Dad,' she explained. 'They're meant to last a season, not a lifetime.'

'Well, maybe they're meant for men who've paid off their mortgage, unlike me!'

In time, both Grace and Michelle had to move on. Grace was seeking full-time work as a teacher, where retail was irrelevant. While she completed her degree, Michelle was seeking part-time work in office administration, where retail was also irrelevant.

I asked my nephew Pierre, who was a partner in an accounting firm, if any of his clients were seeking a part-time office employee. He happened to be searching for one in his own firm. Within three days, Michelle needed a car to get to and from work and uni. I suddenly felt that she resented my lack of capital gains. She knew that I married fresh from street work, unable to afford a lavish wedding reception. She knew that, apart from the house we lived in, I had never invested in property or shares. She knew that I was always an employee, never an employer. She knew what not to do if she wanted to avoid ending up living my sort of life. I knew that she secretly admired other fathers who had a solid backbone of property and multiple sources of income.

She needed a car so I needed to debunk her ideas about me. It was a Sunday afternoon and bucketing rain. We drove to local Toyota car yards, spotted a suitable car within the budget I had hastily drawn up, took it for a test drive, took a photo of the engine, consulted a mechanic friend and signed the contract. Michelle walked arm in arm with me under our umbrella, then drove her new car back home. Just like that.

Risk taking? Spontaneous? Decisive? I hoped my actions would show her my true colours. I had bought Grace a car two years before, but in less dramatic circumstances. After years of investing in dance schools for Grace and Joy, Michelle more than deserved her fair share of the family budget.

'Well, Dad's spontaneous when it's pouring rain,' she laughed later.

'Then I hope it buckets down when I need a car,' warned Joy.

After her first day of work, Michelle left a card on my bed: 'Dear Dad, thanks so much for buying me my first car. I owe you so much and love you so much. From your favourite daughter xo.'

Favourite daughter? I love them all equally! True, I love them all differently, but I have no favourites. It reminded me of Nadia's cards on my birthday, which always started: 'To my favourite husband . . .' It was our in-joke, as if she were a celebrity with many husbands.

Michelle decided to work full time and study after hours so that she could gain solid employment experience. She would return home tired from answering so many phone calls, and her ears would need a rest.

When Grace returned home from work, she had to plan the next school day. My admiration for teachers grew as I saw her stay up marking mountains of assignments and exams, long after my bedtime, long after midnight. And I thought *students* had homework! I tossed and turned until there was no more light seeping under my bedroom door. It felt like only yesterday that she was a student, and now she was a teacher! There is an adage in Arabic, 'They grow up in the blink of an eye', but why would any parent *want* their children to grow up in a hurry?

With two daughters now working full time, the morning rush hour was worthy of a reality-TV show—*Waking up with the Wakims*. It looked like a fast-motion comedy.

Scene One: Action!

Three girls elbow each other to access the one bathroom mirror. Arms cross over to reach for the hair straightener, hairspray, hairbrush, hair dryer, moisturiser, deodorant, face wash, toothpaste, toothbrush and make-up bag. With one vanity between them, they need an accurate aim when spitting out the toothpaste.

The room reeks. Sometimes the sprays miss their target and are inhaled accidentally. The extractor fan makes minimal difference in this congested sauna. I keep my distance, not that there is room for one more person, let alone a male.

Scene Two: Action!

Exasperated with the overcrowding, Michelle (who else?) blows a fuse and storms to her own bedroom mirror, which is larger but dimmer than the bathroom mirror. She cakes on the blush to liven up her face. Suspecting she may have put on too much, she returns to the mosh pit. She elbows her way to the mirror, shoving arms out of the way, only to see that she has, indeed, over-blushed.

'What have you done?' mocks Grace. 'Too much on the forehead, and here . . . you missed a spot . . .'

'Shoosh! I know!' panics Michelle.

After she evens out her make-up, Michelle reaches for the hair-brush for some finishing strokes. When she realises that Joy's blonde hairs have been transferred from the brush onto her own dark hair, she is grossed-out.

'Joy! How did your dumb blonde hairs end up on my head?'

Scene Three: Action!

Michelle marches to my bedroom and 'borrows' my brush because it has no trapped hairs. The brush is innocently waiting for its master to brush his hair (yes, I call it the 'masterstroke'), as he has done the same time every morning for as long as it can remember.

But not today. The brush is snatched screaming all the way to the well-lit main bathroom as I am in my shower. It is 'abused' to de-blonde Michelle's hair and dumped on the sink. The resident rejected hairbrush taunts it.

'Well, well, well, look who's here. If it's not the posh brush from the en suite. Welcome to the real world, brother. Ha ha ha!'

My brush tries to scream but is strangled by girls' hair.

Scene Four: Action!

I dry myself and stand before my mirror for a quick brush but alas, no brush!

'Who's got my brush?'

No answer, of course. The least of their concerns.

Scene Five: Action!

That night, while they are not looking, I tie a string through the eye in the handle of my beloved brush and tie it to my drawer knob. The brush sighs, smiles and winks (or at least would if it only could). I cross my arms and nod.

'That'll learn them!'

৩

When the exodus was over every morning, the bedrooms resembled a battlefield. Their wardrobes became 'floordrobes', as they had no time to return the 'Hmm, not quite right' clothes to their racks. Mountains of clothes formed on the floor, creating trenches for tomorrow's battle. I wanted to remind them of their 'annoying' menswear customers who would dump clothes everywhere for them to refold and rehang, but a little voice whispered, 'Pick your fights, pick your timing.'

The effort required by these young ladies to look presentable and professional was in another world. It took them ten times longer than me to face the world. Did men pressure women to doll up, or did it come from within?

When we went on a *mishwar*, I would lose patience and yell out to them.

Michelle would turn off the hair dryer and yell back, 'What did you say?'

'How much longer? How can I help?'

Armed with the dryer like a weapon, Michelle sighed, 'Every time you yell out, you slow us down.' What she meant was, 'Shut up and wait in the car!'

They had no time for helping with the morning domestic chores, such as hanging the laundry, which once more became purely my domain. While I did that, Joy's routine was to wash the breakfast dishes. We would race to see who finished first.

'What did I do to deserve this? Women have it so tough!' cursed Michelle on a bad hair day.

'What did I do to deserve this? Men have it so tough!' I panted while rushing out to hang the second load of laundry, alone. 'Let's blame Adam and Eve!'

I had heard them singing along to the Beyoncé song, 'Flawless', and pointing to their faces.

'If you're so flawless,' I had asked, 'why do you rush to the mirror in the morning?'

They gazed at each other to decide who would be bothered to respond to my provocation.

'It's a song, Dad!' Joy said, shrugging.

Michelle sighed. 'Dad, there are only three ladies in the world who don't need make-up. You know who they are?'

I thought this was a trick question. 'The Kardashians?'

Her jaw dropped and she raised her left eyebrow. Mayday! She raised her palm towards my face and looked away. 'I can't believe he just said that.'

'*Us*! Your darling daughters!' shrieked Joy.

As professionals, their social life filled their evenings. Dinners with ex-schoolfriends, ex-uni friends, ex-dance friends, church friends, work friends and new friends from touch footy. 'Bye, Dad . . . Hi, Dad . . . Bye, Dad . . . Hi, Dad . . .' Our house became a revolving door.

Was that it? Would all our conversations from now on be reduced to two words? Did we bring children into this world for four words a day? Did adult life mean that we would pass each other like ships in the night? It may have been normal for their friends, but never for me.

Even Sunday masses were no longer a family affair. They loved the 7 p.m. youth mass, where the parish priest and his homily targeted their age group. He touched on social media, relationships, inspirational movies, global events, and linked them all to the weekly gospel. It was no wonder our parish was one of the best attended in all Australia.

But I had outgrown these themes and preferred to keep my Arabic alive, so I attended earlier masses. Besides, they liked to go straight out for dinner after the evening mass and I would have been the only parent there.

One homily in the earlier mass asked when we'd last had family time, with no one else around. I had a lump in my throat. It inspired me to make changes. 'Gals,' I protested once I got home. 'I hear you say "bye" more than "hi" these days. Do we need to make an appointment for family time?'

They looked at me, then at each other and realised I was being serious, not sarcastic. They finally realised what their busy-ness was doing to our family life.

HOW TO MAKE QUALITY TIME

'Just us four?' asked Joy when I broached the subject of scheduling family time.

'But we'll always be here for . . .' began Michelle.

'No, we won't,' I snapped, thinking of Nadia. 'What we have is precious and we shouldn't take it for granted.'

'I didn't mean it that way,' Michelle was offended.

'Let's go out to dinner . . . together . . . once a week,' I suggested. 'To be still. To ask "How are you feeling?" and "How are you dreaming?" and to listen to the answers with all our hearts?'

Michelle rolled her eyes. 'Drama queen strikes again!'

'No, I'm serious,' I insisted. 'We're so polite with our friends and we always make time for them.'

'What do you mean?' asked Michelle.

'Well, you're not a morning person, so it's hi–bye in the morning rush. At night, when I ask you about your day, you give me a mono-syllabic answer. Then I overhear your phone conversations and you give them the long bubbly version, the version I want to hear.'

'No, I don't!' Michelle was defensive and I was jealous.

'And you need to include me, involve me, invite me into more of your life, instead of me having to eavesdrop to find out second-hand what's really happening in my daughter's life.'

'Well, you shouldn't be eavesdropping!'

'And you shouldn't be so angry with the people who love you most.'

Grace wanted to steer us back on track. 'Actually, that would be nice, Dad. We can start our own family tradition.'

And so we did.

The next time I eavesdropped on Michelle's phone conversations, I heard my name: '. . . and Dad said . . . Yeah, of course we have those conversations with my dad, don't you? . . . Well, my dad always says . . .' Really? I was being quoted to her friends? Did she know I was listening?

Being quoted was a humbling experience and revealed my daughter's true colours. I noticed something else, though. The bits she quoted were only ever the first bits of what I had said, the headline. She must have switched off from the lecture that followed and politely pretended to listen. I learnt that it was best to for me to get straight to the point rather than slowly build up to a punchline.

In our 'cosy' house where the bedroom walls were not soundproof, I heard the way my daughters conversed. Many of their sentences began with the words 'I feel' and 'I think'. They opened all valves and vented. Their conversations flowed between head and heart and mouth and ears and back again. Just like our cosy house, there were no insulating walls to create a sound barrier within them.

Many of us men laughed and applauded when we watched the American comedian Mark Gungor explain how men and women's brains are wired differently. He explained how men's brains consist of many boxes that never touch each other and how we often go to our favourite 'nothing box' where we can be brain dead and still breathe. It may be a funny and neat metaphor, but do we really want to be imprisoned in these dark boxes? I would rather refract light as a prism than waste my life in a boxy prison.

Some of us men have been conditioned to think that our compartments should remain separate and that letting our feelings 'leak' out is bad. But what if we are wrong? What if leaking is good? And we have all seen what happens when there is the opposite of leaking. The pressure builds up and penting leads to venting, which sometimes leads to violence, which then leads to counselling, if not prison.

My daughters were uninhibited in sharing their fears and hopes, their likes and dislikes. They listened and empathised, never sitting on a throne, pontificating, but always swapping seats to view life from different angles. 'I never thought of it that way,' they would say. 'Yeah, same . . . I had the same reaction but thought it was just me.' Their definition of strength was based on honesty, not victory.

To the uninitiated, this small talk and chatter was bitching and gossip, but it taught me that I and my 'fellow man' had a lot to learn. Their talk was the middle stage between feeling and action: advanced dialogue instead of primitive sabre-rattling. The male mentors I knew saw it as a weakness to talk about feelings or to talk too much. We were supposed to *act* on our feelings, not *talk* about them. A strong man was a silent man. A strong man was an action man. Less talk, more action. We were trapped in a cage where chirping was deemed futile.

And so it was important to me to *talk* to my daughters regularly. The weekly family dinner would be our regular *mishwar*. They knew the Sydney restaurant scene much better than me, but sometimes the noisy venues they chose did not suit me. As we drove, I wondered if this is what a busy family now needed to do, just to have family time. When we were setting up a mutual 'appointment' to fit into their busy social calendars, Michelle would jibe, business-like, 'Get your people to talk to my people.'

'Is the restaurant bill the new price I need to pay for your precious time?' I joked back.

For me, precious time meant quiet time. Too many restaurants amplified their music so much that we had to yell to hear each other.

'But they're creating a vibe, Dad,' Grace explained when I complained.

'But we can't have a conversation!' I protested, cupping my hands around my ears.

I saw that Joy had her phone on silent but responded to a message with

KK 🌙😀🌙

'What's KK?' I asked.

Joy shrugged, 'It's like K, short for OK.'

I frowned. 'But now it's back to two letters.'

Joy rolled her eyes like I was the one who was absurd. 'Who cares? We understand each other.'

'And what's with the smiley face and the moon?'

'Why are you looking at my phone?' Joy said defensively, learning from Michelle, who probably learnt from me. 'It's just emoji for "Call me later tonight".'

'Emoji?' I laughed. 'Why don't you just pick up the phone and talk, instead of sending these stupid faces?'

'Dad, it's just how people express their mood,' Grace shook her head and defended Joy. 'It's just a new way of—'

'New?' I needed a sarcastic-face emoji. 'We've gone from words to abbreviations to . . . cave paintings. How is that new? That's primitive.'

Was it just a fad, I wondered, or was the new generation 'devolving' from letters to pictures? I once watched a table of four people at a restaurant spend their entire time on their phones. When they finished one message, they peered up, saw that their friends were still looking down, then continued to the next message and the next, thumbing away as if they were thumbing through a book on their own. They were serial text offenders.

One of them suddenly stood up. 'Sorry, guys, got to go, nice catching up with you.'

Catching up? He didn't even *look* up! Was this the new normal? In my view, these phones needed to be issued with an etiquette licence.

I insisted that mobile phones be switched off during our 'sacred' time. 'You know, gals,' I pontificated with my hands joined in a prayerful position, 'they have signal jammers in churches, to make sure people don't text during mass?'

'And your point is?' asked Grace.

I indicated a sign on the window. 'Well, you see how this restaurant offers free Wi-Fi?'

'And your point is?' Michelle echoed impatiently, in a higher pitch. 'Now we know where Joy gets it from!'

'Excuse me?' piped up Joy, offended at the backhanded slap for her long-winded stories.

'I'll ignore you,' I said, raising my palm to Michelle's face. 'A-ny-way . . .'

'*Exactly* like Joy!' laughed Michelle, and even Joy struggled to contain her laughter.

'Come on, Dad, this is torture!' added Grace. 'Do you want a drumroll?'

'Here you go, princess . . .' began Michelle, drumming the table with her fingers, urging me to make my point.

I closed my eyes and turned to the wall. 'I'll tell the wall. It'll listen with respect. Anyway, wall, what do you think of a Wi-Fi-free zone, where there's no Wi-Fi, even if you try? A digital detox where families can have uninterrupted time? What do you think, wall?'

'It won't sell,' Michelle shook her head. 'People have family emergencies and—'

'I wasn't talking to you,' I said, turning briefly to look at her then returning my gaze to the wall. 'I was talking to the wall. So, what do you think, wall? People don't need the phone if their precious ones are with them at the table, right?'

A waitress noticed me talking to the wall and chuckled. My daughters noticed and the laughter was contagious.

'Sorry, he hasn't had his medication today,' apologised Michelle.

'Excuse me, this is a private conversation between me and the wall,' I continued.

By now, Grace had turned to jelly and fallen to the floor in hysterics. Her snorts incited more laughter from Michelle and Joy. The more I maintained a straight face, the more they laughed.

'Dad, we're not laughing *with* you,' squealed Michelle. 'We're laughing *at* you!'

By the end of dinner, I had another dilemma. 'Which is worse, gals, leaving food on your plate and it going to waste? Or forcing yourself to eat and it going to your waist?'

Michelle gave a sarcastic applause. 'Very punny, very punny.'

'That's not a pun,' interjected teacher Grace. 'It's a homophone.'

'Homo what?' asked Michelle.

'You've had too much to drink!' Grace waved her hand at Michelle.

'It's the red wine,' I suggested. 'You know, at the last supper . . .'

'Oh no, not another story . . .' began Joy, imitating her elders. 'Tell the wall again!'

I turned to the wall. 'If the twelve apostles had white wine instead of red wine, would they have fallen asleep when Jesus wanted them to stay awake? What do you think, wall? . . . Really? . . . Oh, that's a good point . . . Yes, I wish I was a fly on the wall at that time . . .'

No one laughed.

'Anyway, Dad,' sighed Joy, 'if your food ends up in the bin, you're not hurting anyone, but if it ends up forced into your stomach, it could hurt you.'

'So I'll leave the food on the plate,' I shrugged. 'Who's driving home?'

'Grace,' responded Michelle, 'she only drank water.'

As she drove home, Grace told me about the offer she had received to work at a new school much closer to home. She felt guilty about leaving her current students, even though she had only been there one year.

'Grace, put aside your emotions,' I advised when we arrived home, 'and put a straight line down the middle of a piece of paper.'

Together, we weighed up the pros and cons, and as a result she decided it was a wiser career move to seize the new offer. Rather than pretending to have all the answers, I encouraged her to speak to veteran teachers, who would know which pros and cons carried more weight.

'Dad, it's all swinging towards taking the new job, but it's the guilt . . .'

'Guilt? Guilt will cloud your judgement and drown you.'

Grace looked surprised. 'But it's true, Dad. The Year 11s need me to get through . . .'

'They don't need. They want,' I insisted. 'Guilt and I are buddies from way back. But it bogs me down and I sit in it without going . . . anywhere. I've been a guilt guru for . . . too long.'

'Maybe I get it from you,' she smiled.

'If we haven't done anything wrong, guilt is a wasted emotion. Sometimes we're better off *doing* something with that guilt, turning it into another emotion that helps us climb out of the hole.'

'Like what?'

'Like anger.' I turned around and switched on the kettle. I still missed my late-night cuppas with Nadia. 'Guilt is a passive emotion. Anger is an active one.'

'But anger at what?'

I remembered my many nights alone and how they emboldened me to move from despair to action. 'At the injustices in this life and wanting to do something about it. It's short term but it . . . moves you.'

'But this isn't about justice. It's about my kids at school.'

'When I worked with street kids and I had probably become the only person they trusted, I still had to leave. I was angry that I was receiving death threats and could not continue my work.'

'So what did you do about it?'

I poured Grace a cup of boiling water and added some filtered tap water, just the way she liked it. For myself, I grated some ginger, squeezed some honey into a cup and poured in the boiling water.

'I let my frustrations out by talking to journalists and exposing the truth about the predators on the streets.'

We both sipped from our hot cups, loudly.

'So how did you leave the kids?'

'It was tough. Some of these kids were already suicidal, but I was honest and told them where I was going.'

'From Melbourne to Adelaide?'

'And from Adelaide to Melbourne three years later.'

'So what happened?'

'Well, some of the kids said I was just like the other people who come and go, in and out of their lives. That hurt. But a couple of them actually followed me, and even tried working with me to get other kids off the street.'

'Did it work?'

'No, not really. They needed what you need.'

'What's that?'

'Professional distance. They were driven totally by their hearts. They were drowning with the kids, in the present, unable to see the future. They saw a flat ocean in every direction. The kids needed more than empathy. They needed hope. They needed a lighthouse that could see the curve of the horizon at the edge of the ocean.'

She rolled her eyes but smiled, 'Do you always have to be so poetic?'

'It comes with wisdom, Grasshopper.'

'Who's Grasshopper?'

'It's from *Kung Fu*, a TV series I used to watch at your age.'

'So you *did* watch TV?'

'Selectively, Grasshopper.'

'So, bottom line, you think I should accept the new offer?'

'With both hands, with bells on, and . . . maybe with dance shoes on.' I stood up and tap-danced on the spot.

'Dance shoes?' she frowned.

'Of course. You have more than eighteen years' training as a dancer and four years training as a teacher. Imagine what you could choreograph for your school!'

Grace's eyes lit up. Her lifelong passion would be dusted off like my guitar.

'Why didn't I think of that earlier?' I mocked myself. 'You'll get three out of three.'

'Three what?'

'The three Ps: passionate, professional and payable. Most people I know manage two out of three. They're good at what they do and it pays well, but . . . there's no passion.' I was thinking of myself. I did have passion for my first two professions with street kids and refugees, but the pay was typical of jobs traditionally done by women. Once I became a father, I separated my life from my livelihood.

The professionals, Grace and Michelle, also clamoured for life— on the weekend—but Saturdays were always our clean-up days. My daughters always groaned at the thought as they went to bed on Friday nights.

'Dad, all this vacuuming under beds can't be good for my back,' protested Michelle.

'And by the time we finish, we're wrecked,' added Grace. 'Like seriously, my friends invite me out and I have no energy. The house-work ruins my whole day, because I have to spend the rest of it recovering.'

'Yeah, Dad,' Joy joined the chorus, 'why don't we pay for a cleaner, like we pay for the lawn mowing? What's the difference?'

'Easy!' I insisted. 'Cleaners make you lazy. I saw the maids in Lebanon and how some people can't even cut parsley for their tabouli anymore.'

'What's a cleaner got to do with tabouli?' asked Joy.

'When you're a parent, Joy, you should teach your children to clean the house. How can they take you seriously if you haven't been cleaning your own?'

The three of them gazed at me as if they were going to charge, nostrils flaring.

Michelle took a deep breath and placed her hand on her heart. 'You're giving me palpitations. Do you seriously think we'll forget how to dust and vacuum and mop and iron?'

'Why do you pay for the lawns to be mowed?' Joy asked, placing her clenched fists on her hips.

Oh, dear. The juvenile judiciary was cross-examining me, again. They may as well have asked, 'How do you plead?' But as I answered and realised that I was echoing Michelle's exact complaint, it dawned on me that they were right. 'Because it was exhausting me,' I said, 'and I needed the rest of the day to recover.'

'And you're a man, and plenty of men do lawn mowing.'

'But our lawn is massive.'

'Now imagine waking up on Saturday, knowing the day is all yours. No stress. No rush.' Michelle was persuasive.

Joy massaged the message: 'And instead of waking up relaxed on one day, you wake up relaxed on two days.'

'And if it helps, we'll pay for the cleaner,' Grace nodded, tipping the scale.

They wanted this so badly and they were completely logical about it. I thought of Nadia and how we learnt together to minimise unnecessary stress in our lives. The six eyes before me were pleading to do the same, for the price of a takeaway dinner.

'You're right,' I nodded. 'It's just habit, and fear, and trust. But if it means we can reclaim our Saturdays, then it *will* feel like our weekend is two days, not one. You're right, Joy.'

And so we did it. Our happiness was more sacred than our house.

HOW (NOT) TO DRIVE

'Stop the car . . . right now!' screeched Michelle on the way to our weekly family dinner.

'W-what?' I asked.

'Just do it . . . pull over here.'

'Why?'

'Aagh! Your driving . . . it's driving me crazy!'

'But what am I doing?' What *was* I doing? I had just been driving, hadn't I?

'You drive with one hand. You keep hitting the brake—for no reason! I feel like throwing up!'

'Am I that bad?'

'Worse! I don't feel safe. You'd fail your licence if you did your test today,' said the darling daughter to her father.

I flicked the left indicator and checked my rear-view mirror. The clenched jaws of all three daughters looked ready to eat me.

Even before I pulled over, Michelle had unbuckled her seat-belt, poised to take over the driving. 'P-plates, please,' she said, holding out her hand. She sounded like a police officer conducting a random breath test.

'Yes, constable!' Really, could she *hear* herself?

As I handed her the green plates and we swapped seats, I grinned at passers-by, pretending I was generously giving my daughter driving experience in my shiny new car. I had to hide the humiliation of being evicted from the driver's seat and relegated to the back seat by a P-plater.

Changing seats reminded me of when each girl was sixteen and I was their driving instructor. Even after driving home from work through 22 traffic lights, I would sit outside and toot so my daughters could come out for a drive and clock up their logbook hours.

They would rush to sit in my seat and be in charge, but it brought out the worst in me. As they drove my company car, I would plant my foot on the imaginary brakes and hang on to the passenger door handle as if my car were the sinking *Titanic*. I could swear we were always about to clip parked cars, although we always missed them by a whisker. My body would stiffen and my palms perspire.

After a slow build-up, my fear would finally escape as a high-pitched gasp: 'I don't feel safe! Pull over!' And now here they were, saying the same thing to me!

'Is this payback time?' I asked, squinting. But it was perhaps best to avoid bringing up recent history. After all, they could bring up ancient history.

Grace simply turned her head from the front passenger seat and reminded me of the Wakim genes. 'Dad, you know what Michelle's like when she's starving. Don't take it personally.'

Either way, it was my fault I had ended up in the back seat. If it was not my unsafe driving, it was my family's 'irritable when hungry' genes. So, nothing personal then!

Joy glanced sideways from beside me on the back seat and raised a brow. 'Well, she is her father's daughter.'

Ouch!

Michelle adjusted the driver's seat forwards. She had usurped my throne, my air conditioner and my sound system. She had usurped my brand-new car—my very first very own car, my fiftieth birthday treat to myself. As she ramped up the temperature from low to 20 degrees, she asked, 'Why do you make it so fricking cold?'

'Male menopause,' I snapped, but no one laughed.

She cranked up the music and my car became a mosh pit with all their long hair whipping the air and their hands accentuating every syllable sung. The speakers were pulsating to the percussive piano of 'Clocks' by our family's favourite band Coldplay. Soon the driver's left hand became a drumstick and her knee became a snare. And they felt unsafe when *I* drove with one hand? They no doubt forgot that I was the one who converted them to Coldplay when they were drifting into rap and crap. But by this point they seemed to 'own' everything in the car.

As the song reached my favourite part, the bridge, where Chris Martin repeatedly sings 'And nothing else compares', I inhaled in anticipation, but Michelle, utterly in charge, suddenly cried, 'I'm over it,' and changed songs. I was left singing the falsetto lines, alone, stripped of the music, like someone singing in the shower with the curtain suddenly drawn. Now I cannot even sing along to my own music in my own car with my own family!

She's her father's daughter? Is that what Joy just said? Really? I sighed and fogged up my reflection in the back window, trying to remember when I had ever behaved like that. Is that what Grace means when she says, 'You don't see yourself?' I sighed again to fog up my re-emerging reflection.

They are their mother's daughters, too. There was Grace's reflection in the front passenger window, an uncanny replica of my beloved

Nadia. 'And nothing else compares', indeed. I missed driving with my right hand and massaging her long fingers with my left while the three children snoozed in the back seat, where they belonged.

When God rested her soul he arrested our pursuit of so many dreams. Thy will be done, I prayed, trusting that 'Our Father' had different dreams for us. Here I was, ten years later, blessed with three mini-Nadias. But no matter how much I loved my blossoming three, it would never be enough to make up for the motherly love that had been stolen from them.

HOW TO LET THEM DATE

'Dad, we're inviting my old schoolfriends over tonight to play cards,' Grace announced.

'Are you asking me or telling me?' I served. What I was really asking was, 'Do you want me to be invisible?'

Michelle animated her left eyebrow, but Grace gave her an 'I got this' look. 'Neither,' she said. 'We're inviting you to join us.' Grace returned my serve without hesitation.

'Yeah, didn't you ask us to invite you, involve you, include you?' All right, love fifteen. Except they were playing doubles—two against one!

My serve again. I bounced the idea in my head and realised that I was the one who should have been more inviting. Why was I playing king of the castle? I whacked the imaginary racquet on my head and my next serve was far friendlier. 'I'll make some snacks.'

'No need, Dad,' Grace said, waving her hand. 'They'll probably bring some junk food.'

'Yuck! All the more reason!' I clapped my hands in excitement. 'Let the game begin!'

They glanced at each other. 'Game?'

'Yeah, your card game!'

'Oh!'

It was April, and it was Lent. As Catholics, I knew that some of Grace's friends might be fasting from meat. While my daughters took showers, I baked nachos, spreading a wooden platter with ingredients, including sliced lettuce, tomatoes, red kidney beans and salsa.

'Oh, yum!' Grace and Michelle cried as they floated into the kitchen and followed their noses. 'You didn't have to!'

'Is this inviting enough?' I boasted.

Joy prepared some nibbles, drinks, plates, glasses and cutlery.

Grace's phone vibrated. 'They're here.'

'Why don't they use the doorbell?' I asked. 'This gen-Y habit will make doorbells extinct and—'

'Dad!' Grace shouted, closing her eyes slowly, like her mum used to do if I had said something stupid. 'It's raining. They texted me for an umbrella from the car to our house.'

'Oh,' I grinned, embarrassed. 'Is it raining? I thought that was your showers?'

'That's because our house is so "big"!' Michelle's sarcasm echoed as they headed along the 'big' hall to play host.

Laughter followed footsteps into the house as two of their peers arrived, followed by another two soon after. There were two boys and two girls. It felt good to hear male voices in my home. It felt good that my daughters had boys as friends.

'Hi, *aammo* (uncle)!' They said, greeting me with a kiss, as is the Lebanese custom.

They were so taken by the wooden platter that they decided to take photos of it. 'Oh, your dad's so cute!' They said it so often that I was half-expecting one of them to come over and ruffle my thinning hair or pinch my cheeks.

Just as Grace had suspected, their friends had brought chocolate biscuits, chips and soft drinks.

'Oh no!' complained Grace. 'I gave up chocolate for Lent!'

'And I gave up chips!' added Michelle.

'And I gave up Coke!' sulked Joy. 'I'm craving it so much!' She got up and put a bag of popcorn into the microwave oven then added a bowl of it to the banquet. 'For those who can't have chips!' she smiled.

'Remember what our priest said,' I waved my finger. 'It's not what goes into your mouth but what comes *out* of your mouth.'

'So, did you give up anything, *aammo*?' asked the louder boy.

'TV.'

Michelle smirked. 'You hardly watch it anyway. How can that count?'

They kept their promise, and involved and included me in their conversations. Grace was not the only teacher in the room. They talked about students who acted out in class because of family problems.

'These days, seriously,' complained one of the girls, 'we have to act as counsellors and nurses, and every second student has ADHD—'

'And we have to remember who's allergic to what—'

'And one of my students at my prac apparently suffers from exam anxiety and needs a break every half-hour!'

'*Haram*, one of my students has diabetes and will need a kidney transplant.'

'We have a friend who's working on heart transplants,' I offered.

'Really?' the loud boy asked. 'Imagine having someone's *actual* heart in your hands!'

I compared their body language. How they sat. How they stared. Who they faced. Who they interrupted. Who they didn't interrupt. Who topped up whose drinks.

'Imagine you had someone else's heart in your chest,' I suggested, 'but that heart still loved the dead donor's . . . partner. And each time you passed that partner, your new heart fluttered because it recognised them and missed them so much . . .'

Why did talking about this give me a lump in my throat? Every April, my body remembers Nadia's anniversary. My bones ache as I am drawn to her shrine. At night, in the light of the moon, when my children and my neighbours cannot see me, I fall on my knees by the shrine, bow my head and seek her blessing. Reliving the events of 19 April has become my annual self-flagellation. But it does hurt my knees and probably hurts Nadia, who would shake her head and tell me to look up and smile.

Even the 'Alstonville' tibouchina that hangs over Nadia's shrine only blossoms in April each year, its vibrant violet flowers a poignant reminder of life, not death.

'Wow! What a story!' the loud boy's eyes enlarged. 'You should write a book, *aammo*!'

'Anyway, time to excuse myself,' I announced. I really meant, 'Time to give you privacy.' I mimicked a posh accent: 'I shall retire to my quarters.' After I closed the door with my theatrical exit, I heard the chatter: 'Cute . . . Wish my dad . . . stories . . . talk . . . lucky . . .' 'Don't flatter yourself,' my inner voice said. 'They're not talking about you.'

From the study room, I vented and wrote opinion columns about injustices and hypocrisies around the world. The steam from my heart evaporated to my head and trickled through my fingers onto the keyboard.

Even with the pouring rain, the deep timbre of male voices reverberated through the white walls of our home, which were tuned to higher pitches. It felt strange not being the only man in the house. I wondered if I felt threatened. The boys laughed loudly. Their baritone notes created the bass guitar and the girls harmonised with their soprano melodies. All I had to do was tap my feet and we would have had a rock band!

I could not decipher all their conversations through the closed doors, but I did not need to. I had always loved anthropology and there were enough clues here to decipher what was really going on. I once read that monogamous birds sing together in perfect unison to fend off those trying to tear them apart. Yes, I could hear who was pairing off and singing bird songs, but to them they were just playing poker. Or was I reading too much into it? When I went to bed, the male voices vibrated my floor, my walls and my ceiling. I tossed and turned and could not sleep. Was it the timbre of their voices, or their mere presence?

In true Lebanese tradition, they had their best conversations when they began their goodbyes. After a long chat in front of my bedroom door, there was another chat at the front door, then the umbrellas came out and my daughters accompanied the four visitors to their cars.

'We should do this more often!' sang out the loud boy.

They were all on such a high that they had forgotten it was past 1 a.m. and might disturb our neighbours.

When the front door was finally closed, I sat up and flicked on my bedside lamp. I called my daughters and they entered.

'You awake?' they asked, surprised.

'No, I'm sleep talking,' I smiled.

'Sorry, were we loud?' asked Grace, sitting on the edge of my bed.

'You're *allowed*, it's your home.'

'Oh, ha ha,' Michelle returned my sarcasm.

'I still can't believe I got my Ls yesterday,' Joy cried. She had celebrated and stayed up much later than usual, revelling in being included in older company. At sixteen, she thought she was entitled to join the adult league. 'I can't wait to get my driver's licence!'

'That's when I get my gun licence,' I muttered.

Michelle frowned. 'What? You, Mr Anti-War?'

'To keep those guys away from my gals.'

They gauged each other's reaction, then Grace spoke on their behalf: 'So, we'll take that as a compliment.'

Michelle twigged as to where I was going with this. 'Dad, they're just friends.'

I smiled, slowly.

'No, really,' Grace insisted. 'They're just friends from school.'

I raised the blanket to my nose and imitated the boy from *The Sixth Sense*. 'I see live people,' I whispered. 'I see what you cannot see. They don't know that I'm listening . . . watching.'

'Dad, stop,' panicked Joy, jumping on my bed to pull the blanket off my face. 'You're scaring me!'

'What can you see?' asked Michelle, who considered herself a natural analyst. She joined her sisters on my bed and crossed her arms.

I squinted. 'I spy with my little eye, someone who was in this house who has his eye on one of you.'

'Who, me?' Grace shook her head. 'But they're . . .'

'Actually, he has his eye on Michelle.'

'Me?' Michelle blushed. 'Who?'

'The one who laughed a lot.'

'No way,' Michelle exclaimed. 'He's just a friend and I like to keep it that way.'

'But he might like another way.'

Grace and Michelle exchanged frowns and looked back at me.

'Based on what?' asked Grace.

'Don't forget that I was a young man, once, and—'

'Yeah, last century!' mocked Michelle.

'I know what it's like when an attractive girl just wants to be friends but he wants more.'

'Dad, you're reading way too much into—' began Michelle.

'Man is a hunter,' I suggested. 'He's excited by a target that's hard to catch instead of too easy. He believes you'll resist at first, but that deep down you know he's your destiny.'

'Whoa!' Grace raised her palm. 'He's nothing like that, and besides, how would you know, after one conversation?'

'Because I've been through it. I know how he feels. It's tough.'

'So you feel for him more than you feel for me?' Michelle was flippant.

'No, but he might need . . . help to guide him with these things. He makes you laugh but he wants to make you love him.'

'Enough, Dad,' Michelle interrupted. 'We'll keep our eyes open.'

'By the way, Dad,' added Grace. 'They really liked you and how you gave us space.'

'Better that you bring friends home and I meet them first-hand instead of hearing about them second-hand.'

'Yeah, but . . . we don't want you to feel like you need to get out of your own home,' confessed Grace.

'Look, if you were out I wouldn't sleep properly until I saw your car headlights and your head was on your pillow. At least here I can sleep.' Well, apart from the baritones!

'Don't you trust us outside the home?' asked Grace.

'It's not you. I don't trust the other drivers, tired, drunk, late at night. And strangers trying to spike your drinks at clubs.'

They glanced at each other.

'You think we're that naïve?' smirked Michelle, 'I've raised you better than that, Joe Wakim.'

I smirked back. 'You mean I've raised—'

'No, I've raised *you!*' she persisted, and her sisters giggled.

'Anyway, get off my bed, say your prayers, and goodnight.'

'You say *your* prayers!' Michelle continued mischievously as they left me alone.

☙

Various bachelor boys were 'extra' nice to me whenever I saw them at church.

'Dad, he's nice to you because he's interested in me,' explained Grace.

'I knew that,' I lied. I had actually thought he was genuinely complimenting my newspaper columns.

'So, don't . . . give him the wrong idea that you're his friend or invite him over.'

'Why would I?'

'Because he told me that you phone him sometimes.'

I realised how odd this was starting to sound: me seeking contact with a guy who was seeking my daughter. 'But it's always about church matters, not about you.' That was not a lie.

'What church matters?'

'I try to open doors to support his volunteer work, and he tries to open doors to have my writing published in the church newsletter. And we have interesting talks about the church.'

'Like what?'

'Like how forced celibacy in the Catholic Church is a bad idea, and they should copy the Maronite Church, which never forced this on its priests.'

Grace sighed. 'Dad, have you thought that maybe he's trying to open another door . . . to me?'

'Dad, how can you be so smart yet so dumb?' Michelle weighed in and slapped her forehead. 'You talk like you have blind faith in him.'

I resented that. 'No way! I only have faith in my ... faith.' Michelle raised her left eyebrow and I knew I had to clarify my point. 'Look, if anyone dares lay a finger on you, I'll—'

'Dad,' Michelle interjected, 'you used to be the protective parent. Have you now become the pushover parent?'

Was I over-identifying with the guy? Yes, I probably would have done the same thing at his age: win over the parents to flick on the green light to the daughter. 'Look, I get that. Especially given that with one parent in our family, you feel more vulnerable—'

'No, Dad, you don't get it!' exclaimed Michelle. 'It's not about us, it's about you. You seem to need to take them under your wing. Do you regret not having sons?'

Ouch! The question rang in my ears and my daughters' faces spun in my eyes. Michelle had held up the mirror and reflected a brutally honest truth. 'Your mum ...' I confessed, but I could not continue until I had swallowed the lump in my throat. 'We had something stolen from us. We all did. Your mum. My wife. And more children. We never decided to stop having children.'

'Until you had a son?'

'No, we never, ever said that! We were so blessed to have you and we knew we should never be greedy. We knew so many couples who struggled to have even one baby.'

My daughters looked at me as if they were not good enough. Even Joy stepped away from His Majesty towards us. They were now mature enough to know my truth.

'I would be a liar if I pretended that I was never curious about fathering a son. I would be a liar if I denied that sometimes ... just sometimes, I feel that there's a pool of ... parenting in me that's just drying up. I feel I have so much to offer sons as well as daughters. Sometimes, I struggle to understand the ... stages you go through and I feel frustrated because I can't say that I know how you feel ...'

Silence.

Sadness.

Stillness.

Grace sighed and picked up one of my favourite fridge magnets. It was the serenity prayer, attributed to St Francis of Assisi. She had brought it back from Lourdes. My daughter now spoke in a gentler tone: 'I've heard you quote this to others. What about saying it to yourself?'

I read it, as if for the first time: 'God grant me the serenity to accept the things I cannot change; courage to change the things I can; and wisdom to know the difference.' I nodded. 'Serenity to accept the things I cannot change.' They were asking me to practise what I preach.

'And what about this?' Michelle pointed to the painting of the prodigal son the priest had given me just after I was widowed.

I remembered the father who was also a mother. Was Nadia pointing out these reminders through my daughters?

'Dad, are you questioning whoever gave you this . . . pool of parenting, as you call it?' asked Michelle.

'Well, I've always believed that we shouldn't waste our God-given talents, whether it's music or—'

'This isn't about music, it's about parenting,' corrected Michelle. 'And who said your parenting is wasted? How do you know when God might call you to use your pool? It might be with grand-children. It might be through voluntary work at the church. As you say, the second half of your life has only just begun.'

I felt the guilt welling up and wanted it to go away. 'You're right,' I conceded. 'I need to be honest about my . . . selfishness. Michelle, you seriously could be the best psychologist ever!' She always tells me what I would say to a friend in need but sometimes fail to tell myself.

'Are you giving yourself a compliment, again, because you think I got this from you?' she said, smiling.

'No, it's from God. It's not about me—'

'It's *always* about you!' she snapped. The sarcasm was back and her sisters laughed, partly in relief that this conversation was over.

But the conversations about dating had only just begun.

'Dad, your daughter has been asked out on a date,' Grace announced one evening as I was engrossed in writing another newspaper column.

She catapulted me from the Middle East wars back to my own sanctum. 'Date? You?' I asked.

'No, your favourite daughter, Michelle,' she grinned and shoved Michelle in my face.

'Sit down,' I smiled at Michelle, who was blushing.

'Well, you always said you don't wanna find out second-hand—' she began.

'And I also promised that I'll never be angry.'

'There's nothing to be angry about,' she continued. 'Actually, there's nothing to be anything about.'

'So . . . let's start with his name.'

They explained that they had met this guy at the gymnasium. He had dropped hints to Grace many times then finally mustered the courage to ask Michelle out.

'So, when is it?'

'Tomorrow night. But don't worry. He won't come in and meet you.'

'Why not?'

'Too early to "meet the parents",' she explained, gesturing with her fingers, 'and it's just a date.'

'Are you interested? Do you feel anything for him?'

'Well, he's fun at the gym, in a group. I'm curious to find out what he's like one to one.'

'Wouldn't it be awkward at the gym . . . if it didn't "work out"?' I reciprocated her air quotes gesture.

'I already mentioned that to him, but we don't always train at the same time.'

'And how do you know if he's . . . decent . . . you know what I mean?'

'Dad,' interjected Grace. 'He wouldn't *dare*. He's shit-scared of upsetting Michelle and puts her up on a pedestal . . . you know what I mean.'

Michelle looked down and grinned, flattered by this admirer.

'Well, Michelle, I trust you and I trust your judgement. People are often very different one on one. You'll peel off a few layers and get to know him better.' Whoops! Bad choice of words! I gritted my teeth and squinted.

'Dad!' screeched Grace.

'You know *exactly* what I mean!' I pleaded.

When he dropped Michelle back home at midnight the following night, I could sense her disappointment from her heavy footsteps. They carried heavy thoughts. I was still up typing and researching my next newspaper column, so I opened the door and invited her in for a debrief. Grace was also awake, so the three of us sat together on the swivel chairs in the study room.

'So?' I began. 'How was your date? Sweet or pitted?'

Michelle wobbled her hand, as if to say fifty-fifty. 'Dried.'

'Why?' I prompted.

Michelle shrugged and looked down. 'A bit of a mummy's boy.' This was ironic coming from a girl growing up without a mummy.

'You mean, very family-oriented?' I asked.

'I wish,' she replied. 'His mum does . . . everything.'

'And his dad?'

'Long story,' she waved her hand.

'So he's the man of the house?'

'I think his mum feels guilty about him growing up with no dad around, so she lets him off the hook.'

That debilitating G-word again! 'How do you know?'

'He was bragging about his mother and how he would love a wife like that.'

I frowned. I wondered whether sons subconsciously end up with someone like their mum, and daughters with someone like their dad. For this guy, though, it was apparently not subconscious. I wondered idly if Nadia resembled my mum. As an assertive and confident woman, yes. But when it came to caring about what others thought, not really.

'So his mum pampers him?'

'He's not . . . well rounded.'

Was she comparing him with me?

Grace sighed. 'What about the chemistry between you?'

Michelle shrugged. 'There was nothing there. No real . . . fire or chemistry between us.'

'Different from a group, eh?' Grace continued.

'Not just that. I realised something else. I like people who have more . . . culture. Like they know who they are and understand traditions. When it's not there, it's like . . .' Michelle looked around, searching for the right word.

'A dry biscuit?' offered Grace.

'Exactly!' Michelle looked up. 'I like richness and flavour. This guy has no connection to and interest in his culture . . . or his religion. We're so . . . different.'

'And you discovered that these things matter to you?' I asked.

She nodded but seemed disappointed in herself. She looked up at me and our blue eyes sparkled at each other. 'Does that make me a racist?'

I frowned. 'Being racist is generalising about a race. You say he's not even interested in his own culture or religion.'

'But is that how you raised us?' she sounded vulnerable.

'I raised you to be non-judgemental. I fight racism in all my newspaper columns. You raised me better than that!' I imitated her and Grace grinned at my retort.

'But you're not like . . . this guy,' she shook her head. 'You're proud of your culture and your religion.'

'Because I know who I am, privately, I can respect others, publicly.'

'So you found him a bit boring?' asked Grace.

'Maybe the poor guy was just nervous,' I jibed. 'First date with the high and mighty Michelle.'

They both turned towards me and frowned.

'You don't even *know* the guy,' insisted Grace.

Maybe not, but I knew myself. As a teenager, I once asked out a girl I greatly admired. I was not sure which aftershave to splash on. I was not sure what to talk about. I was not sure what she was expecting. I spent the night being the person I thought she expected, not being me. It was awkward for me. It was probably awkward for this guy. Here I was, again, caring for my daughter while pitying someone else's son.

As I tried to sleep that night, I realised that my footprint was indelible as my daughters stepped out onto the dating stage. I was the first man they had ever loved. I was the benchmark by which they would measure all future men. These guys would have more boxes to tick than they could ever imagine, God help them! They would need to be 'iron men', pad shoppers and male mannequins who were not afraid to shed tears.

It dawned on me that everything I did, everything I said in front of them, all their lives, had been etched into their template for a man. Sure, they could cut out the bits they did not like, but they probably yearned for familiarity. It felt like a weight on my shoulders: everything I did externally, they could internalise, permanently.

But it was no wonder I was so cautious when it came to anything that might lead to wedding bells. I recalled my first lament to my sister Eva after the surgeon announced the death sentence: 'Nadia will never see our children married . . . My children won't have their mum at their weddings.' I was in no rush to walk anyone down the aisle. I was in no rush to live without my daughters. I had played MC at enough wedding parties to know that that this was a lucrative industry that capitalised on the 'most special day of her life'. How dare anyone put a dollar value on my love for my daughters?

All three had developed an infallible intuition that would not only guide them, but would soon guide me.

HOW TO LET MYSELF DATE

'The longer you leave it, the fussier you'll be, the tougher it will be.' My 'fellow man' kept counselling me on re-partnering. They had been at me for years, and nothing I could say ever seemed to stop them.

Was I just fussy because I kept comparing possible partners with my guardian angel? Actually, the more time I spent alone, the more I became accustomed to my own company.

At some of our weekly family dinners, waitresses assumed Grace was the mother. She was offended by the assumption, but I grinned at the thought that I looked young enough to be her husband.

'How can you catch a fish if you don't put your bait in the water?' my 'fellow man' continued.

Cute metaphor, but what bait, and what water? Did they mean singles bars? Dating websites? Matchmakers? The women who fluttered their eyelashes at me tended to be divorced and to dress up in . . . not much at all. My regular 'fishponds' were either the girls' school or at church.

'Don't even think about it!' my daughters always cried, giving me the death stare. To their mind, teachers and the mums of kids they knew were completely out of bounds when it came to me going out with ladies. They would have found the gossip humiliating. It did not help that I was the chair of the Parents' Association with a regular column in the college newsletter.

Some people in our community saw me as the most eligible and convenient bachelor for the single mums' club. For others, me falling in love would be a fall from grace, from my esteemed widower status. I resented people calling me 'single', and saw divorcees as very different to widows. Nor was I keen to form my own Brady Bunch.

'Dad, just drop us off and go,' Michelle once insisted. 'When people talk to you on the footpath, everyone watches and they . . . talk.'

As my daughters grew up and went out more often, I was alone more often. I did not want them to feel guilty about leaving me alone, so at this stage a companion would have made them feel better. They had reached a point, emotionally, where they could tell me to my face: 'We don't mind you having a friend.'

I was the one who gave myself conditions: 'As long as you understand that no one compares with your mum.'

Just as I could read the bachelor boys who flitted around my daughters, they could read the lovely ladies. Just as I did not want to find out anything second-hand, neither did they. They did not want their friends ever saying, 'I saw your dad having coffee with this lady and . . .' They would want to be able to shrug and say, 'Yes, of course, we know.'

I had not gone 'fishing' since last century, when my younger brother George taught me how to read the signs to reel in a real fish. Now SMS was a reel that allowed me to test the water and read the signs without getting in too deep. I devised my own cruel rules. Speed of response: too fast means desperate; too slow means not interested—not maybe they are at work, in a meeting or have their phone on silent. Length of response: too long means they have too much spare time—something I did not have—not simply that they are keen; too short was actually more attractive for me. Smiley faces were too cute and turned me off. And serial texts when they knew I was driving were not only dangerous, but too teenage for me.

Perhaps my daughters conditioned me to avoid teenage habits. They were mortified if I ever used teen-speak like 'awesome' or 'convo' or 'Lol'. To them, these Gen Y expressions were never cool or cute if I uttered them. It was embarrassing, especially in front of their peers. Once they claimed a word, even if my generation had invented it, I had to back off. It was copyright. I once commented, for example, that Joy's salad 'rocks'.

'Dad, don't ever use that word,' Michelle said, glaring.

'Why not?' I shrugged and lied, 'I've been saying it all my life.'

'Just . . . don't. Trust me,' she shook her head. 'We say it now.'

'Oh, so your generation pinched it, just like that, and now you think you own it? That's theft!'

I never heard them use that word again. They would hate to think they were talking like I did 'back in my day'. They loved all things vintage from the seventies and eighties except if they were uttered by me! Perhaps I could pretend that other 'new' teen-speak words were stolen from my generation, and watch as they were ditched, one by one. But it turned out I was the same. I was not a fan when mature ladies used these fad words in their text messages. It was too 'hip' for me.

If there was chemistry, I stepped into the water, literally. I loved to go to the beach, where we could walk and swim together. There was something about the elements, the energy, the horizon and the infinity that washed away any guilt that I was betraying my wife. I also loved the openness of doing this in the presence of God rather than hiding anything. After working with man-made inventions such as computers and vehicles, I craved God-made beauty.

Each time, I listened to the potential soul sister with all my heart. It was timeless, spaceless, endless. The pores of our skin opened. The wounds of our past were put into perspective. But inviting her for dinner at my home was always going to be awkward, especially with the 'Beit Nadia' plaque near my front door.

'Dad, she's really nice,' my daughters declared in one instance after she drove away. 'She's an independent woman and stands on her own two feet.'

'But rarely returns my calls,' I grumbled.

They gazed at each other. 'Maybe she's busy raising her own kids and has no time.'

'Well, if you're interested, you *make* time, don't you?' I grumbled.

That maxim would come back to bite me. I had no problem being a hunter if she was playing hard to get. But what if she was genuinely not attracted to me? In another instance, we were both raising children but she was still haemorrhaging from a broken marriage and still seething at her ex. I found myself slipping into the role of future helper instead of future husband. Her children were threatened by me because they still hoped their parents would reunite. I was standing on a sacred spot that I knew too well. And she was not interested in standing anywhere near mine.

There were lovely ladies who arrived laden with gifts for my daughters. They did their research and elicited 'Wow! How did you know? You shouldn't have troubled yourself.' These ladies had a generous but lonely heart. Even Nadia had rarely phoned me during the day, but these ladies were constantly sending texts and sharing photos captioned 'Wish you were here'.

It was very sweet but very smothering. I could not keep up with all the messages: 'How's your day going?', 'What are we doing tonight?' We? Are we a *we*? What about my daughters? Are they part of this we?

Their question was innocuous but I would snap back. 'What are you doing tonight? I haven't even thought about tonight as I need to focus on work.'

'What about the weekend?' they asked, oblivious. 'Let's plan something, otherwise nothing will happen.'

'We'll see.' I had always resented this non-committal expression as a child. It always sounded like, 'Well, it depends if I get a better offer than you.' But now it was the best I could come up with.

I felt so suffocated by the 'we' and also by expressions like, 'Oh, Joey, you make me feel so complete.' Only Nadia had ever called me Joey. It felt strange hearing it from another lady's lips. And I already felt complete. I suppose solitude and death do that to a person. The elasticity of the mind enabled me to evolve, to compensate, to survive and even to thrive. But was I locking all the doors and windows to my heart?

I wondered whether I was sometimes sending double messages, without intending to do so, wanting to be close, but not too close. Until one of my daughters was in a relationship, I felt this closeness would always be difficult. What if my daughters saw me as replacing their mother with another woman, and no longer grieving their mother, with them? This guilt was choking me and all my attempts at closeness were half-hearted.

'Have you ever read Gibran?' I asked one lady, pretending to be an expert on this Lebanese American 'guru'.

'Well, I read *The Prophet*,' she shrugged.

'He tells us that we should stay as two parallel strings on a guitar, vibrating together, not one intertwined string.'

She grinned and corrected me. 'I think he wrote, "Sing and dance together and be joyous, but let each of you be alone, even as the strings of a lute are alone though they quiver with the same music. And let the winds of the heavens dance between you.'''

I applauded. 'Brilliant!'

'But Gibran was writing about marriage. Aren't you jumping ahead?'

Later I thought, the winds of heaven dancing between us? Was that Nadia trying to tell me something? No, I could not imagine her doing that. If it came from her, the wind would more likely bowl me over like a tornado! I picked up my lifelong lover and swung her onto my lap. I ran my hand down her smooth long neck and ran my fingers through her long straight hair until she sang for me. My guitar, of course.

I strummed with my right hand and hammered with my left, producing a melody that expressed my confusion. I struggled with a lady who was too available and ever-ready to drop everything to fit me in. I struggled with a lady who was scared of being alone.

My lyrics fell into place:

Every night, there's an excuse to call me
They say they're caring for me
Then seek reciprocation
How can you love me if you do not love yourself?
Confusing fear with love shall
End in suffocation

My 'fellow man' thought that a doting woman was exactly what I needed.

'Really? But she deserves better than that.'

'Better than what?'

'Better than . . . me,' I explained. 'She deserves someone

who . . . reciprocates. Someone who's dying to be with her every minute of every day.'

'Well, if you're interested, you make time, don't you?'

I felt like Peter when the cock crowed after he denounced Jesus. Peter had been warned that this might happen.

Then I was introduced to someone more compatible.

'Don't be too fussy,' warned the matchmaker. 'You're not perfect, either.'

'Of course not!' I was offended. 'It's just a question of whether my broken pieces fit her broken pieces.'

'Yeah, but don't come across like you have no broken pieces, otherwise she'll find no entry point into your . . . life!' Maybe he had a point. If I canonised Saint Nadia, what chance did any mortal woman have of measuring up? He put his hand on my shoulder, like a brother. 'Listen, if you keep delaying, you won't need a wife. You'll need a nurse to help you walk and help you pee!'

I shrugged off his hand. 'If it's meant to be, the real matchmaker will make it happen.'

'Maybe the real matchmaker is sending you all these signs but you're expecting an angel to fall from heaven.'

I looked up and thought of Nadia in heaven. Was she really giving me her blessing?

I met a lovely lady who reminded me of Nadia. I invited her to my home for dinner and I thought it went well. She made an effort and asked my daughters lots of questions. After she left, our honesty pact was reciprocated.

'Dad, sit down.'

'Don't be judgemental,' I began. 'You hardly know—'

'Dad, what do you see in this lady?'

'She reminds me of your mum.' That was enough to put them offside.

'She's nothing like Mum,' Michelle said, waving her hands. 'Not in looks. Not in personality.'

'Dad, this lady is des-pe-rate,' Grace spelt it out.

'No, she's not,' I insisted. 'Maybe she likes me.'

'You sound like a teenager,' laughed Joy.

'Do you want me to be brutally honest?' asked Michelle.

'Well, less brutal, more honest, please.'

'Ha, ha,' she scoffed. 'Did you not hear what the lady said?'

I was confused. What had they picked up on that I had missed?

'You were walking in and out, trying to impress—'

'No, I wasn't.'

'But when we were alone, whatever we said we liked, she agreed, until you came back in. Then she agreed with whatever *you* said, even if she contradicted herself.'

'Oh, that's cruel. You were setting her up!'

'No, we weren't,' Michelle said, raising her left eyebrow. 'I just cannot imagine you . . . happy with someone who always agrees with you. You like someone who challenges you and is honest.'

I swallowed. No argument there. How did I miss that?

'And did you see how much lipstick she wore?'

I waved my finger. 'Now you're getting personal.'

'No, we're getting honest,' continued Joy. 'You keep saying how you hate too much make-up. Didn't you notice?'

'I thought it was natural.'

'Then you need to upgrade your glasses!'

'Dad, we had bad vibes straight away,' explained Michelle. 'We pick up on how women walk, talk, dress, laugh, how they use their eyes, everything. When we see our friends do it, we tell 'em cos it's a girl thing . . .'

I had studied psychology, but perhaps this was the women's intuition I searched for deep inside me but found so elusive. Sure enough, my daughters proved correct and saved me from hurting this lady. It was only the Julia Roberts lips that she shared with Nadia. She didn't seem to have an opinion of her own and kept agreeing with whatever I said. It was humiliating. I dreaded the thought of my daughters ever behaving this way with a man.

'Please . . . stop,' I said, staring into her desperate eyes. 'How can you know me if you don't know yourself?'

'My clock is ticking,' she said, tearing up. 'I can't handle being left on the shelf.'

Were these clichés referring to having babies? Or menopause? Or marriage? Or all three? 'There is no clock,' I smiled. 'And there is no shelf. Smash the clock and just be yourself. You don't want someone to save you, or pity you. You want someone to love you and respect you.'

'But don't you want the same thing?' she cried. This was some-one's daughter. Someone's sister. She needed a hug.

I sighed, knowing that I was capable of being loved and of loving. 'I'm not afraid of being alone,' I replied. 'I'd rather stay alone and widowed than rush into a wrong marriage then get divorced.' The lovely lady knew she was wasting her time with me, and it ended as quickly as it started. She didn't see me as I was. And I didn't see her as she was. It was unfair on both of us.

Nadia was not holding me back. My daughters were not holding me back. I was holding myself back because I was not convinced that I needed a new soul mate to replace Nadia. Where is this replacement rule written? Maybe there was no need to keep on fishing patiently, waiting for Mrs Right, because maybe there was no Mrs Right.

Maybe there would be many different 'right' people to walk with me, swim with me, fly with me, sing with me, laugh with me and dine with me, and I could share what they enjoy. After all, the idea that I was Mr Right for someone, somewhere, out there, may be wrong. Who said that I ticked all the boxes? I was fed up with boxes.

As my daughters grew wings, they flew from the nest more often. Although I was alone more often, I was never lonely.

HOW TO BREAK FREE

In my mind's eye, I lifted the sledgehammer and swung it over my shoulder. It was time to smash the rusty shackles that had tied my feet for so long to prescribed gender roles. They held me back from the intuition mothers exuded when they entered a room. Without a word spoken, mothers effortlessly read a room, gauging its temperature, scanning their children's faces and measuring their heartbeats.

They glanced at the gap between a child's lips and realised that child was seething. They watched the chest rising and falling, how fast and how deeply, and realised that a sibling tiff had just finished. They noticed if there was no eye contact between the siblings and how slowly they blinked. They saw one vertical line on a brow and realised that a child was worried. They sensed discomfort by how the children crossed their legs.

This was the language of love, a language that should not be the monopoly of mothers. It is a language that we men can reclaim and relearn, as it lies dormant within us, waiting to be brought back to life. I was sure that whoever gave women this gift would not have bypassed fathers, in case they ended up like me.

My fellow man and I were not predestined to enter our family home as dopes. Our intuition antennas are inbuilt and just need to be raised. All we need is to learn how to turn on the switch. This is not getting in touch with our feminine side. This is getting in touch with our inner self. We are not shackled to *Banni Adam*, but have always been part of *Banni Hawa* (the children of Eve). It is odd that we fathers see ourselves as *men*-tors to our daughters. I was so hardwired that I spent years thinking it was *me* doing the teaching, but in fact it was often the reverse, just as Michelle had intimated.

My daughters stretched my imagination to straddle not only traditional gender boundaries but also generational boundaries. They gave me permission not to act my age. They gave me permission to be childish and not to suppress our ageless yearning for play and story-telling. This is not getting in touch with our inner child, it is getting in touch with our inner self.

We men miss out on so much if we remain shackled in the prison of traditional gender roles. I have discovered all this by circumstance and by accident, but other men can discover it by *choice* and live a richer life. It does not mean becoming less complimentary to one's spouse. It means sharing more and being more of a well-rounded role model for one's children.

Sure, I could have outsourced the traditional women's work to a paid maid from the start, but this would have been skirting the real challenge. 'In-sourcing' within myself not only completed my family, but completed me. Freed from my shackles, I could now spread my wings and emancipate myself.

It was time for a *mishwar* to celebrate . . . everything. My three ladies fought over the mirror in their bathroom. Yes, even a trip to a restaurant was a special occasion.

I grabbed the keys and yelled, 'I thought you were "flawless"!'

As the chorus yelled back, I bolted out the door and waited on the front lawn.

When they emerged and strutted onto the 'green carpet', I asked, 'Where am I driving you?'

'Who said you're driving?' asked Michelle.

'*I'm* driving,' offered Joy.

'You're on your Ls!' replied Grace.

'So what, I need to learn, don't I? That's why they're called Ls!'

While they were debating, I sat in the driver's seat and started the car.

They fought for the front passenger seat and Grace won.

I crossed myself and reversed the car out of our driveway, looking in the rear-view mirror. I saw my past. I saw my children. I saw myself. Was the man in the mirror their driver, their mentor, their teacher?

So I once thought, before my emancipation. Now I knew they were mine.

ACKNOWLEDGEMENTS

I wish to send 'bouquets' of gratitude to all who radiated sunshine and sprinkled water on this book so it could blossom:

To my guardian angel Nadia, who guides me and whispers to me through our three angels.

To my daughters Grace, Michelle and Joy—you don't need to watch what you say and do anymore 'in case it ends up in the book!'. You will always be my main characters.

To my parents, siblings and extended families who were uprooted by migration and now sow seeds in this fertile land, especially my only Sydney sibling James and his wife Lola, whose strength and family were never taken for granted.

To my publisher Jane Palfreyman at Allen & Unwin whose invitation to write this book prompted me to see my private journey as a celebration worth sharing.

To my editors Nicola Young, and Sarah Baker, who navigated through my head and heart then joined all the dots to stitch a beautiful tapestry.

To Lucy Clark who encouraged and edited my frivolous idea in The Hoopla—you were virtually there at the conception of this 'unplanned pregnancy'.

To my 'sisters' who kept showering me with drops of wisdom and inspiring me, unintentionally—Sister Sayde Bayssari, Judy Saba, Loubna Haikal, Yolla Estefan, Doctor Fiona Hill, Janice Saoud, Dina Mueller, Christine Hanna, Rita Werden and Leeanne Hanna.

To the 'specialists' who are always gracious when I am swimming out of my depth—Jorgio El Zein, Zeina Issa and Juliette Ayoub.

And to the 'One' who was there at the beginning and the end.

ABOUT THE AUTHOR

Joseph Wakim's family migrated from Lebanon to Melbourne by ship when he was two years old. He studied psychology, graduating in social work, and his first job was as founder of the Streetwork Project in Adelaide in 1986–88. He then returned to Melbourne and worked with Middle Eastern immigrants and refugees. Intrigued by issues of race and religion, in 1996 he started 'moonlighting' as an independent opinion columnist for all the major newspapers. Some articles were shortlisted in the 2014 UN Association of Australia Media Awards. His articles culminated in his first book, *Sorry we have no space* (Connor Court Publishing, 2013), which was shortlisted as Australian Christian Book of the Year 2014.

In 1992 Joseph produced the TV documentary, *Zero to Zenith*, and in the late '90s he wrote four satirical comedies that were staged in Melbourne. Joseph was appointed Victoria's youngest Multicultural Affairs Commissioner in 1991. He was granted the Violence Prevention Award by Commonwealth Heads of Government in 1996, and the Order of Australia Medal in 2001 for public campaigns to redress the roots of racism.

In 2001, he completed his Master of Business degree and has since worked in logistics.

Joseph is also a musician and composer and, with his family band, *The Heartbeats*, he has performed and recorded his own songs. He and his family now live in Sydney.

Most of Joseph's opinion pieces can be viewed on his website, www.josephwakim.com.au, and he can be followed on Twitter @WakimJ.